D1006896

HER
DAILY
BREAD

INSPIRED WORDS AND RECIPES
TO FEAST ON ALL YEAR LONG

KATE WOOD

HarperOne
An Imprint of HarperCollins*Publishers*

For my children.
May you come to rely on Him as your daily bread.

FIRST EDITION

Designed by Elina Cohen

Illustration credits: b.highvector/Shutterstock: p. 9: coffee cup; Mureu/Shutterstock: p. 16: cinnamon sticks; Epine: p. 24: basil, p. 61: oregano, p. 218: avocado; Olga Lobareva/Shutterstock: p. 32: carrots; Vectorgoods Studio: p. 39: cheddar cheese, p. 84: bread, p. 232: popcorn; Prokhorovich/Shutterstock: p. 46: mixing bowl; Natalya Levish/Shutterstock: p. 54: pancakes, p. 188: honey; SpicyTruffel/Shutterstock: p. 68: rice; Sketch Master: p. 75: chocolate chip cookie, p. 112: garlic, p. 181: whole peach, p. 371: frosted sugar cookie, p. 385: pecans; Kuzmina Aleksandra/Shutterstock: p. 91: quinoa; NataLima/Shutterstock: p. 98: parsley; artnLera/Shutterstock: p. 105: mint; mamita: p. 127: margarita, p. 331: bourbon; Qualit Design: p. 134: eggs; p. 354: salt in a spoon; DiviArt: p. 142 strawberry; p. 276: pizza; Egor Zakharov/Shutterstock: p. 150: burger; Lina Keil/Shutterstock: p. 158: blueberries; AlexandrLiogkih/Shutterstock: p. 173: dill; Kate Macate/Shutterstock: p. 195: lemon; Istry Istry/Shutterstock: p. 202: cut peach; Dina FR/Shutterstock: p. 225: balsamic vinegar; white snow/Shutterstock: p. 239: chili pepper; nadiia_oborska/Shutterstock: p. 253: whisk; EngravingFactory/Shutterstock: p. 262: apple; Varlamova Lydmila/Shutterstock: p. 285: zucchini; Susann Schroeter/Shutterstock: p. 292: muffin tin; aksol/Shutterstock: p. 300: peanut butter; Siberian Art/Shutterstock: p. 308: bacon; Vasilyeva Larisa/Shutterstock: p. 324: ladle; Katrine Glazkova/Shutterstock: p. 339: butternut squash; Rina Oshi/Shutterstock: p. 346: shrimp; ilonitta/Shutterstock: p. 378 peppermint candy canes; Irina Zaharova/Shutterstock: p. 392: champagne.

Library of Congress Cataloging-in-Publication Data has been applied for.

ISBN 978-0-06-307906-9

21 22 23 24 25   LSC   10 9 8 7 6 5 4 3 2 1

Contents

Recipe Listing

✂ Introduction ✂

Can I tell you a secret? Sometimes I get out of bed in the morning strictly for that first sip of coffee.

I've long been a morning person, but motherhood has a way of making even the earliest of risers sneak out of bed before the sun comes up to capture a few minutes of solitude. When it's just me, the tea kettle, and a French press full of ground coffee beans, I can gently lure my mind and body to awaken, to ready themselves for the busy hours that are to come.

For many years, I did little to prepare myself for the day at hand. After all, you'd be amazed at what a girl can do with concealer and a clean(ish) pair of sweats. I was surviving, but not thriving, and it wasn't until after my second child was born that I realized I needed more than flavored coffee creamer and a fresh schmear of deodorant to make it through the day successfully; I needed real connection with myself, with others, and with the Lord. I needed daily bread, a time spent feasting on the very presence of God Himself, even more than I needed a second or third sip of caffeine. My hunch is you do too.

After a few years of dabbling in the kitchen, I found myself in a full-blown love affair with baking and began my food blog, *Wood and Spoon*, in hopes of becoming a cookbook author. Early on, I didn't anticipate the healing that would come with storytelling or the encouragement I'd receive from readers who identified with the words I was writing, yet each week I'd receive emails from women who appreciated my vulnerability and wanted to share experiences of their own with me.

As they told me about their memories of meals from long ago and the ways they used my recipes to love the people in their corner of the world, it became evident to me that food is a uniting thing, connecting us to our past, our future, and all the people we bump into along the way. At the table, there's an invitation to serve, connect, and give deeply of ourselves, and as I slowly uncovered the wealth of love available to us simply through physical nourishment, I began to wonder how it was all tied to our spiritual nourishment as well. So began this book.

Consider the coming months with this book an extended conversation with a friend. In these pages, I've included a year's worth of scripture passages, personal stories, and life lessons that I'm still wading through myself. I'm about thirty-something years into my own narrative, and much of what I've learned in these recent chapters of my life as a woman, wife, mother, daughter, and friend is reflected in these pages. My prayer is that, by reading about the joys, hardships, and experiences that have brought me this far in my story, you'll pause to reflect on your own. This is an invitation for us to bring our thoughts, questions, and desires to the table to share, together.

There are 365 entries in this book, 52 of which are recipes. Most of the entries are short devotionals about our relationship with God relative to themes like womanhood, motherhood, marriage, friendship, personal growth, and, of course, food. Each week, there are six days of devotionals, and on the seventh we'll pause for a recipe: a soup, a batch of muffins, or maybe even some crazy-delicious ice cream sandwiches. That recipe day is like a Sabbath rest in the midst of a hectic schedule, and my hope is that you'll use it as an opportunity to connect with others in your own kitchen and participate in some much-needed rest.

Many of the recipes you'll find in these pages are connected to some of my most beloved memories; they are dishes I've shared with women who have fed me in ways far deeper than bread alone ever could. Most of us stand on the shoulders of the people who came before us, and that's certainly true for me; these pages are a thank-you to them, the ones who nurtured and nudged and gave so much of themselves for my benefit.

When you read the recipes and words that follow, I hope you'll bring yourself along too, interjecting your own experiences to settle in next to mine. We all have a seat at God's table, and I think it delights Him to no end when we pull up a chair to share in community around it. He's our daily bread, and I can assure you there's more than enough to go around. So let's dig in.

DAY 1: Fresh Starts

For many of us, the new year is an opportunity for change. On January 1, we survey the pages of our lives like a fresh spiral-bound notebook that is ours to fill, eagerly penciling in changes to be made and vows to do better. For most of my own life, I've used the new year as my opportunity to rewrite some of last year's book too, editing pages and scribbling out plotlines that I didn't want included in future volumes.

Although many of us love the idea of reinventing ourselves in pursuit of a better life, we need to remember that God doesn't wait until January 1 to do a new thing. In Christ, there is always hope, possibility, and promise awaiting everyone who welcomes Him as the author of their life. Jesus wants to write a triumphant tale for your days on earth, one filled with adventure and growth and joy and potential. Instead of simply filling our journals or calendars with plans and resolutions of our own, we can press in to the dreams, blessings, and experiences that He has for us too.

As you start a fresh new year, are there areas of your heart you need to surrender to Him today? Maybe parts of your own plan that need to be aligned with His? Rather than settling for an ordinary year, you have the opportunity to lean in to the unimaginable story He is writing. January 1 is as good a time as any to begin walking in new life with Him, so if you haven't already, start today.

 **ISAIAH 43:18–19**

DAY 2: Good Luck

The first January that my husband, Brett, and I were married, my father-in-law brought us a traditional Southern meal to celebrate the new year. I was still new to my husband's hometown of Selma, Alabama, having lived most of my life in Orlando, Florida, and the elements of that meal were a first-time experience for me. There were slow-cooked black-eyed peas, wedges of skillet cornbread, and peppery collard greens that were braised with smoked pork, for both flavor and good luck. As we shared the meal, I learned that those foods are traditional on January 1, as Southerners everywhere fill their cast-iron skillets with foods that are said to bring prosperity and good fortune.

Although we still often enjoy beans and greens on New Year's Day for fun, I remain comforted knowing that God isn't the type to leave anything to a matter of luck. As believers, we don't have to roll the dice, wish on stars, or hope for something favorable in our skillets, because we have been called to rest in the promises of a God who works all things for our good (Rom. 8:28). He's already offered grace that is sufficient for everything we'll face this year, and our primary job is to remain confident in it (2 Cor. 12:9).

Be encouraged: the odds are in your favor with Jesus. Spend some time in prayer today, and ask Him to reveal any areas where you can rest more fully in His provision. Commit the coming weeks and months to Him, and remain hopeful in the blessed assurance that belongs to children of God.

EPHESIANS 2:8–9

DAY 3: Resolving for More

My greatest success with new year's resolutions happened the year I decided to start exercising. For three weeks, I jogged, lunged, and even did push-ups at my bathroom sink, determined that this would be the year I finally decided to love my body. Unsurprisingly, before the month was up, I had burned out and quit, my motivation overcome by an onslaught of shame over my lack of persistence. Since then, I've spent a dozen or so Januarys making the unsteady leap toward the illusion of achievement, starving and straining and guilting myself into perfect misery. Have you been there?

I want to look at resolutions differently. I'm all for goals, but I'd like to work toward them for the right reasons. Instead of thinner thighs, I want more self-confidence. Instead of less debt, I want more financial freedom. Instead of fewer stress-induced gray hairs, I want more of the stuff that brings me life: deep relationships, laughter, and rest.

January may be the perfect time to cut back, make changes, or switch gears, but let's examine our motivations for doing so. Are you searching for contentment in things that won't satisfy, or are you digging deep in order to uncover the very best that God has for you? When in doubt, move toward Jesus. By aligning your ambitions with the Father's heart, you can take manageable steps toward a life that looks more like His. Contentment in Christ is never misplaced, so this year, instead of being motivated by your lack, move toward the God who offers more.

 **PROVERBS 16:1–3**

DAY 4: Planning on Jesus

There's nothing better than cracking open a brand-new day planner, with its crisp edges and fresh pages—a year full of opportunities just waiting for my pencil or pen. I'm that person who writes down every to-do I can think of, no matter how small or silly it may be, because I take so much satisfaction in scratching it off my list, another task fulfilled. The downside to a thorough schedule is that I often fail to make room for the unexpected, the incidentals in the margins of my life that necessitate attention. Instead, I find myself rushing from task to task, rarely looking up long enough to see what I've been missing along the way.

As good as it feels to achieve and accomplish, I know that fulfillment happens when I'm present. In my rush to check off another box, am I missing the opportunity to read a book to my daughter? To answer a phone call from a friend? To pray, or take a walk, or give my husband a hug just because? I'll be honest—most days it's more gratifying to see a page full of check marks than it is to be present, but that's not the story I want to write. I know God has more for me.

Are there areas of your life where you need to cut back? Slow down? Make room for things in the margins? Ask God to show you some places where you can create space for more of the things He has for you, like rest, joy, connection, and growth. Instead of filling your minutes with things that won't satisfy, create room for God to jot love and blessing in the corners of your life. It's all right to make your own plans, but today leave space for His too.

 **PROVERBS 19:2; 21:5**

DAY 5: Learning from Experience

Many of the older women I rub shoulders with learned to cook by watching other people in the kitchen. They weren't reading or following recipes; instead, learning happened by putting their hands into bowls of flour, by smelling the sugar caramelizing on the stove, and by watching chicken skins fry to a crispy golden brown. Sure, you could put those measurements and techniques into words, but these women didn't need them; they learned by experience.

Jesus was all about experience too. He wasn't looking for scholars with head knowledge or lofty answers—He was looking for friends. The Bible shows us time and time again that real transformation happened when ordinary people experienced His extraordinary love, and that same principle applies to us today. We can consume all there is to know about God, but that knowledge alone will never make us holy. Speaker and author Graham Cooke said it best: "God isn't doing anything academic in us. He's not reaching our head; He's teaching our heart to walk with Him."

I don't want to become someone who knows about God but still hasn't truly understood. Instead, I'd like to learn His principles from experience, by doing life right alongside Him and witnessing the transforming power of His presence. Today, instead of just reading about Jesus, experience Him. Spend some time in prayer and ask for a fresh revelation of His love for you. There's so much to learn from God just by soaking in His presence, so dig deep for more of Him today.

 **PHILIPPIANS 3**

DAY 6: Awakened to Praise

On mornings when my husband wakes up before me, when my sheets are warm and my eyes are still heavy from sleep, it's that first whiff of coffee from the kitchen that lures me out of bed. That comforting scent awakens my mind, signaling the nearing of familiar flavors, the taste of something that I know will satisfy. Once I've sensed it, I can't resist—I'm up and out of bed, ready to experience the goodness of that very first sip.

I sometimes wonder if God responds the same way to worship. All throughout scripture, we read about instances of worship summoning the presence of God, as if the Holy Spirit can't stay away when He hears those joyful noises. So often we feel separated or distant from God, but the road map to intimacy is very clear: we get there with thanksgiving and praise.

Make a joyful noise to the Lord today. Sing your songs of praise or whisper sweet words of thankfulness. You can bring your concerns and questions along too, but don't miss the opportunity to worship Him in those prayers. Tell Him who He is to you and proclaim what you know to be true about His nature. God is drawn to a heart that is full of love and gratitude toward Him, so lift up your praise as an offering to Him.

✂ **PSALM 100**

DAY 7: Nutella Coffee

If you ask me, Nutella makes a great addition to just about anything, but the simplicity of this coffee is downright heavenly. A dear friend of ours is a talented chef who first mixed Nutella into my coffee years ago. Now it's something I make myself as a special treat on chilly afternoons that mandate a warm beverage, something to cozy up with when you're stuck inside. This recipe can be easily batched to serve a crowd, but don't skip the whipped cream if you really want a crowd pleaser; just a little on top makes for a seriously decadent treat. (For my favorite homemade whipped cream, see the recipe for Strawberry Shortcakes, p. 142.)

....

NUTELLA COFFEE

Serves 1

12 ounces strong brewed coffee

3 tablespoons chocolate hazelnut spread (like Nutella)

Whipped cream (optional)

Add the hazelnut spread to the coffee in a large liquid measuring cup or oversize mug, and use a milk frother or small whisk to stir it in until all the chocolate has melted and is smoothly combined. Top with a dollop of whipped cream and enjoy!

DAY 8: Remembering the Good Parts

Years ago, a friend asked if I would make her wedding cake. Honored by her request, I instantly said yes and began planning and prepping for the big day. The evening before the wedding, I fussed over the cake for hours, frosting and piping, adding little garnishes to what I had wrongfully assumed would be a simple design. If it could go wrong, it did, and after hours of stressing over the cake's obvious imperfections and shortcomings, I swore I'd never make a wedding cake again.

The bride didn't notice whatever imperfections had kept me up the night before and ended up loving her cake. Before long, another friend asked me to make a cake for her occasion . . . and then another, and another, and another. Each time, the joy of being able to create something for a friend's big day was so compelling that I completely forgot how agonizing the process was. Instead, the gift of being included made everything else a distant, forgotten memory.

Just as my friends overwhelmed my stressed-out memories with their gratitude and love, I believe God wants to overwhelm some of the hard parts of your life with love too. He can use every bit of your life, even the seasons marked by anxiety, fear, or loneliness, and if you'll allow Him to show you His grace in those moments, He will. He has never abandoned you, never left you to fight your battles alone, and has a purpose for every circumstance you find yourself in.

Today, instead of fixating on the imperfections, past failures, or challenges ahead, ask God to use those parts of your life for His glory. Seek His face even in the midst of trial, and watch how it transforms the atmosphere of your mind and heart. The goodness of God far outweighs the brokenness of your circumstances, so press in to His peace and rest there.

 **JOHN 16:16-24**

DAY 9: Eating Slower

My mom tells me that when I was a little girl, I would beg her to take me to Mc-Donald's for, I don't know, basically every meal. On the days she refused, I'd pout and tell her I was going to work there someday, so I could get a Happy Meal whenever I wanted. Truth be told, I still get the occasional hankering for a Big Mac and a Diet Coke, but grown-up Kate is no longer looking for excuses for fast food—I'm looking for reasons to slow down.

So much of our lives is built to be performed on the fly. We have fast food, packaged snacks, and meal-delivery services that will bring us anything we want at any given moment. All of these amenities make life convenient, but is this way of life really nourishing us? Is it feeding our hearts and minds and spirits with the rest and connection we need most?

Having lunch at my desk may allow me to work longer, but it won't refresh my soul. Eating breakfast in the car might offer me a few extra minutes of sleep, but it won't provide the connection I find at the table with my family. After years of rushing from one thing to the next, I'm working on slowing down long enough for the transforming work of the Holy Spirit to take root in my life and to have meaningful impact on my heart and relationships.

Take some time for reflection. Are there opportunities in your day to create a slower pace in your life? To cook a meal with your family, to linger over a plate of waffles, or make a pot of coffee to share with a friend? God is in the minutes we carve out to nourish our bodies and hearts in meaningful ways, so ask Him to slow you down, and offer up those meals as moments for Him to do transforming work in your life and relationships.

 **MATTHEW 11:28-30**

DAY 10: Mothering

There's a reason I drink wine. It's the same reason I go for walks, listen to my favorite records on repeat, and hide little containers of homemade ice cream in the back of the freezer.

Kids. The reason is kids.

Let me be clear: mothering is the honor of my life. I wouldn't trade it for all the perfect hair and front-row tickets to *Hamilton* this world has to offer, but this work we do, mothers—this beautiful, insanity-inducing joy of our lives—is quite often a literal and proverbial poop show, and guess who gets the backstage pass to the whole thing?

Yup—it's the same person who moonlights as a chauffeur and clips microscopic toenails. It's the gal who loses her last French fry to a sassy teenager and who sorts through the trash to find shoes that the toddler "hid" in there. Mothering is a 24/7 job with seriously low pay, and if you're as close to losing your mind as I am at times, let this be a message of solidarity: you are not alone.

If you have children growing up in your home or within your reach, know that, as a woman, you are uniquely qualified to teach and nurture them in powerful ways. Just as God brought them into your life, He will equip you to do the eternal, life-giving work that is motherhood. When the menial tasks and dirty work of parenting feel fruitless, know that your kids are watching you, observing how you move in grace and perseverance, and that your love will mean something someday. Today, instead of becoming overwhelmed by the work in front of you, let it be a gesture of love that points them to Jesus.

 **DEUTERONOMY 4:9; 6:6-9**

DAY 11: Call Out the Wonderful

My kids love to hear about our lives when they were younger. I once told George he was by far my snuggliest baby, and it delighted him to no end. This kid could be the poster child for physical touch as a love language, and those words threw gasoline on an already blazing flame of affection. Now, over a year later, he still regularly perches himself on my lap, looks up at me with eyes glittering with anticipation, and asks me which baby gives me the best snuggles. It's as if he wants to know that he's set apart, that there's a special spot on my lap and in my heart reserved only for him.

Heartwarming and hormonal mommy feelings aside, I think we all want to know what our role is, where we're loved, and where we're known. When we wonder whether our life has actually made a difference in the world, we want someone we love to fly a banner over us that reads, "*I see you! You are amazing!*" George doesn't really care if he's the best snuggler—he just wants to know that his uniqueness is noticed. He wants to know that his presence makes a difference.

Let's start calling out the wonderful in others. Tell them what they mean to you or what special part of your heart is reserved just for them. Jesus told Peter he was a rock for the church, and he went on to shepherd thousands of the very first Christians. Just imagine what a difference your words can make in the lives of the people around you today. Ask God to season your language with love and encouragement, and share His heart today with the people around you freely.

 **PROVERBS 18:20–21**

DAY 12: Leftovers

On days when I'm testing recipes for my blog, I often send finished treats for friends and neighbors to enjoy. After the best of what I have to offer has been given away, the leftovers are stored in the freezer for my husband: broken cookies, half-eaten slices of pie, and melty containers of ice cream.

He doesn't mind the leftover desserts, but I'm often troubled by the other remnants I toss his way: the leftover time, the leftover words, the leftover bits of anger and frustration and tears when my day hasn't gone as I'd hoped it would. While my best efforts are siphoned off by my kids, my work, and my home, my husband is often left with whatever I can muster at the end of the day. In those exhausted, harried moments, we do our best to extend grace to one another, offering compassion and love even when we know that we might not be able to give each other our best that day.

Thankfully, God isn't offended by our leftovers. He doesn't heap us with shame when we miss a quiet time or guilt us when we forget to pray; instead, when we offer our affection to Him, presenting Him the best of our hearts on that day, He readily fills us back up. We're never left depleted when we rely on Him as our bread of life, because His return of love satiates our deepest needs (John 6:35).

Are you giving God the best you have to offer? If not, know there's no shame, only opportunity. True relationship with Jesus is an overflowing cup of blessing and grace that will never leave you dry. Give Him a few minutes of your heart today, and ask Him to fill you up for all you'll encounter.

 **PROVERBS 3:9–10**

DAY 13: Perfecting Recipes

There's a bakery in Birmingham, Alabama, that sells incredible homemade breads. I discovered their cinnamon swirl bread in the earlier part of my first pregnancy and loved it so much that I spent my second and third trimesters trying to replicate the recipe at home. I must have made thirty loaves of bread, tweaking the recipe each time to make the filling a little sweeter, the insides a little softer, the crust a bit more flaky. Finally, weeks before my little one, Aimee, arrived, my cinnamon bread did too, and I stockpiled loaves in my freezer to enjoy or share in the coming months. The dedication of those months of baking had finally paid off.

Most of the things we come to treasure in this life are planted in seasons of longing and matured in perseverance. By testing and retesting, tweaking and changing and growing, we're not just inching closer to our goals—we're developing resilience, a steadfastness that bolsters our hope and makes us even more assured of those desires within our heart.

Some of life's most delightful rewards come with perseverance, so if you, like me, sometimes need a reminder to keep going, here it is. Whatever you're facing today, whether it is a challenge, an end goal, or a million question marks, God will equip you to take it on. Are there circumstances in your life that require your endurance? He has invited you to participate in the work He is doing in your life by persevering, so don't let discouragement diminish how far you've come or take you out of the race. Instead, press on toward the promises, the dreams and desires of your heart, and ask God to partner with you to see it through to the end.

 **ROMANS 5:3-5**

DAY 14: Cinnamon Bread

Cinnamon bread is the ultimate comfort food in our house. I can barely pull it from the oven before the kids are picking sugary pieces from the top and licking up melty bits of cinnamon filling that have dribbled out the sides. The recipe requires a bit of effort, but the reward of two buttery, tender loaves makes the effort more than worth it.

....

CINNAMON BREAD

Makes 2 loaves

DOUGH

3/4 cup whole milk

2 large eggs plus 1 large egg yolk

1 teaspoon vanilla extract

1/2 cup granulated sugar

1 tablespoon instant yeast

3/4 teaspoon table salt

31/4 cups all-purpose flour,
  plus more for rolling

1/2 cup plus 2 tablespoons unsalted butter,
  at room temperature

FILLING

1/2 cup unsalted butter, melted
  and slightly cooled

1 cup packed brown sugar

6 tablespoons granulated sugar

2 tablespoons cinnamon

Pinch of table salt

TO PREPARE THE DOUGH

In the bowl of a stand mixer, stir with a spoon the milk, eggs, egg yolk, and vanilla. Add the sugar, yeast, and salt, and stir to combine. On low speed with the paddle attachment, add the flour, 1/2 cup at a time, scraping the sides of the bowl as needed. Increase to medium speed and begin adding the softened butter 1 tablespoon at a time. Scrape the sides of the bowl and continue beating for an additional 4 minutes. The dough will be soft and slightly sticky. Lightly grease a large bowl with baking spray, place the dough in it, and cover it tightly with plastic wrap. Allow the dough to rest in a warm spot until it has approximately doubled in size, about 1½ to 2 hours. Once the dough has nearly doubled in size, prepare the filling.

TO PREPARE THE FILLING

In a medium bowl, stir to combine the butter, brown sugar, granulated sugar, cinnamon, and salt and set aside. You will use about ½ cup of filling for each loaf.

TO PREPARE THE LOAVES

Once the dough has doubled in size, lightly grease two 8½ × 4½ × 2¾-inch loaf pans with baking spray. Generously flour your work surface and rolling pin. Flour your fist and gently punch the dough down into the bowl once, dividing it in half. Lay half of the dough on the floured surface. Generously dust the top of the dough with flour as well. Using a rolling pin, roll the first piece of dough as evenly as possible into a 13 × 16-inch rectangle. You may need to reflour the work surface if the dough begins to stick. Spread half of the filling on top of the dough, leaving a 1-inch border around the perimeter.

Standing with one of the short edges closest to you, begin to tightly roll the dough away from you, forming a 13-inch log of dough. Gently pinch the dough together at the seam to seal the filling inside the roll. With the seam facing down, use a sharp chef's knife to cut the dough log in half lengthwise, facing the insides of the roll up. Quickly twist the two pieces of dough around each other, and fit the braided loaf in one of the prepared pans. Repeat the process with the remaining half of the dough. Once both loaves have been formed, cover them again with plastic wrap and allow them to rise again for about 1½ to 2 hours. The dough should rise about ½ to 1 inch over the top of the pans. Do not let them overrise.

When the dough is nearly risen, preheat the oven to 350ºF. Bake the loaves for about 40 minutes, or until the internal temperature registers 180ºF. If you notice the tops of the loaves beginning to look too dark before they're done, you can cover them with a loose sheet of aluminum foil. Allow the loaves to cool in the pans on a cooling rack for about 20 minutes, and then remove them from the pans to cool completely.

DAY 15: Enough as You Are

Have you seen all the memes on social media about the overachieving moms? They basically poke fun at the women who take on intense Pinterest-style crafts, made-from-scratch baby food, hyperorganized home rituals, and so on. The jokes are intended to jab at those with supermom tendencies and infer that they're just *really* being a bit too much.

I want to let you know that it's okay to be exactly who you are right now. If you're struggling at home—maybe buried under schoolwork, stressed out from your job, feeling lonely, or slowly going insane with a handful of kids—it's okay. You can be exactly who you are in this season and come into your role as wife, mom, or friend in your own way.

On the other hand, if there is grace in this season of your life to create and play and achieve and thrive, you can embrace that too. You don't need to make yourself smaller because an internet full of memes is telling you your personality or abilities are too big. You be you. We all have grace in our lives for different seasons and settings, and it's okay to flourish in some and be struggling in others. Give yourself some space. Also make room for your friends and the people you rub shoulders with on social media to be exactly who they are, and remember to be kind—to others and especially to yourself. You're enough exactly how you are.

We all have our own special abilities, and God has asked us to use them, in all their strengths and imperfections, to the glory of His name. Set your heart on doing everything—mothering, working, growing, and more—to the best of the ability that He has put inside you, and remember there's grace wherever you find yourself.

 **1 PETER 4:10–11**

DAY 16: **Showing Up**

There are moments in life when words feel inadequate: a death, a diagnosis, a crushing disappointment or loss. Learning how to grieve with another, to press in to our own discomfort and love people through their pain, often feels so impossible. In those moments, I find myself wanting to look the other way to skirt the pain. *What if I say the wrong thing? What if my words make it worse? Maybe I shouldn't say anything at all.*

In those moments, I need the reminder that words usually *aren't* enough. People don't need another Hallmark card one-liner to make it through the impossible—they need love. Sometimes, all you can do is just show up and allow your heart to break with theirs, and that act of being present, both physically and emotionally, is love. Sometimes God allows us to participate in the healing by being conduits of love for Him.

Don't let fear paralyze you from showing up. As believers, we carry a light and a hope that there aren't words for, and your presence and love are the best things you can offer. If you're grieving with a friend in this season of life, ask God how you can best show up for them. We are His hands and feet, and if you ask Him, He'll show you how He wants you to use them.

 **MATTHEW 5:1–12**

DAY 17: Memorable Meals

If tonight's dinner was destined to be my last meal, I would request a giant plate of my mom's baked spaghetti. It's nothing fancy—just noodles, sauce, and a blanket of mozzarella and Parmesan, but no matter how many times I try to recreate the dish in my own kitchen, it's just never quite the same. Over time, I've begun to realize that it's not the recipe itself that I'm so fond of—it's the way that meal brings me back to my childhood, to the warmth and love I felt at my family's table.

For many of us, food is a uniting thing, one of those tangible ways in which we engage and share love with the people around us. Although the flavors and textures often do make a difference, the love within those relationships usually ends up being the thing that feeds people the most. Eating my mom's spaghetti brings forth nostalgic memories of home and the ways I felt loved and nurtured around her table, and my guess is that you have memories like that too.

Who are the people moving through the food memories of your past and the ones you're currently making? I encourage you to use meals, whether it's baked spaghetti, take-out pizza, or a special homemade recipe of your own, to love the people in your circle. The table offers you an opportunity to nourish people with love, connection, and time spent together. Welcome Jesus into that space, and ask Him to show you how you can become a person who serves love.

 **1 PETER 4:8-9**

DAY 18: On God's Time

I've been in a phase of waiting for most of my life: waiting to get my driver's license, waiting for college, waiting for graduation; waiting to find love or have kids or become financially stable. In a way, it's as if I was crossing off requirements on a self-imposed scorecard of milestones and achievements that absolutely no one was demanding of me. I took pleasure in checking each box, but I was constantly rushing to the next thing, always evaluating my pace in comparison to those of the people around me.

I've heard people say that life is what happens while we wait for the next big thing, and I'm finding that to be true. In fact, many of the times in my life when I experienced great personal growth were those seasons when I felt as though I was actually *behind*. Whether I was watching friends get married while my relationships fell apart or colleagues get recognition while I struggled to keep it together, I see now that God used those painful moments as opportunities for growth. In retrospect, the periods of life in which I felt lonely, disconnected, or left behind were always ones that stretched me and prepared me for more, because God shared His strength with me and I came out all the better for it.

Although I still tend to rush from one phase of life just to get to the next, He's teaching me how to live expectantly right where I am. Today, let the same be true for you. Press in for more of Him wherever you find yourself. The rush of life and that next big achievement can wait, but His presence is always on time.

 **PSALM 27, ESPECIALLY VV. 13–14**

DAY 19: Following Directions

I grew up in the era of Food Network, during the rise of celebrity chefs and TV food personalities. During college, I'd skip class to watch Ina Garten prepare a Sunday brunch in the Hamptons or to see if Rachel Ray could *really* eat through Italy on less than forty dollars a day. One semester, I watched an entire season of *Cake Boss* and was convinced I had garnered enough know-how to make my own homemade fondant. What started as a hopeful attempt ended with me sitting on my mom's kitchen floor, covered in powdered sugar, corn syrup, and tears. Turns out I'd skipped some of the directions and, in the process, completely blown the recipe.

Directions are good, particularly when it comes to recipes, road trips, and things like IKEA furniture, but some of us still get caught trying to do things our own way. Consider the story of Jonah, the guy who was sent to Nineveh on a mission from God but decided to do things his own way instead. Although it's unlikely that our failure to follow directions will find us, like Jonah, inside the stomach of a whale, there's no denying that God's way is still the best choice for our lives, always.

Are there areas of your life where you've been running from God or trying to do things on your own? God loves His children to partner with Him to achieve His purposes in life. He doesn't give directions or commands because He likes to see us work, but because He knows what we need in every circumstance (Matt. 6:8). DIY projects are fun, but working alongside God is where you'll find the love, purpose, and fulfillment your heart desires. Today, consider where you can partner with Him to pursue the hopes and dreams of your heart, and listen in closely when He gives you directions—they're always there for a reason.

 **ISAIAH 55:8-9**

DAY 20: Comfort Foods

When winter rolls around, I tend to rely on comfort-food recipes that warm from the inside out: a tender roast, a hearty soup, or any other rich, savory bowlful of deliciousness. In colder months, few things satiate my belly like the robust yet soothing flavors of those slow-cooked meals.

In the same way, I know a lot of people who are like comfort food to me. Relationship with them is nourishing and life-giving, because they show up with authenticity and love every time. Conversation with them has depth, and the words they say carry weight because each one is sincere and thought through. There's a simplicity in how I'm welcomed into their homes and conversations, because they're not there to dazzle or put on a show—they're just there to love. Looking back, I can now see that their love for me came from the overflow of their affection for Jesus; it was His presence in their lives that made the difference.

There's a comforting peace that comes from spending time with the Lord, and I'd like more of that for myself. Rather than some flash-fried version of Christianity, I want the simmer of a rich and steady relationship with Jesus that softens and saturates my soul. Today, ask God to begin transforming your heart into one that is nourishing and comforting to others. Soak up His goodness, soften to His direction, and let the overflow of that relationship be a sweet aroma to the world around you.

 **2 CORINTHIANS 2:14-17**

DAY 21: Simple Pesto Risotto

Risotto is one of those intensely comforting dishes that many people shy away from, because they believe it's more difficult than it actually is. I'm here to tell you *you can do this*. This simple risotto makes a terrific side option for all sorts of proteins (try it with Balsamic Grilled Chicken, p. 225), or Blackened Snapper, p. 210), or you can also bolster the dish with extra cheese and your favorite roasted vegetables to make it an entrée.

....

SIMPLE PESTO RISOTTO

Serves 4 as a side

¼ cup unsalted butter, divided

1 small sweet onion, diced (about ½ cup)

2 cloves garlic, minced

¼ teaspoon black pepper

1 cup Arborio rice

3¼ cups chicken or vegetable
    stock, divided

¼ cup dry white wine
    (or additional chicken stock)

6 tablespoons fresh grated
    Parmesan cheese

3 tablespoons prepared basil pesto

Table salt and additional pepper to taste

Preheat the oven to 375°F. In a 4-quart Dutch oven-safe saucepan with a lid, melt 2 tablespoons butter over medium heat. Add the onion and cook, stirring occasionally, until softened and translucent, about 3 minutes. Add the garlic and stir until fragrant, about 1 minute. Stir the pepper, rice, and 3 cups stock into the pan. Cover the pot with the lid and place it in the oven for about 25 to 30 minutes. Carefully take a test bite of the risotto to see if it is al dente—it should be soft to the tooth with zero crunch or sogginess. If done, add the remaining chicken stock, wine, remaining butter, Parmesan cheese, and basil pesto. Stir for a few minutes until the butter and cheese have melted, and add salt and pepper to taste. *Buon appetito!*

DAY 22: Being a Cheerleader

For much of my adolescence, I saw other people through the lens of my own self-doubt. It was so easy for me to admire the talent, beauty, and success I saw in others, but I found it harder to appreciate those same qualities in myself. Those years were heavy with jealousy and shame, and although they were painful to my own heart, the thing that disappoints me most is that I missed opportunities to whole-heartedly celebrate the people I loved.

When we encourage others as they pursue their ambitions, we become invested in their success. It's like being a coach or benchwarmer on a championship team—even if we're not the one scoring the goals, we still get to partake of the victory. If we allow our own insecurity or jealousy to prevent us from cheering on the sidelines, we'll miss out on the joy and camaraderie that comes with the process. Fortunately, we do not need others around us to fail so that we can succeed at our own dreams. We can partner with our peers to help them realize their own ambitions while simultaneously pursuing our own, because, truly, there is enough blessing and success to go around—especially when it comes to God's kingdom.

Take time to check in with your heart this morning. Has fear or insecurity whispered lies to you about who you are or what you are capable of? Have those voices caused you to remain silent or resentful on the sidelines of someone else's story? Submit those feelings to the Lord and remember there is more opportunity for victory, both personal and shared, when we partner with one another in the pursuit of our ambitions. Be proud of God's work in your life, and use His voice of love to encourage others.

 **MARK 9:35; GALATIANS 5:13–15**

DAY 23: Every Morning

Every few weeks or so I have one of those days when I get out of bed anxious about the day ahead of me. When there's too much to do, when I'm dreading a task, or when a relationship in my life is struggling, sometimes it's all I can do to wake up and face it again. In those messy, challenging minutes of everyday life, I'm encouraged to remember this promise from scripture: His mercies never come to an end; they are new every morning.

When you have to clean up yesterday's mistakes...

His mercies are new every morning.

When another sleepless night leaves you running on coffee and two hours of sleep...

His mercies are new every morning.

When it's time to clear the air and address the conflict that's been looming for days...

His mercies are new every morning.

When the work is piling up...

His mercies are new every morning.

When discouragement reminds you of the loss you're facing...

His mercies are new every morning.

When you're fighting the same senseless battle again...

His mercies are new every morning.

When you're starting back at square one...

His mercies are new every morning.

Taking comfort in this promise from God's Word reminds me that I'm not alone in my struggles. God isn't frustrated when we approach Him with needs again and again, and He certainly isn't running low on kindness. Instead, His mercy is fresh and alive, appropriate for every circumstance you'll face today, tomorrow, and until the end of time. Call out to Him today—He is faithful and equipped with new mercy just for you.

LAMENTATIONS 3:22-24

DAY 24: Keep Sowing

My mother insisted I take piano lessons as a kid, so for two years I fumbled through elementary renditions of "Für Elise" and "Silent Night" until my fingers cooperated. Eventually I quit, until just last January when I inherited that old piano and began taking lessons again for the first time in twenty years. Within weeks, I was playing old familiar tunes, revisiting the notes my fingers had memorized all those years ago. It was surprising to find that there were parts of my childhood lessons that had stuck despite years of no practice and that with a few attempts those skills came back to me as if no time had passed at all.

The same is true in other areas of our lives. Many of the seeds we plant in our own life or the lives around us, whether skills, wisdom, love, or even habits, will take root at some point. Although we don't always see immediate fruit, we can plant them anyway, knowing that God is able to use those actions in big and powerful ways. Ephesians 3:20–21 says He has the power to do exceedingly more with our offerings than we could ever imagine, so I have to believe that if I sow seeds, He has the power to make them grow.

If there are relationships or areas of your life where you've been sowing seeds for years with no sign of fruit, this is a message of hope: keep going. You never know when those skills, prayers, or acts of kindness will take root. Pray and love and serve in whatever capacity the Lord calls you to, knowing that He can do marvelous things with offerings made in His name.

 **LUKE 8:4–15**

One Piece at a Time

Winter is my favorite time for puzzles. If I find myself on a Sunday afternoon with napping children or a quiet home, I occasionally make a pot of coffee and spend a few hours poring over a puzzle, using the colors to help me fit the pieces together one by one. Early on, my table is overwhelmed with little piles of chaos for me to make sense of, but as the day goes on, the picture becomes clearer and better defined, and I'm able to work through small sections one at a time until the puzzle is complete.

Quite often, life feels rather scattered, with its own kinds of bits and pieces. Without order or some idea of what the end product should look like, it can feel overwhelming to try to make sense of the piles of chaos that lie before you. The poet William Wordsworth famously wrote, "To begin, begin," meaning there won't always be a clear starting point, but you can still make that first step and take on the mess piece by piece. We begin simply by biting off small sections and piecing together what we can until that confusing pile has dwindled and turned into a finished shape.

Are there things in your life that feel overwhelming or difficult to make sense of? Maybe you're facing a problem or task that seems too big to accomplish? Thankfully, you don't have to have all the answers to begin picking up the small bits and connecting them one at a time. God is the One holding the box—He knows what the final outcome looks like and is delighted when you invite Him to join you at the table. Ask Him to partner with you, and He will make a finished work out of any mess you face today.

JOHN 16:33

DAY 26: Really Good Gifts

When I tuck my children in at night, they love to stall bedtime by negotiating the following day's breakfast: "Can it be doughnuts, Mom? How about eggs and biscuits? Oh, and chocolate milk!" They're like me in that way—always looking ahead for what's next, always eager for a good meal. Can you blame them?

I love the idea that God prepares things for us that will exceed our expectations. He gives really, really good gifts. While I'm busy worrying about tomorrow's breakfast or finishing that last load of laundry, He is actively at work on my behalf, conjuring up possibilities and blessings far greater than what I can dream up for myself. The older I get, the more I realize how fun our God is: He never stops connecting our loose ends and dotting our stories with little happies along the way.

I believe God takes care of us in those small ways, because He wants us to experience His love on a grand scale. He exceeds our expectations by showering us with a love that is wider and deeper and higher than our arms and minds can reach or understand. Are you expecting something from the Lord today? You should—if you look for His goodness in your life, you definitely won't miss it. Ask for a fresh show of His glory and prepare your heart for an awakening of His love in the coming days.

 **LUKE 11:9–13**

DAY 27: Love in the Time of Grief

We started praying for her as soon as we learned of the diagnosis. The cancer was progressing, but she was young, a new mother with her whole life ahead of her, and we were confident that, with prayer and treatment, all would return to normal. She was a friend of a friend, a woman I'd only met twice, but her story felt so close, so seemingly attached to mine, that I couldn't help but become deeply invested. Less than a year later, I walked into her best friend's home with a pot of beef bourguignon and a sympathy card. I was awkward and unexperienced with death, but when there aren't words, there are tangibles, things like hugs and tears and cards and food, the kind of gestures that let people know they're not alone.

Loving people through their grief is hard. Most of the time, I'm tempted to shy away from it, to step back and allow someone closer or wiser to fill in the blanks for the rest of us, but when grief shows up at your back door, you can't run or look the other way as it shatters the hope and hearts of the people around you. Your only choice is to show up, in all your awkwardness and insecurity and fear, and to wrap your arms around the brokenness that's right in front of you.

The Bible says, *The Lord is near to the brokenhearted* (Ps. 34:18), and I think that's our calling too. Attach yourself to the people you love with invisible strings of prayer and love and support, so that when tragedy rolls in to sweep away the peace and certainties of their story, they can remain connected to a lifeline. You might not have the words, but you can still show up and be a source of hope in the midst of grief. Are there people who need your love and support today? Be the one, be the set of hands and feet, to carry Jesus's love and walk in His truth.

 **PSALM 46:1–3**

DAY 28: Beef Bourguignon

Ina Garten's beef bourguignon is the near perfect dish I love to share when the times call for comfort food. Her recipe is flawless as is, but this is the version I lean on in my own home. The simplified steps and ingredients make preparation less time-consuming, and fewer onions and mushrooms make this a favorite for meat lovers like my husband. Give this Beef Bourguignon a try on winter days or when you need a meal that feels like a hug—this one will do just that.

....

BEEF BOURGUIGNON

Serves 6

2 tablespoons olive oil

3 pounds boneless beef chuck roast,
    cut into 1^1/$_2$-inch cubes

1^1/$_2$ tsp salt

1 tsp pepper

2 large yellow onions, chopped
    (about 2^1/$_4$ cups)

1 pound peeled carrots, cut into
    1-inch pieces (about 2^1/$_2$ cups)

6 tablespoons unsalted butter,
    at room temperature, divided

2 teaspoons minced garlic

1 (750 mL) bottle dry red wine
    (such as Cabernet Sauvignon,
    Pinot Noir, or Merlot)

1 tablespoon tomato paste

1 to 2 cups beef broth

8 ounces sliced white mushrooms

3 tablespoons all-purpose flour

3 tablespoons fresh parsley,
    finely chopped

Preheat the oven to 250ºF. In a large Dutch oven, heat the olive oil on medium-high. Season the beef cubes with 1^1/$_2$ teaspoons salt and 1 teaspoon pepper. Cook the beef in two batches, stirring occasionally, until browned on all sides, about 6 minutes per batch. Once browned, use a slotted spoon to remove the beef from the pan to a bowl.

Add the onions, carrots, and 2 tablespoons butter to the pan and cook for about 10 minutes, stirring often, until the onions are softened and translucent. Stir in the garlic and cook for an additional minute. Add the red wine and stir, scraping up the browned bits on the bottom of the pan. Add the meat back to the pan along with the tomato paste and just enough beef broth to almost cover the meat (I usually add 1 cup). Put the lid on the pot and place it in the middle of the preheated oven to cook until the meat is tender, about 1½ hours.

Just before the stew is finished cooking, melt 2 tablespoons butter in a sauté pan on medium heat and cook the mushrooms, stirring frequently until lightly browned. In a small bowl, use the back of a fork to cut the remaining 2 tablespoons butter into the flour. Once the beef is tender (be careful while taste testing!), stir the flour mixture and mushrooms into the pot and then cook on low for about 10 to 15 minutes, or until barely thickened. Stir in the parsley as well as additional salt and pepper to taste.

DAY 29: Taking a Breather

For most of my life, I was an extrovert. Social gatherings, attention, and quick conversation fed me like an addict. The more I got, the more I wanted, so I said yes to every outing, every party, every opportunity for more.

Later in life, that part of me shifted. Marriage, motherhood, and adult relationships found me as a different person, one who was more comfortable with solitude and in desperate need of the quietness my new life with busy toddlers was lacking. For a while, I considered it nothing more than a funk—*Why wasn't I ready for as much fun and adventure as I used to be?* But when I finally offered myself the freedom to be who I needed to be in that season, I began to rest confidently in my identity and what I had to offer as an individual.

There are seasons of life where you just need a breather. You don't have to be who you were last year, last month, or even last week, if that's not who you are right now. It's perfectly acceptable to take a step back and care for yourself, and knowing when you need a breather from rigorous relationships and social activity can be really healing.

Pray and assess where you are right now. What is on your plate and how much of it are you able to manage? Is this a season where you need to do less in order to be more? Today, ask the Holy Spirit to reveal some areas where you may need to reallocate your energy and resources, and know there's no shame if a change is needed. Instead, let Him guide who you are in this season.

 **ECCLESIASTES 3:1–15**

DAY 30: When the Brook Runs Dry

Last year, my parents moved out of their home of twenty-one years. It was strange to watch them consolidate decades' worth of memories into corrugated boxes, as if that whole season of their existence could be stuffed into a single truck. But when the time came for them to close on the house and say goodbye to the neighborhood, there was almost a sense of relief. It was a great home, one that had welcomed new babies, countless birthdays, and a million other big life milestones, but although God had provided for that season, it was time for something new.

Saying goodbye is rarely easy, but God doesn't always intend for us to stay in one place. Often, He gives us homes, jobs, and even friendships intended to serve us for a time until He's prepared something new. A story in the Bible describes a time that the Lord provided for Elijah during a season of drought. He offered him a brook with water to drink and even commanded a flock of ravens to bring him meat and bread for food. But one day, the brook dried up. With that, Elijah knew it was time to move on, and he looked to God to show him where.

If you're in a dry-brook kind of season, know that God still has more for you. His promises and provision never dry up, and if the curtain is closing on this phase of life, you can be confident He has something special in store. Instead of moving us backward, God always draws us forward, closer to Him, closer to eternity, closer to the beautiful abundance He has waiting for us. Whether you're saying hello to a fresh season or bidding adieu to an old one, look to the Lord for the guidance and provision He has promised you.

 **1 KINGS 17:1–7**

DAY 31: Sons and Daughters

Last year, our dear friends adopted the son they had fostered since birth. The ceremony was more of a technicality, a dotting of i's and crossing of t's, because he had been a part of the family for years. A party was organized for after the ceremony complete with balloons and banners and sprinkle cupcakes to celebrate the occasion—a day that changed their lives and future forever.

Although I regard myself as a daughter of God, I often forget that I got there by adoption. We are all separated from God by sin, bound to our lengthy list of insufficiencies, until the day we are rescued by the blood of Christ. I like to think that, in that moment when a human goes from sinner to daughter or son, there's got to be an epic party happening in heaven. Just as we huddled in my friends' house, ready to explode with joy and photos and hugs at their arrival home with their son, all of heaven is holding its breath, waiting to welcome in the new brother or sister. God loved us like children long before we ever welcomed Him in, but on that day it was official, signed in crimson ink. We are His and He is ours, forever.

Let this sink in: you are a child of God. Your identity is no longer "sinner"—just "daughter." Spend time in thankfulness this morning and praise Him for this gift of adoption into the family of God. Doesn't it make your heart glad to know you are a part of a beautiful, holy family? Let that reality bless you today.

 **GALATIANS 4:4–7**

DAY 1: A Good Measure

It wasn't unusual for Jesus to speak in parables, those stories that spoke to deeper truths. He knew that the best way to speak to our hearts was to relate to the concerns of our daily life—our stomachs, our workplaces, and our pocketbooks.

Luke is full of great parables, but one of my favorites is in 6:38: *Give, and it will be given to you. Good measure, pressed down, shaken together, running over, will be poured into your lap. For with the measure you use it will be measured back to you.* Here Jesus is instructing the disciples not to concern themselves with judgment or condemnation of others, but, instead, to offer forgiveness and goodwill to the people around them. He uses the measuring cup as an example, illustrating that God's return for such benevolence is generous and full to the point overflowing, a packed measuring cup that spills over. This is no ounce-for-ounce reward—it is rich blessing in return for our smaller contribution.

I don't know about you, but I like the sound of God's measuring system. I'm all for a Father who takes pleasure in exchanging our meager, human offerings for an overflowing helping of His goodness. Take time to consider how you can love people with Jesus-size spoonfuls of kindness, forgiveness, and grace, and don't hold back. As believers, we can share all we have freely, because God always returns our offerings with abundance.

 **LUKE 6:27–38**

DAY 2: Making Sense of Disorder

I have a fabulously organized spice cabinet that my kids like to make look like a junk drawer. They rifle through the jars and bottles and bags, picking up the familiar containers for a shake or a sniff. They think cumin smells like tacos and cinnamon smells like their morning toast. Bay leaves and star anise elicit a string of questions, and sprinkles of kosher salt end up, well, everywhere. I love that they're interested in food, particularly since it's such a big part of my life, but for a type A woman with a passion for order, this disassembling of my orderly spices is a constant test of my patience. I'm told this is a common theme in parenting, so please—pray for me!

I'm finding that the sooner we get comfortable with our own discomfort, the better. If not kids, it will be spouses or coworkers, pets or pandemics that wreak havoc in our lives. There will forever be moments of disassembly, instances when our work, our plans, and our preferences get jostled around and thrown into disorder, and although this reality of life is inconvenient, it's a reminder to me that the only sure thing I've got is Jesus.

Have you found yourself in the midst of messy circumstances, trying to make sense of the disorder? Maybe you've been burdened with broken plans, a disappointing loss, or an unexpected season of unknown? Cling to Jesus. Hope in the steadfast love of God that has promised to never leave or forsake you (Deut. 31:6). He alone can make sense of our shuffled plans and purposes, so take comfort in knowing that you can lay them at His feet today.

 **PROVERBS 19:21–23; ISAIAH 54:10**

DAY 3: Bread of Life

On some days, particularly during these frigid winter months, a craving will strike for a taste of something warm and comforting. You know the feeling, right? In those moments when we're starved for a meal that is rich and nourishing, nothing else will truly satisfy.

There are other kinds of cravings too. As humans, we were all created with desires that can only be satiated by the love of God, but somehow we often settle, stuffing our mind, body, and heart with temporary things that won't meet those needs. The world's offerings of love, connection, and joy aren't sufficient to meet the deep needs of our soul, and if we attempt to satisfy those longings on our own, we'll remain forever starved for something more. Jesus called Himself the Bread of Life because He knew that feasting on things from heaven was the only way we'd experience meaningful satisfaction, and His gift to us, as believers, is to fill and nourish our souls with His everlasting goodness. Praise the Lord!

Are there places in your life that need nourishment? Any areas that are craving the rich heart-filling that comes from time spent with Him? If you find yourself trying to fulfill your desire for authentic love with things that won't satisfy, know that Christ is always available, ready and waiting to meet that innermost need. Today, take time to fill up on the ultimate comfort food: the Bread of Life.

 **JOHN 6:26–40**

DAY 4: Southern Cheese Grits

Cheese grits might be the best-kept comfort food secret of the South. Truly, you haven't lived until you've had *really* good old-fashioned grits. I love to serve Southern Cheese Grits as a starchy side for hearty dinners, but you can also make these into a meal by topping them with roasted veggies, legumes, or hearty meat.

....

SOUTHERN CHEESE GRITS

Serves 6 as a side

4 cups water

½ teaspoon kosher salt

1 cup old-fashioned corn grits

1 cup shredded cheddar cheese

3 tablespoons unsalted butter

2 to 4 tablespoons whole milk
   or half and half

Salt and pepper to taste

In a medium saucepan, bring the water and salt to a boil. Slowly pour the grits in, whisking constantly. Bring the mixture back to a boil and then reduce the heat to low. Allow the grits to simmer, stirring frequently, until they have absorbed most of the moisture and are well cooked, about 20 to 25 minutes, depending on the coarseness of the grits. Add in the cheese and butter and stir until melted and combined. Add milk or half and half until the mixture comes to your desired consistency and then adjust the salt and pepper to taste. I usually add a heaping ¼ teaspoon salt and ⅛ teaspoon pepper. Serve warm!

DAY 5: Nailing It

My kids love a show on Netflix called *Nailed It*. On the program, amateur bakers are presented with professional-level baked goods that they are to re-create in a short span of time. For thirty minutes, we watch as contestants fumble through the recipes and present finished products so terrible, so far from the original, that it's hysterical. In the end, they uncover their finished cakes and cookies, declaring a loud and sarcastic, "Nailed it!"

Some days, I feel as though I'm living an episode of this show, except instead of burned cupcakes or slouchy fondant, my imperfections show up in my attitude and words to the people around me. Sometimes, it looks like an impatient conversation with my kids, a selfish reaction to something my husband has said, or an uncomfortable interaction with a friend; sometimes it looks like obnoxiously passing a slow driver in the left lane or making a snide remark in passing to a family member. We all have these "nailed it" moments, except there are no cameras or television host, just a load of awkwardness and regret.

I think God wants to relieve us of shame and fear of embarrassment. He's seen our imperfections, a whole lifetime of them, in fact, and you know what? He's loves us all the same. Jesus came knowing we'd mess up again and again, but He still wanted union with us; He came to offer us a better way.

Where are you carrying shame or embarrassment? Are there places you feel downright uncomfortable with what you are able to do or offer? Today, ask God how He feels about your mistakes. He's not disappointed, but He does want more for you. We can look at our mistakes and failures with grace, because that's how God sees them.

 **ROMANS 5:6–8**

DAY 6: Go, Love, and Make Disciples

Early on in my Christian walk, when I was still figuring out who God was and where I fit in the equation, I made a mess of some relationships with friends by trying to push my new beliefs on them. Although my heart was in the right place, my execution was all wrong, and after some flailing attempts to introduce them to Jesus went awry, I backed away from some of those friends because we were different. How could I stay friends with people who didn't share my beliefs? Wasn't I supposed to be set apart?

Our call to "be in the world but not of the world" is an interesting challenge. Although it would be easy to take Jesus's words to mean that Christians are supposed to insulate themselves from the world within the cushy confines of churches and small groups, I believe the opposite is actually true: we're sent into the world to be carriers of light and love, exposing our surroundings to the glory of God. Sure, our home is in heaven, but so long as our location is planet Earth, our calling is to go, love, and make disciples.

Take some time for reflection: Are there people in your life who need to experience the love of God? The world is starved for the freedom, love, and grace found in Christ, and although the calling isn't always easy, it is quite clear: go, love, and make disciples. Today, thank God for the love that lives inside of you, and ask Him to show you how to offer it to the world for His glory.

 **MATTHEW 28:18–20; JOHN 17**

DAY 7: Making Room for Yes

Brett and I always wind up trying to be doers, the kind of people who can wear all the hats and handle anything. Saying no to social, volunteer, and work opportunities is a real challenge for us, because, when a good cause knocks on our front door, it's hard to say no to the need in front of us.

Our marriage counselor once told us that learning to say no is necessary, because it makes space for the yeses that are more important—yes to family, yes to real connection, yes to more of what God put on our plate. God has assigned unique gifts and purposes to each one of us. Each of our yeses (and our capacity for yeses!) will look different, but if we needlessly fill our plate with opportunities that don't align with His purposes, we may end up missing out on rewarding things He has in store for us. Ultimately, we want to be available to the calling He has on our lives, and if we've maxed out our capacity for impact on things that aren't within the range of our gifts, we're bound to miss out!

Today, remember that every good opportunity is not *your* opportunity. Even the good things—the church groups, the jobs, the charitable causes—can be distractions from what God really has in store for you. Ask God what's on your plate right now. Have you said yes to some things that are pulling you away from what He has laid out for you to receive? Has your yes meant a no to a gift that He's already called you to use? Say yes to what the Lord has in store for you, and give yourself grace when it comes to the rest.

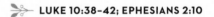 **LUKE 10:38–42; EPHESIANS 2:10**

DAY 8: Hearing in the Quiet

Saturday mornings are sacred in our house. With nowhere to be and a house full of babies, I find myself intentionally stretching out every possible moment. We linger in bed longer and get dressed a little later, allowing extra time to sip an extra cup of coffee (or two!). Monday through Friday, heck, even Sundays are often rushed with things to do and places to be, but on Saturdays we go solely at our own pace.

I think God speaks the loudest in those quiet moments. I don't always hear Him in the rush of dressing kids and stuffing lunchboxes, when I'm refreshing my email box for the millionth time or zeroing in on yet another thing I just "have" to do. Instead, I hear Him when I'm still in the warmth of my covers, when I sit still for nothing more than to linger in His presence.

Thankfully, God's ability to speak is not dependent on our ability to listen, but we may miss out on the opportunity for relationship when we fail to slow down. Take time today to quiet yourself before the Lord—maybe go for a walk, spend some time journaling, or find a quiet corner in your home. What is He saying to you? How does His presence affect your heart? Are there things you need to share with Him? God longs for intimate relationship with His children, so quiet the noise of your world and listen for the sweet things He has in store for you.

 PSALM 131

DAY 9: The Other Side of Vulnerability

It took me many years to be able to tell people what they really meant to me, because deep down I was insecure about the certainty of our friendship. *What if this relationship is one-sided? Maybe we're not as close as I think we are. What if they laugh at my affection?* I'm sure that over the years my lack of vulnerability robbed me of opportunities for relationship, but thankfully I eventually learned that the reward for putting yourself out there is worth the risk. Every once in a while you find yourself a friend.

Vulnerability is hard. So many of us live behind the closed doors of our heart, because it's less painful to ignore all the voices in our lives than it is to sort through for ones that come from love. I don't discount the painfulness of broken relationships or a hurtful word from someone who was supposed to be on your team; I've been there, and I know—it sucks. But the beauty of vulnerability is that, sometimes, our sincerity is met with the open arms of mutual desires and common ground. Your offering of a shared heart or a kind word has the potential to evolve into a genuine life-giving connection that could bless the pants off you for years to come.

As believers, we're called to be carriers of truth and love and kindness. To me, that looks a whole lot like being a friend. Ask God to show you people in your circle who could use some of that kindness, and be brave enough to open your heart to new relationships. You never know what He has waiting for you on the other side of that vulnerability, and He is honored when you're willing to use your heart and life to love people well.

 **ROMANS 12:9–21**

DAY 10: One of a Kind

If you've ever walked into a charming bakery lined with glass cases of pastries, you know: there's something delightful and exciting about the possibility of discovering the new flavors within those treats. Even when, from the outside, rows of doughnuts or layer cakes or little chocolate squares look exactly the same, each one has its own offering, a hidden, delicious surprise on the inside that sets it apart from the rest.

Today, I want to remind you that you're one of a kind. You have been fashioned with unique characteristics and ideas hidden deep within your heart that are wholly yours. Those intricacies, although different from those of others around you, are to be celebrated and enjoyed, because God intentionally fills each one of us with purpose. God knows the flavor you've got deep inside of you, and He says, "It is good."

The things that make you *you*—your physical features, your personality, the questions and dreams and cries of your heart—contain beautiful reflections of our heavenly Creator. To catch a glimpse of Him, look no farther than the mirror, because you were prepared in His image. Take time this week to celebrate His handiwork by enjoying the hopes and passions He put inside of you, and thank Him for pouring out His creativity on you. You are a prize, a beautiful offering of heaven, and God is absolutely captivated by you.

 **SONG OF SOLOMON 4:9–15**

DAY 11: Weeknight Red Velvet Cake

I absolutely love to make cake, but I cannot, in good conscience, be the one to eat all the leftovers. My solution? Weeknight Red Velvet Cake. Here we have all the flavor, all the color, all the tender texture of a normal red velvet cake, but at half the size. The cocoa-scented layers are complemented by a sweet and tangy frosting that keeps this cake moist and ridiculously tasty for days. The finished product is a beautiful red treat that is perfect for just about any holiday (but especially right around Valentine's Day!).

WEEKNIGHT RED VELVET CAKE

Makes 1 small cake

CAKE

6 tablespoons unsalted butter,
  at room temperature

¼ cup canola oil

1 cup granulated sugar

1 large egg plus 1 large egg yolk,
  at room temperature

1¼ cups all-purpose flour

1 tablespoon unsweetened cocoa powder

¾ teaspoon baking soda

¼ teaspoon table salt

⅔ cup whole milk, at room temperature

2 tablespoons white vinegar

1 teaspoon vanilla extract

1 tablespoon red food coloring (optional)

FROSTING

¾ cup unsalted butter,
  at room temperature

4 ounces cream cheese,
  at room temperature

2½ cups confectioners' sugar

¼ teaspoon table salt

¾ teaspoon vanilla extract

TO PREPARE THE CAKE

Preheat the oven to 350°F. Lightly grease one 8- or 9-inch square pan and line the bottom with parchment paper cut to fit.

In a large bowl or the bowl of a stand mixer, beat the butter, oil, and sugar on medium speed for 3 minutes, scraping the sides of the bowl as needed. Add the egg and egg yolk, stirring to combine. Scrape the sides of the bowl. In a separate bowl, gently whisk together the flour, cocoa powder, baking soda, and salt. In a large liquid measuring cup, combine the milk, vinegar, and vanilla. Add half of the dry ingredients to the butter mixture and stir on low to combine. Add half of the liquid ingredients and stir just to combine. Scrape the sides of the bowl and then repeat this process. Add the red food coloring and stir on low only until the color is evenly distributed. Pour the batter into the prepared pan and bake for about 35 minutes, or until it is puffed and set and a toothpick inserted comes out clean. Allow the cake to cool completely before frosting.

TO PREPARE THE FROSTING

In a large bowl or the bowl of a stand mixer, beat the butter on medium speed for 2 minutes until light and creamy, scraping the sides of the bowl as necessary. Add the cream cheese and beat to incorporate for an additional 30 seconds. Add the confectioners' sugar, salt, and vanilla and beat on low speed until incorporated. Scrape the sides of the bowl and continue to beat until well combined. Do not overbeat, as this can cause the cream cheese to loosen. If needed, add a tablespoon at a time of water or milk to get the frosting to the right consistency. Refrigerate as needed to thicken the frosting.

TO ASSEMBLE THE CAKE

For a sheet cake, simply spread the frosting on top. For a small two-layer rectangular cake, remove the cake from the pan and use a serrated knife to level the cake. Cut the cake in half to create two 4 × 8-inch pieces. Smooth a small amount of frosting on a cake board or plate and center a single cake layer on top. Spread a thick layer of frosting on top, extending it just beyond the edge of the cake. Stack the second cake layer on the first and frost the top. Spread any remaining frosting on the sides of the cake and decorate as desired. The cake will keep in the fridge covered for up to three days.

DAY 12: Eating Crow

Admitting you're wrong can be painful. There are few dishes that can feel more nausea-inducing than a steaming plate of crow, and I should know—I eat it regularly. Owning your part in a matter is always the right thing to do, but sometimes I find it so uncomfortable that it elicits a physical response from my body—I'm talking nervous belly, curled toes, and every hair on end.

Here's the thing with responsibility: it's almost always someone's to own, and when we fail to clean up after our mistakes, we're often leaving that mess for someone else to manage. Although humility is a terribly uncomfortable posture for those of us who like to believe we're always right, I'm finding there's a freedom that comes with owning your part. It means you can unpack that burden, move on, and allow closure to be your first move toward healing.

Don't be afraid to look at your mess and call it like it is. In Christ, there is no condemnation for your mistakes, and He'll give you the grace to make it right with the people here on earth too. Be honest with yourself—are there places you've shorted yourself or others by not owning your part? Are there any uncomfortable conversations you need to have today? I'm not saying it will be fun, but I believe you'll find freedom in the process. Choose that freedom today.

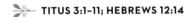 **TITUS 3:1–11; HEBREWS 12:14**

DAY 13: Moving Toward Jesus

Early on in my marriage, I spent a lot of time trying to fix everything in our relationship. I thought if I tried harder, explained myself more thoroughly, or provided specific examples of his *obvious* wrongdoings, we could work through the issues. Maybe we could plan more date nights or go on better vacations; perhaps the solution was a matter of more time, more effort. Well, I've invested a lot of energy looking into these "solutions," and I'm here to tell you, there's only one surefire remedy.

The best way to move toward a healthy marriage is to get close to Jesus. I'm learning to see every dispute, painful exchange, and unresolved issue as an opportunity to lean in to God; I can inch toward Him in every moment, for better or for worse, in hopes that, one day, Brett and I will wind up at the same place—together at the feet of Jesus.

There's a big learning curve in marriage, and no amount of experience or premarital counseling will prepare you for the snags you're bound to face. Thankfully, even when you can't fix yourself, your husband, or the situation, you can move toward Jesus. He has the hope, solutions, and grace for all you'll face in marriage, so today, instead of holding tight to control in your relationship, let go and cling to Jesus.

 PSALM 63

DAY 14: U R LOVED

When I was a kid, Valentine's Day was the opportunity to tell your friends how cool they were. I'd buy bags of candy conversation hearts and set aside my favorite phrases for my closest friends and the cutest boys. After all, there's no more embarrassing way to land a middle-school boyfriend than to write his name all over your notebook and announce your feelings with a purple candy heart that says, "U R CUTE." (Cue my inner cringe.)

I think God has special conversation hearts for each of His children too. All throughout the Bible, you see Him calling out the good characteristics and the strength of character in His people—He's all about telling His children why He loves them. Unfortunately, we often bypass His loving words for the opinions of the world. Instead of listening to the Father's heart, we cling to the criticism we receive from others, magnifying our shame, our doubt, and our every insufficiency.

Don't underestimate the amount of love your Father has for you today. Worthwhile messages of love, admiration, and encouragement can be found all throughout scripture, revealing His heart for you. Who has God said you are? Does the way you see yourself contradict what God has said about you? Today, instead of looking for a conversation heart to suggest that you are special, cling to the heart of your Heavenly Father, who has loved you all along.

 **PSALM 36:5–10**

DAY 15: Box of Chocolates

We all remember that scene in *Forrest Gump* where Tom Hanks likens the unpredictability of life to a box of chocolates: biting into one of those morsels, you never know what you're gonna get. Life is filled with a hodgepodge of flavors, and, to be honest, some days are more palatable than others. It's easy to delight in days that seem to be dripping with the goodness of a promotion, a thriving marriage, encouraging words, or personal success, but the truth is, there will always be ones that taste more bitter than sweet.

I often find myself questioning the chocolates in my box, picking through moments with puckered lips and a sour face while comparing my portion to the treasures I see others savoring. In those moments, I'm thankful to know that my joy is not dependent on the contents of my life, but on the unwavering goodness I have found in Jesus Christ. As believers, we have been given the grace to remain thankful, even in difficult, uncertain seasons of life, knowing that God is an ever-present source of joy (Ps. 28:7). Hallelujah!

Spend some time in thankfulness today. Thank Him for the gift of sweet days and for His provision during the hard ones. Thank Him for the steadfast nature of His love and goodness and for His grace that allows your heart peace in undesirable circumstances. If you're tempted to question the chocolates in your box, fix your eyes on His joy and let that be the sweet song of thankfulness that satisfies your heart.

 **COLOSSIANS 3:15–17**

DAY 16: Self-Care

Have you ever found yourself in a funk? Sometimes, when life feels hard and discouraging circumstances land in my lap, I find that blah feeling really hard to shake. Sometimes, the cure is as simple as a chat with a friend, a good laugh, some rest, or a change of scenery (or, if all else fails, I can wholeheartedly recommend the crispy rice treats on p. 269), but in other moments, I need to step back to consider how I can take better care of myself.

Self-care has gotten a bad rap as a trendy excuse for self-indulgence, but there's something to be said for taking good care of all your parts. For me, self-care looks like shushing my doubt to appreciate the person I am. It looks like receiving grace and forgiveness when I mess up again. It looks like replacing my inner monologue of criticism with encouraging words, particularly in areas where I'm a work in progress. The mental exchange we engage in day after day can make or break our spirits, and I think we owe it to ourselves, to the Christ in us, to exercise a bit more kindness.

I don't know who out there needs to hear what a treasure they are, but here it is: You. Are. Great. Not because of your appearance, abilities, or attitude, but because of who you are in Christ. You are made in the image of a great God, so be good to yourself and celebrate the work of God by taking care of His creation in you today.

 PSALM 104

DAY 17: Life Without Sprinkles

I made the mistake of introducing my children to sprinkles early on. For some time, pancakes, cookies, and cinnamon rolls were treats best served with sprinkles on top, and even today my kids don't understand why restaurants fail to speckle their meals and snacks with those colorful nibs of sugar. I get it—sprinkles make just about anything feel a little happier, a little more festive.

I wonder how often we fail to see the goodness in our story just because it doesn't seem to have any sprinkles. Nestled in between all the big achievements, milestones, and extraordinary life events are delicious nuggets of beauty and sweetness that often get overlooked. Those small, everyday victories are still victories even if they don't come trumpets blaring, right? A cinnamon roll without sprinkles is still a cinnamon roll, right?

Are there places in your life where you may need to realign into a posture of gratitude? Where is there untapped treasure in your everyday life that may benefit from a heart of thankfulness? God has filled your life with opportunities to give thanks, so take time this morning to offer up your heart in appreciation for His sweetness.

 **PSALM 34:1–10**

DAY 18: Sprinkle Pancakes

We are not healthy breakfast eaters in our house. Instead, we take more of a "no carb left behind" kind of approach, and my kids usually end up being the guinea pigs for all the breakfast pastries I've tested all week long. Don't you dare judge me.

These Sprinkle Pancakes garner loads of excitement from my kids. The clear vanilla extract offers a flavor that is delightfully reminiscent of Funfetti boxed cake mix, but in a pinch you can use regular vanilla. Just don't scrimp on the sprinkles—that's where all the fun is.

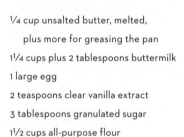

SPRINKLE PANCAKES

Makes 9 small pancakes

¼ cup unsalted butter, melted,
   plus more for greasing the pan

1¼ cups plus 2 tablespoons buttermilk

1 large egg

2 teaspoons clear vanilla extract

3 tablespoons granulated sugar

1½ cups all-purpose flour

2 teaspoons baking powder

¼ teaspoon baking soda

½ teaspoon table salt

⅓ cup rainbow sprinkles

Toppings: butter, pancake syrup,
   whipped cream

In a large mixing bowl, whisk together the butter, buttermilk, egg, clear vanilla extract, and sugar until well combined. Add the flour, baking powder, baking soda, and salt and stir together with a spoon or spatula until combined but still a bit lumpy—do not overmix. Fold in the sprinkles and allow the batter to rest while you preheat the pan.

Heat a griddle or nonstick pan on medium (about 325ºF) and lightly butter it. Use a measuring cup to scoop out a heaping ⅓ cup of batter onto the griddle or pan for each pancake, depending on how many will fit, and gently smooth them out into 5-inch circles. Cook until bubbles appear in the center of the pancakes and the edges no longer look glossy. Flip the pancakes and cook an additional 2 minutes, or until the bottoms are golden brown. Serve with additional butter, syrup, and whipped cream, if desired.

DAY 19: The Richness of Community

There was a time when my relationship with God was a private thing. Beyond singing in church or praying over a meal, I didn't feel as though my connection with Jesus was anyone's business. Vulnerability with God was one thing, but was I really supposed to welcome other people into that part of my heart too?

When my husband and I married, we joined a small group of believers for our Sunday worship. There were no fancy sermons, no stage-lit bands, no paid clergy on staff—just a ragtag group of people who wanted more Jesus. I met women who seemingly made it their job to love and welcome me into their time with the Lord, and I experienced firsthand the rich, unifying treasure of intimacy within the Body of Christ. We shared in each other's blessings, held one another up in prayer, and allowed that time to expand our perspective and knowledge of who He is. It was there that community deepened my faith and stretched my capacity for more of Him.

Community and Jesus go hand in hand. Like champagne with oysters or Merlot with a rich stew, few things enhance the experience of Jesus like sharing it within the body of believers. Sure, there are moments that are intended just for you and God, but don't discount the rich blessings that come with a community of faith. Instead, get connected to women who will come alongside of you and bolster your faith, listen for the voices that speak to your life in love and truth, and stay connected to people who point you to Jesus—you'll see how well community and Jesus go together.

 **MATTHEW 18:19-20**

DAY 20: Dreaming Outside the Box

My kids make some wild dinner requests. Things like cheddar cheese and popsicle, suckers and watermelon, or French fries with chocolate milk are not unlikely combinations. There's no rhyme or reason to their choices, and you can't tell them that these foods aren't legitimate options for dinner; in their minds, the possibilities are limitless, and if it's delicious, why shouldn't they enjoy it?

Obviously, as their mother, I turn down those meal orders regularly, but it does raise the question: How often do we miss out on experiences because they don't fit within the confines of our thinking? Are we skipping over dreams, pursuits, and opportunities for adventure because they don't align with conventional modes of thought?

I think God puts crazy dreams in each of our hearts and takes delight when we are wild enough to pursue them. Each spark of an idea may not end up blazing, but I think some of them, when brought into the light of His desires and purposes, just might ignite. God is the One who equips us with vision and provision for the dreams He puts inside of us, but our job is to be bold enough to step out in faith toward them.

Are there any wild, God-size ideas in your heart? Although they may seem big or farfetched, if it's a desire He's given you, He won't leave you to accomplish it on your own. Today, test your dreams against His word, and be brave enough to go after them.

 **JUDGES 6–7**

DAY 21: Forgetting the Rules

I used to think being a Christian meant following a bunch of rules. As a longtime people pleaser, this didn't bother me so much, and if getting into heaven meant wearing a purity ring and being home by curfew, I was fine with that. In retrospect, I can see that I was performing for God rather than responding out of love for Him, and the condition of my heart reflected as much.

When I truly experienced the love of Christ for the first time, it changed my relationship with Him forever. It was as if the fullness of His heart for me had cracked through the stony, religious exterior of my own, and I was free to pursue relationship over religious aptitude. His love compelled my heart to surrender in obedience to His ways and desires, and where I once felt obligated to follow rules, I now felt freedom in honoring Him with my life by yielding my own plans to His. This is the paradox of Christianity: we find our lives when we lose ourselves in Him.

The response to a real encounter with the Father's love is a heart that overflows back to Him. It doesn't look like adhering to a set of rules or checking all our religious boxes; it looks like loving God and others as hard as we can out of the overflow He's already provided to us. If you've found yourself in a relationship with God that is driven by performance rather than love, take time today to unpack the burden of doing everything right. Instead, fill up on God's love, and let that be the overflow you carry with you.

 **1 JOHN 5:1-5**

DAY 22: The Least of These

Truly, I say to you, as you did it to one of the least of these my brothers, you did it to me (Matt. 25:40). I used to read this scripture and immediately picture myself ladling bowls of chili at a soup kitchen or handing a couple of bucks to a guy holding a cardboard sign. Every time I donated a box of clothes or passed out toothbrushes on a mission trip, I felt a little surge of pride, as if I was checking off my call to love in Jesus's name for the year.

Recently, I was reminded that the physical, spiritual, and emotional needs of the fallen humanity we live among are not limited to the teeny, tiny worldview I'd like to pack them in. Sometimes, loving the least of these looks like befriending the girl who is difficult to love. Sometimes, it looks like offering grace for the hurtful words a neighbor said in passing. Sometimes, it looks like engaging thoughtfully and generously with the family member whom you'd rather just ignore. If loving the "least of these" was limited just to those wearing tattered clothes or prison jumpsuits, what would God have us to do with all the needy friends, lonely outcasts, and inconvenient family members we're bound to rub shoulders with from time to time?

The Holy Spirit is using this scripture to remind me to be gentle, generous, and loving with everyone, even when it's uncomfortable to do so. He's reminding me that God's love has always been available to all of us, even in our most broken and unlovable seasons of life; and in the places of our story where sin abounds, thankfully His grace does too (Rom. 5:20).

Take time to consider what loving the "least of these" would look like in your life. If it feels sticky or uncomfortable, you're on the right track. Thankfully, as a believer, you have the opportunity to love and serve out of the overflow He's already filled you with. You're not loving people from your own strength—you're loving from His.

 **MATTHEW 25:31–46**

DAY 23: Dreaming Big Dreams

I toyed with the idea of a blog for a long time before I finally dove in. Fear kept me on the bench with whispers in the back of my mind that told me why I couldn't do it: *I don't have time. My voice won't make a difference. Maybe I don't have anything valuable to say.* Countless people around me were taking chances, stepping into new adventures, and pursuing their dreams in ways that inspired me, but I just wasn't sure I had a seat at the table. Maybe my dreams weren't worth the risk.

If you're reading these words today from the sidelines of your own world, I urge you to jump in. Make a list of your dreams, strategize, and go for them, ignoring the doubt, the fear, and any person or thing that belittles your ideas. You never know what kind of joy you'll find when you finally step into something that you're passionate about, and you can't predict how much your story might change when you decide to be the one who writes it.

God puts big, beautiful desires in our hearts, but it's our job to step into them. Walking into a new thing is usually not without fear or challenges, but that doesn't mean you're not still intended to pursue it. Allow yourself the freedom to dream big, improbable things, and thank God for the opportunity to try. If you've been waiting for someone to believe in you or say your dreams are worth their salt, let me be the first. Get it, girl. You can absolutely do this.

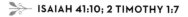 **ISAIAH 41:10; 2 TIMOTHY 1:7**

DAY 24: Finding Treasure

They say that kids grow up too fast, and you know what? It's true.

Aimee is my oldest child, and I'm always surprised by how grown she is. The baby who was just kicking in my belly is now the one who helps me stir pots of soup on the stove and toasts her own bread. She used to be a toddler, but now she's jumping off of swing sets, cracking witty jokes, and caring for her young brothers. Where does the time go? It feels as though day one was just yesterday.

As Aimee's mother, I have a unique vantage point in her life. I've seen the full spectrum of her existence, from birth till now, and have witnessed her physical and emotional growth firsthand. I see her strengths and personality emerging, even now as a child, and from where I sit her future is like a chest brimming with possibility and treasure—hopes and truths, successes and joys she could one day come to realize. I've gotten a front-row seat to her life and see her exactly as she is, and I just want it all for her.

In the same way, God knows every bit of you, His child, and deeply desires that you would step into every gift He has for you. It's as though He's prepared for you a future of possibilities and passions that are already tagged with your name on it, and all of heaven watches, waiting for you to step into those treasures that are yours. God desires for you to taste and see how good He is, leaning in to the future He's planned for your life and trusting Him enough to welcome every gift as your own. Press in to Him today. Ask to be on the receiving end of every single blessing He has for you, and praise Him in advance for the treasure it most certainly will be.

 **EPHESIANS 2:4–10**

Go-To Chili

Aimee calls herself a "bean girl" because it's her favorite vegetable. I know she may read this in a few years and be totally embarrassed, so let me just go ahead and apologize—I'm sorry, little bean girl. My Go-To Chili is one of Aimee's favorites.

....

GO-TO CHILI

Serves 6

1 tablespoon olive oil

1 large yellow onion, diced

1 large green bell pepper, diced

3 large stalks of celery, diced

4 cloves garlic, minced

1 pound ground beef

3 bay leaves

2 teaspoons paprika

1½ teaspoons dried oregano

1½ teaspoons kosher salt

¼ teaspoon cayenne pepper

4 cups beef stock

1 (28-ounce) can diced tomatoes, undrained

1 (28-ounce) can crushed tomatoes, undrained

3 tablespoons tomato paste

2 (16-ounce) cans kidney beans, drained and rinsed

¼ cup plus 2 tablespoons packed brown sugar

Salt and pepper to taste

In a large Dutch oven or heavy-bottomed pan on medium, heat the olive oil and sauté the onion, bell pepper, celery, and garlic, stirring occasionally until softened, about 3 minutes. Add the beef and cook until browned, breaking the meat up with a spatula. Add the bay leaves, paprika, oregano, salt, and cayenne (if you like a *really* spicy chili, add up to an additional ½ teaspoon) and stir while cooking for 2 minutes. Add the stock, diced and crushed tomatoes with their juices, tomato paste, kidney beans, and brown sugar. Bring to a boil and then reduce the heat to low. Simmer uncovered for 2 hours, stirring occasionally, until slightly reduced and thickened. Add salt and pepper as desired and enjoy!

DAY 26: Nose to Tail

A few years ago, my brother and I enjoyed a fabulous meal at a trendy restaurant in Chicago. We were told that the chef wanted to celebrate every ingredient, every portion of the animal, nose to tail, by letting nothing go to waste, and our dinner reflected this. Somehow, she made something delightful out of pork cheeks, duck tongues, and goat livers, as well as a number of other dishes that I tried not to ask too many questions about. After all, I'm an adventurous eater, but I do have my limits.

If you had offered me those foods years ago, I would have quickly passed them over for something that sounded more palatable, maybe a filet or a roasted chicken breast, please and thank you. But that evening, I was reminded that sometimes the stuff we pass over or view as waste can actually be repurposed into something beautiful.

Jesus doesn't let much go to waste either. When He fed the five thousand, a meal he rendered from a single person's scraps, He made a point of collecting the leftovers: *Gather up the leftover fragments, that nothing may be lost* (John 6:12). The miracle was done, the people were fed, and the crowd had recognized Him as something special, but He still made use of the crumbs. Even the unused, forgotten parts had purpose.

Our stories sometimes have gristly bits that may feel completely unpalatable, but not a single bit is wasted in the hands of the Lord. He uses every part, every painful word and lost hope, to the glory of His name and for our good (Rom. 8:28). He has a purpose for every bit of your life if you'll entrust Him with it.

If there are parts of your story that feel painful or unnecessary, ask God to show you how He's using them for good. He's promised to celebrate every part of you with dignified purpose, so you can trust that He is making all things good in His time.

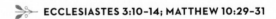 **ECCLESIASTES 3:10–14; MATTHEW 10:29–31**

DAY 27: Having God's Faith

Recently, a friend told me about a time He followed God into what felt like an impossible situation. By all human perspective, there was little hope. Even though it was God who had brought Him into his position, my friend couldn't see beyond his circumstances and, quite frankly, had lost faith.

He told God that it all felt too big. He was grasping for the faith that he wanted to have, but it just wasn't there. Do you know what God told Him? "That's okay. You don't have to have faith for this, because I do. Will you trust me?" And that was it. It wasn't my friend's job to muster up more faith or provision—He just had to trust that God had more than enough for the both of them.

I have a lot of conversations with God like that now. When there's a situation I want to have faith for, trust God with, or believe in, I just tell Him where I'm at. I ask Him to help my unbelief and trust that when I press in, rely on Him, and place the whole thing in His hands, He has enough faith for the two of us. He has the power, the kindness, and the care to accomplish it all.

What are the things in your life that you're struggling to have faith for? Are there uncertain circumstances, relationships, or hurdles that you're feeling discouraged about? Take the weight off your own faith and ask God to share His portion instead. He has the authority to work against all odds, so you can trust Him with any impossibility you face today.

 **MARK 9:14–29**

DAY 28: Enough to Go Around

Bedtime is an all-out war in our house. The kids run wild, no one wants to brush their teeth, and "just one more story" turns into a forty-five-minute brawl over book titles and stuffed animals. Even after we get the kids down, the battle continues, as Brett and I fight over the remote, the temperature in the room, and even the residual space in our bed.

Some of us are wired to be ever in combat, fighting to stake out our territory. We want esteem in our workplace, authority in our home, and more money, more social invitations, more stuff. These mini wars we wage feed an incessant inner need to take what is ours in order to protect our own comfort and affluence. Fill in your own story here—can you relate?

The truth is, there's more than enough to go around. With the exception of bed space (because any woman with raging hormones and body temperatures knows that's a finite resource), we're rarely in a position where there isn't enough room to go around. When we exert so much energy trying to one-up or out-perform our neighbors, we risk running ourselves ragged in a rat race that we will never actually win.

With Jesus, there's always enough to go around, because God's grace is wide enough for both you and your neighbors. Instead of fighting for your own agenda, you can move forward with kindness and generosity, knowing that God is always at work on your behalf. He's a God of infinite resources and is nowhere close to running out of love and blessings, so instead of battling for an extra inch of territory, rest in what He's already supplied.

 **PHILIPPIANS 2:3-4**

DAY 1: Balancing Act

One of my favorite things about a terrific meal is how a balance of tastes and textures, enough bitter with sweet or just the right amount of fat with acid, can transform simple ingredients into a composition of flavors that are tastier together than they are on their own. Too much salt, lime, butter, or sugar can make just about anything unpleasant, but there's a sweet spot in between, a balance that can be downright heavenly.

Life requires balance too. Our days can't be made up of just work or play or service or sleeping, but a combination of those things, activities that simultaneously feed our heart and utilize our skills, creates a sustainable framework for our lives. God calls us to a life that reflects both work and rest, both pleasure and responsibility, because there's a place and time for all of those things in His agenda. Even in the work of creation, God set aside specific time for rest, and if He made room for balance, then we're called to that too.

Does your life reflect balance? Is God calling you to step back from anything to make room for something else He's called you to? If you've gone overboard in one area of life, accept this opportunity to be more intentional with your time. Take inventory of your life, and don't be afraid to reconsider where you're allocating your time and love. God will help you to figure out where your time is best suited, so if you're unsure where to start, begin by handing it over to Him.

 **EPHESIANS 5:15–16**

DAY 2: Saving the Best for Last

We keep a strict "dessert every night" rule in our house. If you're willing to eat your supper, you're welcome to dessert, no questions asked. There are plenty of dinners where my kids pick at their remaining brussels sprouts or salmon, reluctantly eating bit by bit because they know the best is coming. We always save the best for last.

I love the story in John 2 about the wedding party that ran out of wine. In distress, Jesus's mother informs Him of the predicament, and in an act that would later become known as Jesus's first miracle, He turns water into a fine wine. This was no dollar-store box wine or cheap imitation; this wine was the real deal. The master of the banquet declared, *You have kept the good wine until now*, and His disciples were in awe over the glory Jesus revealed in that moment. (Can we stop and raise a glass to a God who knows every party needs great wine?)

The point is, God never withholds good gifts. The Bible says He is always at work on our behalf and never turns away from doing us good (Jer. 32:40). He doesn't give up on us or ignore our needs—He eagerly meets them, completing every good thing that He has begun (Phil. 1:6). In the story of the wedding party, Jesus revealed his glory, yes, but He also revealed His desire to meet our needs, even the nonessential ones.

We serve a God who always saves the best for last, so if you find yourself in a place of lack, look for Him in your story where He has promised to be at work. How is God meeting your needs today? Where do you need to trust Him to provide for you this week? Ask Him to align your desires with His, and remember that you can trust Him with all the details of your life.

✂ JOHN 2:1–12

DAY 3: Southern Hospitality

In college, I had a friend whose mother was the picture of Southern hospitality. Her home was always as bright and welcoming as she was, and it was within those walls that I began to dream of what it would be like to open my own home to others someday. Each time I stayed the night, she put fresh flowers in my room and filled little glass candy dishes with my favorite treats. Over the years, she passed on cookbooks to me, shared snipped recipes from old magazines, and taught me that homemade salad dressing is always worth the effort.

Tragically, this sweet woman died just after I graduated from college, and for a little while a tiny piece of me did too. I had grown to love her like a mother and was devastated to lose the warmth of that relationship. Through candy dishes and conversations and meals around the table, she taught me about hospitality and what it looks like to welcome people into your heart and home. Every single bit of it was her offering of love.

You don't have to be Southern to extend hospitality. Just pull a few more chairs up to your table, fill a candy jar, and seek out opportunities for intentionality and connection. You'll find that hospitality isn't just an *outward* expression; instead, there's always a sharing of warmth and memories when hospitality is offered as a means of love.

Who can you welcome with hospitality today? Is there anyone in your life who needs the encouragement of a thoughtful gesture or a kind word? Even the little things make a difference, so ask God for a fresh infilling of His love that you can offer to the world around you.

 **EPHESIANS 5:1-2**

DAY 4: Chicken and Shrimp Paella

This Chicken and Shrimp Paella was in regular rotation at my friend's mother's home before she passed. She served it with buttered slices of French bread and leafy salads that always looked like the ones in magazines. If you can tolerate extra heat, increase the cayenne pepper by $1/4$ teaspoon.

CHICKEN AND SHRIMP PAELLA

Serves 6

1½ cups long-grain white rice

3 tablespoons olive oil

1 large white onion, diced

1 clove garlic, minced

1 tablespoon paprika

1 tablespoon instant chicken bouillon

2 teaspoons kosher salt

½ teaspoon black pepper

¼ teaspoon turmeric

¼ teaspoon cayenne pepper

3 cups water

1 (14.5-ounce) can diced tomatoes

3 cups diced cooked chicken

1 pound medium cooked shrimp, peeled and deveined

1 (13.75-ounce) can quartered artichoke hearts, drained

1 cup English peas (frozen or thawed)

Pour the rice into a fine mesh strainer, rinse with cool water, and allow it to drain.

Pour the oil into a large sauté pan over medium heat. Add the onions and cook, stirring occasionally, until they are translucent, about 3 minutes. Add the garlic, paprika, chicken bouillon, salt, pepper, turmeric, and cayenne, and cook, stirring constantly for an additional minute. Add the water, tomatoes, and rice, and bring the mixture to a boil. Cover, reduce the heat to low, and cook for about 20 minutes, or until the rice is tender, and most of the liquid has been absorbed. Add the diced chicken and shrimp and toss to combine. Cook to warm through, about 5 minutes. If you notice the mixture is dry and sticky, you can add an additional ¼ cup water at this time. Toss in the artichoke hearts and English peas and stir to combine.

DAY 5: I Love You Back

One of my favorite things about mothering a newborn is knowing as sure as anything you're that baby's favorite person. Baby looks at you with eyes that twinkle with equal parts wonder and adoration, taking in your features as if they were a work of art. In those intimate moments, my love for the child is overwhelming, but the fact that he or she loves me back... well, that's enough to bowl me over.

I wonder what it does for the Father's heart when we mirror His love back to him? In Romans, it says, *God's love has been poured into our hearts through the Holy Spirit* (5:5), so any love we share, whether inwardly, outwardly, or heavenly, comes directly from a reservoir that He is filling for us. We're never at risk of running out, sharing too freely, or giving more than we have, because His love knows no end. When we truly encounter God's love, the response of our heart is to love Him back, as if to say, "God, your love is so big and so real and so good. Thank you for loving me, God. I love you back."

Take a minute to reflect on God's love in your life. How has He revealed His love to you in the past? Are you aware of His love in your life today? If you need an extra dose of His love today, tell Him. Ask for a fresh revelation of His heart for you, and out of that overflow love Him back.

 **JOHN 7:37–39**

DAY 6: Stop Apologizing

Full disclosure: I'm a recovering apologizer. For me, "I'm sorry" has become some-what of a blanket statement that covers over any mistake or insufficiency I might unknowingly expose. It goes something like this: "Sorry the vegetables are over-cooked!" "Sorry my house is such a mess!" "Sorry I didn't dress nicer!" Somewhere over the years, I bought into the lie that my emotions and flaws were too much for people to handle, and they'd think less of me if they saw my imperfections. *Will people like me if they see who I really am?*

It's kind of ridiculous for me to assume that people care about my frizzy hair or soggy vegetables. People won't always notice if your mascara is smeared or if your sink is full of dishes, but they will recognize when they feel loved. If we allow our mess, our shortcomings, and our "flaws" to keep us from engaging honestly with others, we may miss out on the opportunity to participate in an exchange of love with them. Instead of apologizing for who we are, God wants us to be proud, engaging in authentic relationships with a vulnerability that lets people know that we love them enough to share our truest selves.

God saw you from the beginning of time and said, "It is good." He's seen the messes you make and loves you all the same. Stop apologizing for what you think you're not, and rejoice at the goodness God says you are.

 PSALM 139

DAY 7: Never Too Late

What is that dream deep in your heart? Is it learning a new skill? Having a child? Getting a certain job? Maybe you've dreamed of learning guitar, a second language, or how to prepare your own homemade bread. (Check out my Mom's Homemade Bread, p. 83, to cross that one off your list!)

In the shuffle of life, it's easy to forget about our dreams or believe they're not worth pursuing. Instead, we put them on the back burner for another day or allow the words and judgments of others to snuff them out. If you find yourself with deferred hopes flickering in the deepest corners of your heart, let me be the one to tell you: it's not too late. You're not too old or too young or unqualified. You didn't miss your shot when you got married or when you were passed over for that internship—your time has not run out.

God puts desires in our hearts to achieve His purposes. Right now ideas are alive in you that fall in line with His plans, and those passions, even the secret, seemingly silly ones that you haven't told anyone about, *matter* to Him. He desires for us to experience joy and fulfillment, even on this side of heaven, and sometimes that's not nearly as far-fetched and serious as it sounds.

Test your hopes against His word. Ask Him to plant His desires in your heart, and be brave enough to watch them grow. He has beautiful things in store for you, and it's never too late for God. If you're on His watch, your dreams are always right on time.

 PSALM 145

DAY 8: Possibilities

Watching my kids transform from babies into tiny humans reminds me that we don't begin our lives with feelings of fear or shame or speculation. Unrestricted by adult logic or cynicism, children exist in total freedom, willing to laugh and play and dream. Their hearts are open to curiosities and wonder and possibility, and, to be honest, I really long for some of that myself.

I'd like to not be so trapped within my own understanding and reasoning. I'd love for my heart to be open enough to trust and hope even when all logic says to do otherwise. Jesus contends for that kind of childlike faith throughout the Gospels, and observing my children in action helps me to understand why.

God wants us to trust Him in the impossible and hope for the improbable. He wants us to believe He's as big and kind and present as we say He is and to live our lives as a reflection of that faith. He wants us to be looking for His grace around every corner, expectant that He will provide and make His goodness known in every circumstance.

Next time you see young children, watch them. Observe how they explore and marvel and free-fall into the world around them. Just think: this is the freedom that is yours in Christ. You have the opportunity to trade your doubt, logic, and fear for the free and lightened load of a generous Father. Today, offer God the weight of adulthood, and ask for a fresh infilling of some childlike faith.

 **MARK 10:13–16**

DAY 9: ## Small Intentions

I'm a creature of habit: two cups of coffee in the morning, a carbonated beverage at lunch, and a fresh glass of water before bed. I have a favorite spot on the couch, a favorite burner on the stove, and a regular sequence of scrubbing each time I get in the shower. The confines of routine and predictability suit me, but unfortunately that means I also suffer when I allow bad habits to become a part of my daily life.

Whether intentional or not, our lives are often built around the habits we fill them with. If I regularly nag my husband, that shapes our relationship. If I'm constantly short-fused with my kids, that changes how we engage with each other. If I make a habit of eating a dozen cookies every night without also making a habit of eating fresh produce and exercising, I probably won't fit in my jeans next month. At the end of the day, our lives will reflect the sum of all our habits, good or bad, and I gotta tell you, I just really want all the good stuff. Don't you?

Let's start small today. We probably won't change our marriage, our career path, or our bodies overnight, but those little habits make a difference. Plant a good habit this week—maybe a change of routine, an extra minute or two with the Lord, or a kind word to your friend or yourself—and watch for the fruits of that effort. Don't get discouraged if you don't see it right away; instead, give it to God and press in for more. He longs for us to live full and healthy lives in Him, and it starts with small intentions.

 **MARK 7:14–23**

DAY 10: Hiding His Word

To this day, I can still recite my childhood best friend's phone number by heart. Even though, thanks to Siri, I haven't had to dial it for years, I spent so many of those formative years tapping her number into my parents' landline that I could probably still whisper those seven digits in my sleep. Newer numbers are an entirely different story, and without my iPhone, I'd be totally lost. Because I haven't *had* to memorize any phone numbers in recent years, I truly don't know a single one of them.

We memorize phone numbers and songs and directions, but there's something to be said for becoming familiar with God's Word too. When the promises and lessons from His Word become our second nature, we can approach the challenges and conflicts of this world with confidence, because our foundation is secured to Him. Instead of flailing in the chaos of uncertainty, we can respond boldly with the truth and power of heaven, His Word acting as a sword against the doubt and darkness around us. The Bible isn't just a story—it's a tool intended to strengthen our hearts and minds, to fill us with hope and remind us of the victory we have in Him.

Psalm 119:11 tells us to hide God's word in our hearts (NIV). The truths and encouragement and wisdom found in the Bible are pertinent to and able to serve you in every circumstance of life. There is a word there for you today and every morning, and if you will hide some nuggets, seeking to understand them with your whole heart, those truths will emerge when the you need them most. Spend time in His Word this week, and when He speaks to you, hide those words in your heart. They're living, powerful, and a mighty source of hope for your life today.

 PSALM 1:1–3

DAY 11: Freezer Cookie Dough

When I was growing up, my mom told me if I ate raw cookie dough, I'd get sick. Miraculously, I've been consuming copious amounts of chocolate chip goodness for years with little to no side effects. How could this be, Mom? Surely you weren't holding out on me??

Now, in my own home, I keep frozen rounds of cookie dough in my freezer "just in case." I take comfort knowing there are a dozen or so cookies in the freezer ready to be baked, shared, and devoured at a minute's notice. When friends pop by for a glass of wine or when one of my kiddos needs a little happy after a hard day, warm, homemade cookies are just the kind of thing I love to make magically appear.

In place of chocolate chips, you can substitute your favorite baking chips, nuts, or other mix-ins. Toffee bits and pecans are favorites in my house, but nothing feels quite as comforting as regular old chocolate chips. Regardless of whether you listen to warnings about eating raw cookie dough, you will undoubtedly enjoy every last one of these when they are fresh from the oven.

....

FREEZER COOKIE DOUGH

Makes 36 large cookies

1 cup (2 sticks) unsalted butter, at room
    temperature

3/4 cup granulated sugar

1¼ cups packed brown sugar

2 large eggs

2 teaspoons vanilla extract

3 cups all-purpose flour

1 teaspoon baking soda

3/4 teaspoon baking powder

1¼ teaspoons table salt

2 cups semisweet chocolate chips

In a large bowl or the bowl of a stand mixer, cream the butter, granulated sugar, and brown sugar together for 2 minutes on medium speed. Scrape the sides of bowl and add the eggs and vanilla extract. Mix on medium speed until just combined. Add the flour, baking soda, baking powder, and salt and stir until combined. Add the chocolate chips and stir on low. Use a medium-size cookie scoop or a large spoon to scoop 3-tablespoon-size balls of dough onto a parchment-lined baking sheet. Place in the freezer to firm up briefly, about 30 minutes, and then place the dough balls into a freezer-safe container or bag. Freeze for up to two months.

When ready to bake, preheat the oven to 360ºF. Place the frozen dough balls on a parchment-lined baking sheet at least 2 inches apart and bake until the edges are golden and the cookies are set, about 14 minutes. Allow the cookies to cool briefly before sharing.

NOTE: To make smaller cookies, scoop 1½-tablespoon-size mounds of dough and bake them for about 12 minutes.

You can also bake the cookies immediately rather than freezing the dough—just knock 2 to 3 minutes off the baking time.

DAY 12: Open Table

I love that Jesus frequently told parables involving food. The theme of hospitality, of serving one another and welcoming everyone to the table, shows us that God's idea of community doesn't look like a closed supper club with limited invitations; it looks like a generous, abundant table where everyone has a seat.

Take a minute to consider what community looks like in your life. Are you sharing generously with the people in your circle? Are you pulling out chairs for the people who look different from you, who are uncomfortable to love, or who have nothing tangible to offer you in return? Admittedly, this is often easier said than done. I'm most comfortable sitting at familiar tables within the social bubble I'm accustomed to, and welcoming people who aren't usually at that table often requires more stretching of myself than I care to do. Instead of feeling guilty, I'm slowly learning to be honest with God about those feelings and asking Him to show me where there is room for kindness and love in my heart to expand my table.

Don't be afraid to invite newcomers to your proverbial table. You won't end up being best friends with every new person who pulls up a chair, but no generous act of love goes unnoticed. Your open arms and that extra place setting have potential for impact both on yourself and on the world around you. Ask God to provide opportunities to love people within and just outside of your reach in big ways.

 **LUKE 14:7-24**

DAY 13: Saturated with Jesus

I know the Bible says we're all a reflection of His image, but sometimes I get the feeling He gave some people an extra dose. You and I both know them—the people who bubble over with so much love and joy and beauty that you immediately know they're filled with something special. I have a handful of people like this in my life, and I always find them so inspiring—they're so saturated with Jesus that you can't help but be drawn to them.

I'll be honest, most days I feel more saturated with my own humanity. Conscious of my shortcomings, I become hyperaware of every bad attitude, slipup, and shameful thought, and instead of resting in the Lord, I hop on the exhausting mental hamster wheel that is condemnation. It's like the enemy amplifies the sin in my heart, and instead of listening to who God says I am, I'm just reminded of all that I'm not.

Sister, let's just let that go. When God looks at us, the beauty of His Son in us is enough to overwhelm any shortcoming we bring to the table. We have an opportunity to live in freedom from the guilt and shame we were previously attached to, and I gotta tell you—the weightlessness of that freedom is beautiful. Disentangled from our own depravity, we can fully experience the love, joy, and peace that is so attractive in others.

We're bound to make mistakes and experience shortcomings in our lives, because, after all, we're human. But with Christ in us, every minute on earth is an opportunity to welcome heaven into our circumstances and to abide more fully in Him. You're already saturated with a full dose of Jesus in you, so today be someone who lets it shine.

 **ROMANS 8:1-11**

DAY 14: Confidence in God's Faithfulness

One Friday in March 2020, I picked up my kids from school and headed home for the weekend, not knowing that we had just said goodbye to friends, teachers, and life as we knew it for months to come. My story isn't unique: COVID-19 overturned the infrastructure of our lives and world in ways most of us never anticipated.

Seasons of change are hard, particularly ones marked by the ambiguity of threat and fear. When the very ground beneath our feet shifts from day to day, we can stand with confidence on the faithfulness of the Lord. We can be strong and courageous, because He is with us (Josh. 1:9) and we can wait in expectation for His goodness, trusting that He will provide in every circumstance (Ps. 27:13–14).

Are you struggling to trust God with the events happening in and around your life? Are there places of ambiguity that need the hope and clarity of an all-knowing Father? Wait on the Lord. Look everywhere for His goodness. Seek out the evidence of His power moving on your behalf. It's there, because it's who He is and He's working in your story, even now.

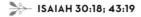 **ISAIAH 30:18; 43:19**

DAY 15: Needing Each Other

During the pandemic, one thing became crystal clear to me: we desperately need each other. For the first few weeks of the quarantine, when there wasn't pressure to go and do, I enjoyed the luxury of staying in with my kiddos. After a while, though, the challenge of working and parenting from home became heavier and lonelier. I'm not the only one; isolation left many of us feeling, well . . . isolated.

In those months, I was reminded how deeply nourishing relationships can be. They serve as a source of encouragement and joy and laughter, and that time spent connecting with one another offers a sense of comradery and understanding that provides hope, support, and comfort.

On our first night out of quarantine, as I sat socially distanced around a table with a few dear friends, I couldn't help but well up with tears. The gratitude and affection for one another was so thick in the room, it was almost tangible. Every inch of me felt covered in love, because I knew I was reconnected to people who were just as eager to spend time with me. I was reminded of how good it felt to be seen, known, and loved.

We weren't meant to do life alone, so today ask God if there are ways you could be better connected with your friends and loved ones. Do you need to set aside more time for relationship? Maybe offer a little more vulnerability? Is there someone you've lost touch with or a neighbor who may need a friend? Let God show you how to use your time and proximity as a means of love to the people within and outside of your circle today, and remember that the best relationships are the ones into which we welcome Him.

 **ECCLESIASTES 4:9-12**

DAY 16: Built to Last

One of my best friends is a woman who I was once at odds with. We had been friends for years when a series of poor choices found me dating the guy she was in love with. It was about as crappy as it sounds, and although I didn't win any awards for "friend of the year," I will forever remember that season as one of tremendous growth.

For some reason, she forgave me. It wasn't instantaneous, and there was certainly a lot healing that needed to happen, but, still, it was there—grace. In the middle of mess and heartache and betrayal, she gave out what little bits of forgiveness she could offer, and that was enough. We slowly rebuilt our friendship, and, to our surprise, it wasn't stuck within the flimsy confines of the relationship we once knew—it was stronger. In that season, one of the hardest and loneliest of my life, she presented me with a little grace, and it blew the walls off of my heart.

Don't underestimate God's infinite capacity for grace or His ability to work in your impossible circumstances. He can use those moments to make room for your growth, so you become more dependent on Him, and to rebuild the brokenness that exists in your story. He won't leave you where you're at, because He desires to remove the things that were lost to sin and replace them with portions that are double what you expected.

Today, instead of shying away from your mess, look for opportunities to give and receive grace. God can make a lot of beauty from your ashes if you'll let Him.

 ISAIAH 61

DAY 17: On Baking Bread

Baking homemade bread always feels like a holy activity. It's a slow process in which humble ingredients are made into something of substance by sifting and stirring, kneading and waiting, a transformation that results in change and rising and growth. What starts as a handful of grain, after a little work, time, and rest, in the end looks and tastes an awful lot like bread.

We, as humans, are full of talents, interests, and personalities, and as children of God we've been invited to bring it all to Him. He does the work by stirring up dreams and sifting through our thoughts. He kneads us and softens our heart to create one that has the strength and potential for growth. Our part is to wait and rest in Him, because His timing is the only way to make something life-giving and beautiful—something that looks like Jesus.

Are there circumstances in your life that are in process? Maybe relationships, ideas, or areas of personal growth that feel as though they have a long way to go? You can present it all to God today. Give him your dreams, your abilities, and all the stuff that looks like crumbs. Let Him mix up something delightful and worth serving to a world that desperately needs Him. He's eager to make something wonderful out of all that you are, so you can lay it in His hands today.

 **PROVERBS 3:5–6**

DAY 18: Mom's Homemade Bread

I grew up eating out most nights of the week. Seriously—the people at Outback Steakhouse and Macaroni Grill knew my family by name, and those were only two of the restaurants in our weekly rotation. Shortly after I left for college, my mom turned into a seriously healthy eater and even began milling her own wheat for fresh loaves of bread. Most kids came home from college to bum a few dollars off Mom and Dad, but I just wanted some homemade bread to bring back to my dorm room.

This is a simplified version of the recipe my mom used. The recipe yields two fluffy loaves that taste terrific for sandwiches and even better toasted. I make a lot of my own bread these days, but whenever I smell these loaves, all I think about is Mom. That's probably why I like the recipe so much.

....

MOM'S HOMEMADE BREAD

Makes 2 loaves

1¹/₂ cups lukewarm water

¹/₄ cup olive oil

¹/₄ cup honey

1 large egg

2 teaspoons table salt

4 cups all-purpose flour, plus more as needed

¹/₄ cup flaxseed meal

1 tablespoon instant yeast

In the bowl of a stand mixer, stir to combine the water, oil, honey, egg, and salt. Add 2 cups of the flour, the flaxseed meal, and the yeast, stirring to combine. Add 2 more cups of flour, and, using the dough-hook attachment of the mixer, begin to knead the dough on medium speed. If you notice the dough is still very soupy and loose, you can sprinkle in a little more flour 2 tablespoons at a time until it comes together into a soft, stretchy dough. Knead for a total of 6 minutes, or until the dough stretches slightly when you pull the dough hook out of the bowl. Lightly grease a separate large bowl with cooking spray and dump the dough into that bowl. Use plastic wrap or a large tea towel to cover the top of the bowl and set it aside in a warm area of your kitchen to rise until doubled in size, about 1¹/₂ to 2 hours total.

Once the dough has puffed and risen to double its size, lightly sprinkle a counter with flour and dump the contents of the bowl onto the prepared work surface. Use a knife to cut the dough into two equal-size pieces. Lightly spray two 8½ × 4½ × 2¾-inch loaf pans with baking spray and begin to shape the loaves. Gently pat a single piece of dough into a small rectangle and fold the bottom third of the dough up toward the center as if you're folding a letter. Fold the top part down and gently pinch the dough to seal the seam shut. Gently roll the dough over so the seam is on the bottom and use your hands to carefully work the dough to form it into a log roughly the shape of the pan. Put the log of dough into the pan, and repeat the process with the second piece of dough. Once each log of dough is in its respective pan, cover each with a piece of plastic wrap and set them aside in a warm area of your kitchen for a second rise, about 45 to 60 minutes.

Preheat the oven to 350°F. Once the loaves have risen and are barely doming over the lip of the pan, put the pans in the oven to bake for about 25 minutes, or until the loaves are golden and a thermometer inserted into the center of the loaf registers 190°F. Allow the loaves to cool in the pans for 20 minutes and then remove them from the pans to cool completely. Cooled loaves can be enjoyed immediately or wrapped in foil and frozen for up to six months.

DAY 19: Layers of Love

I'm that crazy birthday-planning mom. I can't resist the ritual and wonder and excitement of it all. I mean, just think about the first time a kid sees a piñata . . . *Candy raining from the sky?* I want to be the parent responsible for that kind of magic.

I made each of my kiddos a smash cake for their first birthday. They sat in their highchair wearing nothing but a bib and a smile while I urged them to dive into the cake in front of them. As expected, they all started out slow, gingerly raking a single finger through the outer layer of frosting. After a few bites, they became more excited and ravenous for the sugary flavors they were experiencing for the first time. The deeper they shoved those chubby little paws into the cake, the more eager they became for another taste.

Life with Jesus is lot like this. Every time we see another side of His face or experience a new flavor of His love and personality, we're like a kid tasting birthday cake for the first time. There's so much depth, so many layers to uncover, that we never quit finding new kinds of goodness as we dig deeper below the surface. We'll never come to the end of what He has to offer, because He continually reveals His glory in fresh and intimate ways.

Today, ask God for a new peek into His heart and character. Consider who has He been in the past to you and how you are experiencing His affection in the present. The Father has a wealth of wonder for you to uncover within the layers of His love, so dive in like a baby with a birthday cake—there's more than enough sweetness for you there.

 PSALM 65

DAY 20: The Potter and the Clay

My friend Taylor is a potter. It's amazing to watch her finesse a block of clay into beautiful cups and bowls, ornaments and vases. I know from experience that it's not as effortless as it looks, which makes it all the more incredible when she uses water and scraps of clay to form vessels that can hold something of substance.

We sometimes see ourselves as that plain lump of clay, don't we? While those around us appear to be fashioned into delicate objects and useful containers, we may feel clunky and inept, lacking any purpose. We call out the good and beautiful in others, but sometimes struggle to find the same good and beauty in our own lives.

I want to see myself the way God sees me. The Potter, with His creative ideas and capable hands, works and manipulates every bit of potential from our scraps. He shapes us with purpose and beauty, willing life and identity into even the dried-up remains of our old selves. Friend, you may be a work in progress, but you are being formed by the skilled and safe hands of a Heavenly Father. Today, welcome God into the undefined and messy parts of your story. Let Him design something whole and beautiful from all that you have to offer.

 **ISAIAH 64:8**

DAY 21: Asking the Hard Questions

My mom has had the same best friend for as long as I can remember. As a kid, I often resented her, because every time the two of them got together, they were inseparable. Now that I'm an adult, I totally get why my mom loves her so much—she saturates the people around her with a love that is downright infectious. She has the kind of personality I just can't get enough of, so now she's not just Mom's friend—I'm claiming her as mine too.

One of the things I appreciate most about this woman is her honest introspection. She's not afraid to get down to the nitty-gritty and ask the hard questions. She picks apart and challenges and digs deep, because she doesn't want to leave people where they are—she wants to see them grow. She wants more for me, for herself, and for the people around her.

Jesus never shied away from the hard stuff, because he knew growth and change could only happen when people were authentic. He asked the hard questions, not to uncover dark secrets or shame, but to encourage others to get real and evaluate their own hearts. Staying honest with yourself isn't always easy, but I'd encourage you to bring Jesus along to those conversations. He never condemned or shamed people for what He saw in them—He just wanted them to experience better. Today, find a friend you can be real with, and don't forget to bring the honesty and kindness of Jesus.

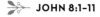 **JOHN 8:1-11**

DAY 22: How You Got Here

When my husband and I got married, I started making annual family photobooks to capture the memories from each year. They've become some of my most prized possessions, not because they're fancy or beautifully done, but because they're a reminder of where we've been, how we've changed, and the million things we have to be thankful for.

Although our big life milestones tend to get all the glory, it's important that we remember our big God days too: our conversion, the day we were baptized, an answered prayer, or a moment of healing, breakthrough, or revelation. Those transformational minutes in our walk with God have eternal significance, shaping not just our own lives but even the kingdom of heaven itself. We can rely on those moments of transformation as a testimony of who God is and how big His love is, serving as landmarks not just for ourselves, but for others too. Each moment speaks to where we've been and how God has met our needs along the way, and when we share our testimony, our words have power to offer encouragement and hope to the world around us.

Think back on some of your big God days. Whether that moment was yesterday or twenty years ago, let who you were or where you've been be a story of God's grace in your life even now. Today, take time to reflect on how far you've come with the Lord, and ask Him what more He wants to do in your life. Let the testimony of His love in your life be one that blesses you, your relationships, and the world around you.

 **PSALM 71:15–18**

DAY 23: Leaving a Legacy

My great-grandmother died a few years ago at the age of ninety-seven. She lived a special life, one marked by kindness and joy, wisdom and love. In the days following her death, I found myself quietly inspired, desperately wanting a similar kind of grace in my story. Knowing that it's possible to live as beautifully as she did filled me with so much hope.

I'm sure you know people like this—the ones that make it count. These are the people who use their lives to make the world around them a better place. They love their families fiercely and spur their neighbors toward goodness, and in the end, the enormity of their legacy for the lives they touched is profound.

Our legacy isn't the sum total of our titles, achievements, and bank account figures; our legacy is enduring the race set before us beautifully for the benefit of the world around us. Today, take time to consider the legacy you want to leave, and ask God to show you ways to begin sowing those seeds for the future, even now. As believers, we have the opportunity to carry on the legacy of Jesus Christ by loving and serving a world in need, fulfilling one of the final commandments He offered while on earth: *Love one another* (John 13:34, NIV). To begin running a race that counts, that's the best place to start: love.

 **HEBREWS 12:1–2**

DAY 24: Discipline

I won't even lie: I'm totally the person who works out to consume more food. I know there are people who love a great workout for its own sake, people who stretch, lift weights, or cycle for fun. I've tried coaxing my body into a routine of enjoyable exercise, but the truth is, some people's bodies like exercise while others just want cookies (cue me raising my hand). Either way, for fun or for cookies, any kind of healthy lifestyle always requires discipline.

Many things pertaining to a healthy Christian lifestyle require discipline too. Beyond the obvious disciplines of prayer, reading scripture, and worship, there's all that extra stuff about keeping commandments and loving your neighbor and making disciples. It's not always a walk in the park, but I've found that those efforts offer the strength training needed to produce a solid foundation in Christ. Just as I balance my love for cookies and caramel with a healthy dose of vegetables, there's balance within our faith too. Those disciplines like praying and reading and worship are catalysts for spiritual growth, and it's in those spaces where our hearts are bent toward God and our spiritual muscles are stretched in preparation for greater intimacy with Him.

Please hear me: this isn't a legalistic thing. This isn't checking spiritual practices off an invisible list as a means of making an A+ in Christianity. Discipline comes from a heart that knows God has more for us beyond the surface stuff, and we press in out of desire for a strong, unshakable faith within the confines of a love relationship with God. Today, feed yourself, both inside and out, with the good stuff that will make you grow.

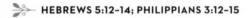 **HEBREWS 5:12–14; PHILIPPIANS 3:12–15**

DAY 25: Mediterranean Quinoa Salad

My kids will randomly decide they don't like certain foods. On Monday they eat strawberries, but by Thursday they hate them. Don't ask—it's a mystery to me too. When my daughter decided she forever loved this Mediterranean Quinoa Salad, I jumped on it. I'm still not sure she understands this is a reasonably healthy dish, and I don't plan on telling her.

You can enjoy this salad as a side, or bump it up to a hearty main with the addition of fresh greens and the protein of your choice.

MEDITERRANEAN QUINOA SALAD

Serves 6 as a side

3/4 cup quinoa, rinsed in a
  fine mesh strainer

1 1/2 cups vegetable or chicken broth

1 medium cucumber,
  diced (about 1 1/4 cup)

1 large red or orange bell pepper,
  diced (about 1 cup)

1 cup cherry or grape tomatoes, halved

1/3 cup finely chopped red onion

2 cloves garlic, minced

1/2 cup fresh dill, chopped

1/3 cup fresh Italian parsley, chopped

1 (16-ounce) can garbanzo beans,
  drained and rinsed

1/4 cup lemon juice

1/4 cup olive oil

2 teaspoons granulated sugar

2 teaspoons cumin

1 teaspoon kosher salt

3/4 teaspoon black pepper

In a small saucepan over medium heat, combine the quinoa and broth. Bring it to a boil, and then cover the pot, lower the heat, and simmer for 15 minutes until done. Remove the pan from the heat and fluff the quinoa with a fork. Set it aside to cool to room temperature.

In a large bowl combine the cucumber, bell pepper, tomatoes, onion, garlic, dill, parsley, garbanzo beans, lemon juice, olive oil, sugar, cumin, salt, and pepper. Mix in the cooled quinoa, add additional salt and pepper as desired, and place in the fridge. Serve chilled.

DAY 26: Overriding with Truth

When fear and darkness move in from all corners, I'm the first to jump ship. I cower, I panic, I go down the rabbit hole of a million what-if scenarios. I read the news, deep-dive into statistics, and make a mental calculation of how long I've got until my rope runs out. This world is full of terrifying things that are big and painful, and it's impossible to just pretend everything is always fine and dandy when, frankly, it's just not.

Someone recently reminded me that faith doesn't ignore the facts; it just overrides them with truth. My faith in God's sovereignty doesn't make things like war or cancer or loneliness less real, but it does shrink them in comparison to His glory. Hate might ravage my city, but it won't defeat the kingdom of God. Disease might destroy my body, but it won't outlive Christ in me. I may walk lonely roads, but the Holy Spirit will never leave me. At the end of the day, the realities of a fallen world are only overwhelming if we leave the One who has already conquered it out of the equation.

Instead of ignoring the ugly truths of this world, meditate on the One who holds it all in His hands. What does God's Word say about sickness? About pain? About fear? Fix your heart on His truth, which is far bigger than anything you'll face today.

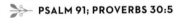 **PSALM 91; PROVERBS 30:5**

DAY 27: Tiptoeing to Jesus

Most days, my two oldest kids tiptoe down the stairs in the early morning hours shortly after I've woken up. With wild hair and eyes that are barely open, they crawl into my lap and snuggle their still-warm bodies into mine. Those few minutes, before they're truly awake and the morning has begun in earnest, are some of the purest moments of my day. I love that, even at ages six and five, they're never too old to come in close and find rest in my arms.

Some of the words in the Bible that touch my heart the most are those that name God as our Father. I picture Him sitting in His chair, waiting patiently for me to tiptoe into His presence, climb onto His lap, and find sanctuary in His arms. As His child, I have access to the love, protection, grace, help, and instruction of a good and loving Father, and it's not just for me—it's for you too.

You're never too old, too much, or too far gone to find rest in the arms of God the Father. You can bring it all to Him—your bed hair, the bad dreams, the worries and the messes from yesterday, and no matter what kind of earthly father you wound up with, you can always find comfort, safety, and love in the arms of your Heavenly Father. Crawl up into His lap today, and let those few minutes be the ones that carry you through your day.

 **PSALM 68:5; EPHESIANS 1:3-10**

DAY 28: Transparency

I have the tendency to overshare. It's safe to say my closest friends know absolutely way too much about me. Some people leave things behind closed doors, but anyone with the pleasure (or displeasure) of listening to me gets the inside scoop on just about every area of my life.

This way of communicating is not for everyone, and certainly there have been times when I've found myself with foot in mouth. I have found, though, that this kind of vulnerability, this willingness to bare yourself to others even at the cost of exposing too much, makes room for others to do the same. I want to be known as someone who is real and who means the words she says, and I believe people will know we're friends by my willingness to be transparent. Sometimes being 100 percent yourself empowers other people to do the same and offers the comfort and feeling of belonging.

We serve a God who knows everything about us. He knows our deepest fears and the things we only whisper to ourselves, and He still asks that we come. He wants us to trust Him enough to be transparent, and His desire is to engage in a close, face-to-face relationship that is full of sincerity and love. There are no limits on what we can bring to His wide-open arms.

Don't walk—*run* to the Lord. He's big enough to handle the transparency and honesty of your thoughts and feelings, and He's got all the time in the world for you to share them with Him. Open your heart to Him and experience the love He's waiting to share with you.

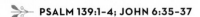 **PSALM 139:1–4; JOHN 6:35–37**

DAY 29: Finding Freedom

Throughout life, my definition of freedom has shifted and evolved with my changing circumstances. When I was a kid, it meant extra dessert, staying up late, or getting my ears pierced, but as I grew older, freedom included other things: more time, more money, or more control over my schedule, lifestyle, and decision-making. Deep down, as a believer, I recognize that even my adult definition of freedom remains lacking, and what I most desire is the freedom found in Christ.

When we became united with Christ, He released us from the bondage of sin. No longer do we have to remain attached to fear, unbelief, shame, or discouragement, because He took that yoke to the grave. Instead, freedom in Christ produces joy and allows us to live beyond ourselves in a way that honors God and others: with peace of mind, hope, and contentment, regardless of our circumstances.

Have you experienced that kind of freedom? Have you felt the weightlessness of having joy in the midst of sorrow, rest even in tumult, or hope when your own plans fail? The freedom found in Christ is yours and mine to participate in regardless of the earthly constraints and conditions of our stories. Today, if you find yourself needing more of that kind of freedom, offer the circumstances of your life at the feet of the Lord, and ask Him to set your mind on the desires of His heart. Allow Him to transform and renew your mind, and rest in the joy of His freedom.

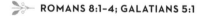 **ROMANS 8:1–4; GALATIANS 5:1**

DAY 30: Preparing the Soil

Spring in Alabama is a tricky thing. It's hot, it's cold, it rains, it freezes. Some springs we enjoy cool afternoons of flowering trees and chirping birds, while others are barely there, as winter melts straight into summer. In our neck of the woods, spring is planting season. My husband spends March and April weeding, tilling, fertilizing, and planting, so we can enjoy the fruit of that labor all summer long. We look forward to a harvest of fresh tomatoes and peppers and corn, but it doesn't come without some attention in the spring.

The same is true for our spiritual lives. We grow where we've been nurtured, and that requires readying our spirits for the new by weeding out the dead stuff: pride, bitterness, busyness, and distraction. God is the One who grows us in wisdom, love, joy, peace, and faith, but it's our job to prepare the soil. He readily pours out gifts and understanding, but if our hearts haven't been readied, we might miss the opportunity for the fullness of growth that He has for us.

The wonderful thing about God's harvest is that it's always abundant when planted in good soil. Whatever is sown with God is sure to produce way more than we could hope for on our own. Take some time, even today, to prepare your heart for what God wants to do in the coming season. And if you need help, ask Him where He wants you to sow more of His heart in the world around you.

 **2 CORINTHIANS 9:10–11**

DAY 31: Being Enough

I spent a lot of my life on the side of the road where the grass wasn't as green. Although I always had a supportive family, good friends, and a host of other things to be grateful for, I struggled with little insecurities and wasted a lot of days with a measuring stick in hand, trying to determine where I stood in the lineup of people around me. Even today, as a thirty-something-year-old woman, I find myself tiptoeing onto the scale of comparison, because somewhere inside is a whisper of doubt that says who I am is not enough.

Do you feel this? Is your life riddled with doubt and shame? Do you find yourself filling up secret, lonely places with the weightiness of jealousy? Even small, seemingly insignificant areas of self-doubt can create mountains of pain in the strongest of humans, and it happens to me so frequently that I'm certain I'm not alone in this; some of you are struggling to stay afloat in this boat with me.

I want to remind you today that your life is significant. The things that make you who you are—the hopes and the history, your personality and your passions, every curve of your body and outline of your words—those things have value. There is beauty spilling out from every corner of you, and with an ounce of confidence and joy to back up that grace in your life, the world around you won't be able to stop watching. Your gifts are a unique contribution to the universe, a reflection of your Heavenly Father, and they *matter*.

Today, we need to say no to the head games, no the measuring stick, no to the scales of comparison. We say no to the voices that second-guess, shame, and doubt. We say no the whispers of "You're not enough." Instead, we say yes to what God says about us: yes to joy, yes to purpose, yes to beauty and passion and individuality. Today, we declare that we have been created with intentionality and precision, and we will rest knowing that we are lovely simply because God says so. Let this truth repeat in your brain and heart all day, every day, until you believe it.

 **PSALM 139:1–12**

DAY 1: Springtime Chicken Noodle Soup

As the weather shifts from winter to spring, I like to make this chicken noodle soup, a dish that offers the comfort of a winter soup with the bright, refreshing flavors of spring. Here, lemon juice and fresh parsley awaken simple noodles, broth, and chicken to create a meal that is light in flavor, yet hearty.

....

SPRINGTIME CHICKEN NOODLE SOUP

Serves 6 to 8 as an entrée

2 tablespoons olive oil	1 bay leaf
1 large yellow onion,	2 teaspoons dried thyme
diced (about 1¼ cups)	Salt and pepper
3 large carrots, cut into ½-inch dice	2 quarts low-sodium chicken stock
(about 1½ cups)	1½ pounds boneless chicken
3 large celery stalks, cut into	2 cups egg noodles
½-inch pieces (about 1 cup)	¼ cup chopped fresh parsley
4 cloves garlic, minced	3 tablespoons lemon juice

In a large pot, heat the olive oil on medium. Toss in the onion, carrots, and celery and cook, stirring occassionally, until the onions have barely softened. Add the garlic and cook for an additional minute or until fragrant. Add the bay leaf, thyme, 1 teaspoon salt, ¾ teaspoon pepper, and the stock, and stir to combine. Bring to a boil, and then add the chicken. Immediately lower the heat and cover the pot. Simmer until the chicken is done, about 15 minutes for tenders or 25 minutes for larger breasts. Remove the chicken and allow it to cool briefly; then shred or chop it.

In the meantime, turn the heat back up to medium-high, bring it to a boil, and add the noodles. Cook for 5 to 7 minutes, or until the noodles are done. Turn off the heat and stir in the chicken shreds, parsley, and lemon juice. Carefully taste and add additional salt and pepper as desired. I usually add another ½ teaspoon salt and a pinch of pepper.

DAY 2: Never Tired of Us

It only takes about twenty-four hours of nonstop, hard-core parenting for me to realize I'm not as sane as I thought I was. The noise, the mess, and the chorus of tiny voices chirping *"Mama! Mama!"* is enough to make me feel as though I've been transported to the Twilight Zone. As humans, we need space and a time to reset and unplug, but motherhood . . . motherhood is a different animal. Yes, it's the joy of my life, but, honestly, it's kinda exhausting.

I'm so thankful that God never tires of hearing our voices. Unlike a tired mother, He's not burdened by our needs or frustrated when we make the same mess all over again. We can't drive Him away or exhaust Him with the sound of His own name, because He longs for His children to come to him and live a life that is dependent on His presence.

I think the enemy would like us to believe that we're too much for God. He'd like us to think that our concerns and cries are burdensome to God, or that we're wearing Him thin with our human neediness. Sister, this notion is a lie. God delights in our willingness to come to Him. He longs for relationship with us and is pleased when we rely fully on Him.

Present yourself as a child to the Lord. Trade your questions and needs and pains for the love of a sufficient Father. Trust Him with the details of your heart, and rest knowing that He has more than enough time, patience, and love to spend on you.

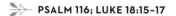 **PSALM 116; LUKE 18:15–17**

DAY 3: In the Middle

I have a love-hate relationship with Swiss meringue buttercream: love, because it's heavenly, and hate, because I'm terrible at making it. Typically, right in the middle of the process, things start to go terribly wrong, and even though I've learned that these malfunctions usually correct themselves with a little time or change of temperature, there's no redeeming my spirits when it feels as though the wheels are falling off. I'm already frustrated, defeated, and swearing to never make Swiss meringue buttercream again.

I'm reminded that it's hard to judge the circumstances of our lives when we're wading through the middle of them. *Where is God when the contents of my life are going wrong? Where is His faithfulness when I'm struggling? Can I trust in His goodness even when I haven't seen the breakthrough?* In those moments of uncertainty, God's gentle commandment is for us to be still—to quiet our minds and the noise of the world and shift our focus back to Him. It's there, in the waiting, where God brings clarity to our mess and the events of our lives come together with purpose and intentionality.

Have you found yourself somewhere in the middle, a hazy unknown of life that seems to be falling apart? Are you waiting for a breakthrough or an answer to the questions in your heart? Be still. Wait for Jesus. He is a God of peace, not confusion (1 Cor. 14:33) and His words will always offer direction and understanding (Ps. 119:130). Look for Jesus in the middle of your process—He's in the waiting.

 **PSALM 46:10**

DAY 4: My Big Mouth

We were out having dinner with friends when I did it again—I caught myself saying something I really shouldn't have. We were at a private dinner table surrounded by people who know my heart, but the instant I said it, I knew it was wrong. Some words simply aren't necessary.

As I get older, I'm realizing that my words don't just shed light on who I am—they reflect on Jesus too. For a long time, any tongue biting came from a desire to protect my own reputation, guard my own secrets, or make myself appear more put together than I knew I was, but lately the Holy Spirit has been letting me know when my tongue is doing more harm than good.

The Bible says, *Death and life are in the power of the tongue* (Prov. 18:21). As believers, we are uniquely positioned to bring life-giving hope to the world around us that is starving for the goodness of Jesus. We are a lifeline, a rope to pull them from the churning waters of this world and onto the shores of heaven, but when they meet us, do they see Jesus? Are we the salt and light, or are we dark and flavorless like the rest of the world?

Sister, there's no condemnation here. We're all a work in progress, but if your words and life don't point to Jesus, there's an opportunity to press in closer to Him. Are there areas of your life that are lacking salt and light? Ask God to fill your heart and mind and mouth with beautiful, life-giving words that look and sound like His. Rely on Him to do the transformation, and He most certainly will.

 **COLOSSIANS 4:6**

DAY 5: Pot vs. Kettle

Marriage has a way of knocking you down to size real quick. It seems as though every time I think I've been wronged, I wind up in a game of pot calling the kettle black. In those moments, more often than not, I march into battle armed with arrows of accusations and proof of wrongs, only to limp away feeling most wounded by my own pride and shame.

I don't have an answer for every quarrel that occurs in marriage, but I am slowly learning to check my pride at the door. In marriage or friendships, at work and at home, I'd rather be humble than falsely assume that I'm right. Owning your part, even when the other person fails to do so, will always be the right thing to do, and there's a freedom that comes from acknowledging the plank in your own eye instead of pointing at the fleck in someone else's. I might still enter a few fights not worth engaging in, but I'm striving to be a person who finishes them all in love.

Are there relationships or situations in your life that have become messy because of pride? It's not too late to own your part. Things don't always get better right away, but you'd be amazed at the weight that lifts when you humble yourself long enough to lower your pride. Ask God to help clear up any confusion in your heart and to scrape off anything not of Him. When you prioritize humility over winning the fight, you make room for God to grow in your life. Let Him do just that in your relationships today.

 **COLOSSIANS 3**

DAY 6: Making Lemonade

Sometimes, life is just *really* good, isn't it? It's easy to celebrate when life gives us new friends, a good hair day, or an extra drizzle of caramel at the bottom of our Starbucks cup. When life hands us a flash sale at our favorite store or a long-awaited answer to prayer, everything in us rejoices, shouting, "YES! Thank you, God! Hooray!"

But then we find ourselves with a broken relationship, bad test results, or that feeling that we're two steps behind everyone else. We might encounter failure or get a load of disappointing news we weren't counting on. On those days, we just have to roll up our sleeves and make lemonade with whatever fruit we've got, but let's be honest—that's often easier said than done.

In those undesirable moments, I'm reminded of my need for grace. When days are overwhelming or different than we imagined, grace is our portion, the thing that fills us up and allows our hearts to rest exactly where we find ourselves. God has promised that His grace will abound when we need it most and is most effective when we're at our lowest, and isn't that encouraging? Doesn't it give your heart hope to know that God has made a way even on our hardest days?

God's grace is sufficient in every circumstance, so wherever you find yourself in life today, you can rest knowing that He's got it covered. His grace is big enough to make lemonade with whatever you've got, so give it all to Him. Rest in Him today.

 **2 CORINTHIANS 4:15; 9:8**

DAY 7: Being True to Yourself

I love that Southern cooking is unabashedly true to itself. It doesn't require frills and furbelows, fine china, or precise measuring or chopping; instead, Southern food has the unique ability to be as buttoned-up or -down as it wants to be, and there's an element of comfort found with the confines of its simple ingredients and techniques.

Jesus has invited us to live the same way. There's no cleaning up or fancy rhetoric required to come before the Father; He's not asked us to memorize a bunch of scripture or learn elaborate prayers to be accepted into His kingdom. Instead, He welcomes us all—the weary, the burdened, the sinful, and the thirsty—to present our bodies and lives as living sacrifices to His cause. Rather than striving to conform to some idealized image of what a "good Christian" should be, God has called us to use each day as an opportunity to become more and more like Jesus.

Your Heavenly Father created you with specific purposes in mind. The unique nuances of your life offer reflections of His creativity and image, so you can confidently embrace your quirks, ideas, and abilities, knowing that He can use all things that are submitted in His name. Today, take time to thank Him for everything that makes you *you*, and be proud of the work God is doing in your life.

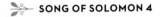 **SONG OF SOLOMON 4**

DAY 8: Mint Sweet Tea

One of my college roommates grew up close to campus, and every once in a while we would eat supper with her parents in their home. Although I hadn't yet acquired a taste for Southern sweet tea, her mother's mint variety was out of this world. This Mint Sweet Tea is exactly how I remember hers being: sweet, flavorful, and altogether refreshing.

....

MINT SWEET TEA

Makes 2 quarts

MINT SIMPLE SYRUP

1 cup granulated sugar

1 cup water

1 cup fresh mint leaves, not packed

TEA

8 cups water, divided

2 family-size (7 grams each) bags of black tea

¼ teaspoon baking soda

1 batch simple syrup

TO PREPARE THE MINT SIMPLE SYRUP

Combine the sugar, water, and mint in a small saucepan over medium heat. Stirring occasionally, bring the mixture to a gentle boil. Once the sugar has completely dissolved, remove the pan from the heat and allow the mint leaves to infuse into the syrup for 20 minutes. Strain the mint from the syrup and store the syrup in the fridge in a heat-proof container or jar until ready to use, up to two weeks in advance.

TO PREPARE THE TEA

Bring 4 cups of the water to a boil in a medium saucepan or tea kettle. Once it has reached a gentle boil, remove it from the heat and add the tea bags to the water. Allow the tea to steep for 5 minutes. In the meantime, add the remaining 4 cups of cold water to a pitcher along with the baking soda and the simple syrup. Once the tea is done steeping, add it to the pitcher as well and stir. Refrigerate the mixture until cold, up to about six days.

DAY 9: Your Identity

During these past few years of motherhood, I've slowly begun to realize that my life and agenda are no longer my own. My schedule, my belongings, and every single inch of privacy and personal space have been wildly (and wonderfully!) invaded by the children living under my roof, so much so that it has become hard to distinguish any semblance of my own life outside of theirs. In the whirlwind of school calendars, breastfeeding schedules, and the wants and needs of my kids, I've found myself losing track of, well, myself.

Although people always say that motherhood is instinctual, I'd argue that most of it is still really hard to figure out. Finding a balance between who I am as Kate Wood and who I am as Aimee, George, and Charlie's mom feels like a teeter-totter that is difficult to steady. Part of me feels incredibly selfish for wanting to maintain some semblance of self-independence from my children, but another part knows that, in order to stay sane, I need to know how to still be *me*. So how do you do that? How do you fully embrace a life you've chosen, one that is truly a gift, while maintaining an identity that is even remotely recognizable?

If you have children, I want you to remember that your identity is not just "mother." Nor are you just an employee or a wife or a young single woman. You're not just a middle child or daughter or widow or whoever the world has said you are. Your identity is child of God. Everything that you are—your talents, your desires, your personality—it's all just a reflection of the King of heaven. Your identity is one that is made in His image, and it should free you to no end to know that all that you are can be wrapped up entirely in Him.

 **1 JOHN 3:1–10**

DAY 10: One Big Family

Every year, my college friends and I get together for a weekend away with all our families. The years we have shared together have been filled with change and self-discovery, knitting us together into something that looks like a big, messy, extended family. Our reunion weekend is like a rerun from the past, and for a few days we are resurrected versions of our old selves, somehow grown up but entirely the same.

The person I am today is, in large part, a product of the lessons and experiences I shared alongside those friends. Watching them laugh and move and play like the eighteen-year-olds I once knew reminds me that, for as much as we grow and change over time, we can still be unabashedly ourselves in the company of true friends.

Have you experienced this? Do you have a friendship that is so deeply rooted in your story that you can't tell what parts of you are yours and what parts are simply imprints of their life in your own? This is a small glimpse into how the Father is connected to us. He sees our truest selves and knows us better than we do. For as much as we have been marked and transformed by our human relationships, God's glory, grace, and love have impacted our story even more. Isn't that incredible?

Take time today to thank God for the friends in your life who sharpen you, nudging you closer to Him. Ask Him to use your relationships on earth to point you toward heaven, and, most important, offer Him thanks for the solid friendship you have in Jesus.

 **1 JOHN 4:7–12**

DAY 11: Simple Bread and Simple Wine

On those weekends away, my college friends and I have a tradition called the "Big Fat Italian Dinner." It started with student budgets and spaghetti noodles for ten college kids but has since grown to include spouses and children. We look forward to the dinner each year, all those familiar faces laughing and chatting in a scene that has come to look and feel and taste like home.

There's something powerful about honoring old traditions by participating in them again and again. Every Italian dinner night is different, but each one evokes a sense of belonging, as we recollect and relive our years together by sharing stories from all the suppers that came before it. In a way, those nights are a time of remembrance, and right there, with our paper plates and cheap wine, something holy happens, as though we're participating in something bigger than a meal.

When I think about Jesus's Last Supper, I know it's not by coincidence that He chose simple bread and simple wine to connect us to the power of His life and death. I used to think it was all about remembering His death, but now I understand there's something much more powerful happening. When we partake, we can relive His power and love, experiencing them again and again, knowing that the cross is big enough to impact and transform us each time we participate, even now.

Don't miss the beauty of coming to the table, both in your own home and in God's. He has offered an invitation there to receive and belong, and intimacy comes with breaking bread. Do you have people, maybe family or friends who feel like family, whom you can welcome into your home? Are there life-giving relationships you can share around the table? Don't miss out on that blessing—participate again and again.

 **MATTHEW 26:26–28**

DAY 12: Celebrating the Eggs in Our Own Basket

My kids dyed Easter eggs on their own for the first time this past year. It was like a wonderful, messy, magic show, and all of my kids were delighted by it, especially George. I watched as he dipped his eggs into every single color, each shell transformation his immediate new favorite. He was so proud of his work that morning until he got a glimpse of Aimee's eggs. She had a bright teal egg with specks of neon purple, and suddenly it didn't matter how proud he was of what he created—he only wanted the eggs in her basket.

We do that as adults sometimes. Often, the things we create and work hard on look dull in light of what someone else has brought to the table. We overlook our gifts, our talents, and the goodness right in our own lap, because we're so consumed with what everyone around us has. In the distraction of someone else's story it can become difficult to remain grateful for our own.

Today, take time to celebrate the eggs in your basket—maybe a talent, a child, or a dream. Maybe you have a big heart, deep understanding, or a refreshing relationship with the world around you. Forget about what is in everyone else's baskets and, instead, celebrate the colorful, life-giving stuff that you have right now. You never know when you might acquire a few new eggs, but don't forget to love the ones God has already placed in your life.

 **1 CORINTHIANS 12:4–31**

DAY 13: Abiding

We built our home on a tract of land brimming with nature: wild deer and turkeys, pine trees and water oaks, native grasses and even a natural well. At the end of our first spring there, we witnessed a happy surprise when a big patch of thorny bushes suddenly produced bite-size berries that, over the course of a few weeks, grew and turned from red to a deep, dark blue. Dewberries! That year, we picked to our heart's content, and even now, at the end of every spring, we ride to that one area where the bushes come to life with a small offering of fruit.

I love how the dewberries grew even without our help. They didn't need fertilizing or trimming or an added irrigation system, because each branch had exactly what it needed within the vine. The success of their growth is wholly dependent on the vine, and even though there were thorns and overgrown grasses in the area, the branches still produced fruit.

As Christians, we often try to rely on ourselves in our walk with God. When our relationship with Him becomes mostly about striving and getting it all right, we can forget that our only role is to abide. Our job is to stay connected to the vine, and God, the Vinedresser, tends to our growth. The harvest in our lives is fixed solely on our ability to remain close to Him.

Be encouraged this morning: abiding is your purpose. You need only to stay fully attached to the vine in order to produce a fruitful, fulfilling life. Today, ask God to show you any areas of your life where you may be striving as a means to achieve spiritual growth, and allow Him to replace that work with rest. In Him, there's no list of extra to-dos or spiritual prerequisites; we simply abide, and our faithful Vinedresser will guide us through the rest.

 **JOHN 15:4-11**

DAY 14: Feeding Our Temple

I often trick myself into buying food at the grocery store that I don't really want to eat. Some days, I fill my cart with greens and peppers and citrus and seeds, even though I'm pining for the containers of leftover take-out chicken and fried rice that are waiting for me in my refrigerator. Deep down, I want to feed my body well and find a place of moderation for everything else, but there are moments (more than I'd care to admit) when the heathy options don't even stand a chance.

Eating well often feels like a battle of good versus evil, but I don't want to be a slave to my own desires. Instead of feeling the weight of shame every time I set the table, I'd like to begin seeing food as both a source of nutrition *and* a source of enjoyment, something that satiates my body *and* my desires. The Bible says we are God's masterpiece (Eph. 2:10), a creation made in His image (Gen. 1:26–27). We have a fresh opportunity each day to make choices that will serve our bodies well, and although I have a long way to go, I deeply desire to take better care of my body.

What is your relationship with food? Do you live to eat or eat to live? Good nutrition is a balance, and it's okay if you haven't figured it out yet. Consider some ways you can take better care of His temple this week. Is it exercise? Including more healthy options? Opting for moderation rather than overindulgence? Ask Him to show you some places where you can make changes, and make those good choices an offering of your love and worship to Him.

 **1 CORINTHIANS 6:19–20**

DAY 15: Simple Shallot Vinaigrette

If you've never made homemade salad dressing, this is a call to action. Homemade dressings, particularly vinaigrettes, are a simple and tasty alternative to store-bought varieties. This Simple Shallot Vinaigrette, made with shallots, garlic, and white wine vinegar, pairs terrifically with salads of all sorts. If you're running low on time, skip the cooking and simply shake all the ingredients together in a Mason jar. This recipe will keep well in the fridge for up to a week and is enough to top a family-size salad.

....

SIMPLE SHALLOT VINAIGRETTE

Makes 1 cup

6 tablespoons extra-virgin
   olive oil, divided

1 large shallot, minced (about ¼ cup)

½ teaspoon minced garlic

2 tablespoons white wine vinegar

2 tablespoons honey

1½ tablespoons lemon juice

½ teaspoon kosher salt

½ teaspoon black pepper

Warm 2 tablespoons olive oil in a small pan over medium heat. Add the shallots and garlic and cook for a few minutes, stirring frequently, until the shallots are translucent and the garlic has turned golden and fragrant. Scrape the contents of the pan into a small blender or food processor and add the remaining oil, vinegar, honey, lemon juice, salt, and pepper. Blend until smooth. You can chill it in the fridge or serve it warm.

DAY 16: Princess in the Kingdom

At our fanciest, Aimee and I don brightly colored dresses, rhinestone jewelry, and plastic crowns. We sip lemonade from doll-size teacups and eat candies and crackers off of coordinating plates. My heart is so tickled; I can't wait for the day she discovers it's not make-believe—she's actually royalty.

We are children of the King of heaven, and our inheritance in Christ is one of power, revelation, and heritage. It's not just a fairy tale—it's who we are in Him. As sons and daughters, we have access to all the riches of His heavenly kingdom, right here, right now, because we have been adopted into His family. We're not waiting here on earth until we die and the real party starts in heaven; instead, we get a front-row seat for the spectacular show of His power and dominion here on the Earth. Let the full glory of this mysterious and wonderful grace settle in your heart: we are His *children*.

Someday Aimee will understand that the crowns and jewels were fun, but the one inheritance worth its salt isn't a fairy tale—it's her reality. Sister, it's yours too. Take some time today to thank God for making you a part of His family. Ask for a deeper revelation of His plans for you in His kingdom, and pour out a heart of gratitude.

 **EPHESIANS 1:3–14**

DAY 17: Reasons for Wonder

Last year, we took our big kids to Walt Disney World, and I went into the weekend with a level of anticipation that is normally reserved for Christmas Eve. *What would they think?* I wondered. *Would they love "It's a Small World" as much as I did as a child? Would they dance in the parade? Be chosen as a volunteer in one of the shows?* I couldn't wait for them to experience the wonder and excitement of all the things that used to captivate me as a child, because I just knew that, within those gates, awaited a trip of a lifetime.

Well, they did love it. They loved the hotel breakfast and chasing birds and splashing in the puddles after one rainy morning. One afternoon, they bypassed rides to spend hours at one of the park's playgrounds, and after about an hour they both wanted to go back to the hotel to watch TV. Over the course of two days, they laughed, made memories, and had the time of their lives, but that joy had absolutely nothing to do with the magic I was trying to manufacture for them. When I quit trying to force my own ideas of the experience on them, I saw they were finding their own reasons for wonder.

Most of us, at some point or another, fall victim to the belief that our greatest life experiences are wrapped up in some big moment like a trip to Disney World, landing a job, or getting the guy, when, in reality, there are treasures just around the corner in our everyday life. We don't have to fly to Florida to find magic when God has placed wonder and blessings in our story, right here, right now. There's an abundance of wonder, adventure, and joy in Christ, and we have the opportunity to tap into them each and every day of our lives.

Are there places in your life where you may be overlooking the goodness of God? Today, ask Him to point out the rich and joyful life experiences that reside just out your back door. Don't miss what God is doing in this chapter of your life; instead, find those chances for gratitude and give Him thanks for the wonder of His kindness.

 **PSALM 107:8-9**

DAY 18: Course Correctors

Some days, I spend all morning recipe testing—baking bread, forming pie dough, or piping messy swirls on colored cakes. The perfectionist in me prefers the days with successful taste tests, but with so many proverbial (and literal) pots on the stove, there's usually a flop or two in the mix. Failure is discouraging, and I have to confess, in that moment I tend to fixate on the errors rather than enjoying the other delicious things that come out of my kitchen.

We often do the same thing with our ambitions. When considering our dreams, it's easy to become distracted by hurdles rather than taking inventory of how far we've come. We overlook our accomplishments, the things that are working in our favor, and get hung up in the itty-bitty potholes we've hit along the way.

Friend, let me remind you that God has given you really big and beautiful dreams. He's assigned you a purpose and has fully equipped you to achieve whatever it is He's called you to. The enemy would love to derail those pursuits with discouragement; instead, let's acknowledge our errors, the failures we encounter along the way, and learn from them.

Wherever you are today in your journey with work, relationships, or yourself, remain tender toward God's grace and love. He can transform setbacks into teachable moments and use your failures as course correctors. He's not surprised or disappointed by a few slipups, and if you're following His lead, you can be encouraged knowing you're well on your way.

 **PSALM 32:8; HEBREWS 10:35–36**

DAY 19: Amuse-bouche

Brett and I have had the pleasure of dining at some over-the-top restaurants, and I love it all—the impeccable service, the crisp linens, and the plates of food that possess as much beauty and detail as they do texture and flavor. One of my favorite parts of those kinds of occasions is the amuse-bouche—a small, usually bite-size taste of food that comes at the beginning of a meal to rouse the appetites of the diners. That little plate of food welcomes you into the experience and offers a small taste of what is to come.

For a long time, I struggled with searching for that initial taste of a deeper spiritual relationship with God. I knew I wanted more of God, but I had no idea where to start. There were days where I'd open my Bible and scan the pages, hoping something would captivate me and satisfy that craving for more. Sometime later, a friend of mine showed me Psalm 100:4: *Enter His gates with thanksgiving, and His courts with praise!* In short, gratitude, worship, and an affectionate heart bring us into deeper intimacy with God. Since that time, I see a thankful, worshipful heart as a spiritual amuse-bouche—a glorious prelude to that first taste of the courts of heaven.

God isn't hiding; we don't have to find Him or lure Him into our hearts. But if you're struggling to settle into your quiet times with Him, remember the amuse-bouche: we enter into His presence with a worshipful heart. Today, let your affection and praise set the tone for your quiet time with the Lord. Bring gratitude into those moments with Him this week, and savor the love and goodness flavoring the experience that follows.

 **HEBREWS 11:6**

DAY 20: Wide-Open Love

Sometimes I watch my children from afar as if the whole moment is happening in slow motion and black and white. I see little faces wrinkled with smiles, heads thrown back with laughter. They move wildly, chasing each other around the kingdom of our backyard as if they could run anywhere in the world. Every once in a while, we lock eyes, and no sooner than they've whispered "Mama," they come running toward me—arms open and voices shrieking, in a knock-you-over kind of embrace. All at once, I'm covered in sticky hands, sweaty faces, and all of their love. It's wonderful.

I've lost a lot of my childlikeness, the parts of my heart, mind, and body that used to move with freedom, unhindered by the practicality of the world, but I know God still sees me as His daughter. I wonder what joy it brings Him to see His children experiencing His creation freely, running toward Him with a reckless love that is full of passion and vulnerability and joy. Most days of the week, I fail to pursue Him with that much zeal, but I really want to. I want to love Him the way my kids love me, and more so, the way *He* loves me.

Bring your messy, wide-open love to Jesus today. Knock Him over with your excitement and adoration, with every bit of freedom and joy you have in you. On days when it's not there, ask Him to stir up a heart that burns for Him (Luke 24:32). He loves us deeply, even more than a parent loves a child, and His deepest desire is for us to love Him back.

 **1 JOHN 3:1-3**

DAY 21: A Story for Our Collection

When I was growing up, my nana would take me to Joseph-Beth, a local bookstore, and we would peruse the store for hours (no joke). After we'd picked out our favorite books, I'd carry my little stack to the register, and Nana, without fail, generously bought me each and every one of them. She taught me to treasure the fresh pages of a beautiful book, and in a way my love for storytelling and writing began with her. What she may have seen as a shopping trip or simply time with her granddaughter had lifelong impact, quite literally changing the narrative of my life.

I doubt we'll ever fully appreciate the impact all our little actions have on the world. Each day, we fill the shelves of our lives with stories and thoughts and feelings, making a few contributions to the collections of others along the way. All of those words we share and choices we make have the potential to change the way our shelves look forever. In the end, our love—time spent, conversations, and the gifts and interests we rub off on others—have the potential to shape the world around us forever.

Today, embrace your potential for impact. Love the people within your reach as hard as you can, and ask God who else needs some kindness added to their story. You don't need a pulpit, a degree, or a title to have impact—you just need love.

 **LUKE 19:1–10**

DAY 22: Brookies (Brownie Cookie Bars)

On our bookstore days, Nana and I would eat lunch at a local restaurant where our special tradition was to eat dessert first. Our go-tos were tall slices of banana cream pie and the brookie, a brownie cookie bar topped with ice cream and whipped cream. In retrospect, it wasn't the food that made the tradition memorable—it was the company.

These Brookies are a combination of brownie batter and chocolate chip cookie dough, prepared together in a square baking pan. Once baked, each bite offers a bit of cookie and a bit of brownie, equal parts chewy, chocolatey, sweet, and salty. If you're a girl who just can't choose between brownies and cookies, don't—make Brookies instead.

....

BROOKIES (BROWNIE COOKIE BARS)
Makes 16

BROWNIE BATTER

¼ cup unsalted butter

⅓ cup granulated sugar

⅓ cup packed brown sugar

1 large egg

1 teaspoon vanilla extract

⅓ cup all-purpose flour

⅓ cup unsweetened cocoa powder

¼ teaspoon table salt

⅓ cup semisweet chocolate chips

COOKIE DOUGH

6 tablespoons unsalted butter

½ cup packed brown sugar

⅓ cup granulated sugar

1 large egg

1 teaspoon vanilla extract

1 cup all-purpose flour

1 teaspoon baking powder

½ teaspoon table salt

½ cup semisweet chocolate chips

Additional chocolate chips for decoration (optional)

Fleur de sel (optional)

TO PREPARE THE BROWNIE BATTER

Preheat the oven to 350°F. Line an 8- or 9-inch square baking pan with aluminum foil, pressing it into the corners and up the sides, leaving a 2-inch overhang on two sides. Lightly grease the foil with baking spray.

In a small saucepan over medium-low heat, stir the butter, sugar, and brown sugar together until melted and smooth. Pour it into a medium-size mixing bowl and allow it to cool slightly. Whisk in the egg and vanilla. Add the flour, cocoa powder, and salt and stir with a wooden spoon until almost combined. Add the chocolate chips and stir until the ingredients are well incorporated. Spread the mixture on the bottom of the prepared pan. Use lightly moistened fingers to pat it out evenly.

TO PREPARE THE COOKIE DOUGH

Melt the butter, brown sugar, and sugar in a saucepan over medium-low heat, stirring until smooth. Pour into a medium-size mixing bowl and allow to cool slightly. Whisk in the egg and vanilla. Add the flour, baking powder, and salt and stir with a wooden spoon until almost combined. Add the chocolate chips and stir until the ingredients are well incorporated. Spread the mixture on top of the brownie layer. Dot the batter with a few additional chocolate chips, if desired, and bake for about 30 minutes, or until a toothpick inserted just barely comes out clean. Allow it to cool on a wire rack for about 20 minutes before lifting the bars out by the foil edges. Once cooled, slice into squares and sprinkle with fleur de sel, if desired.

DAY 23: Cancelled

My younger sister attempts to keep me cool. She regularly sends me songs and memes, taking time to explain new trends and turns of phrases to me. Years before the word "cancelled" took on a life of its own in pop culture, my sister used it to describe a fleeting trend that was no longer relevant, and I was intrigued. Although "cancel culture" can be complicated and not always positive, I do like the idea of cancelling things from our own lives that no longer serve us.

Take a moment today and think: Are there things that you'd like to "cancel" about your past or present? How about fear or anxiety? Maybe a set of habits or a lifestyle that has become painful or unhealthy? What about the hateful words someone spoke about you, or the ones you've whispered about yourself? Are there some things in your world that you wish you could just cancel forever?

Often, we carry those heavy parts of us, because we don't know what else to do with our burdens or we feel like a fraud when we try to shed the past. But friend, consider the lengths Jesus went to remove the pain in your story. He took it all—the doubt, the shame, the wounds, the stains—and He cancelled it. It's all been washed away with His blood. Jesus has cancelled the weightiness of your sin and the sins that were committed against you, and He's offered to shoulder the entirety of your load if you'll just hand it over to Him.

Ask God to show you if there are some things in your life you need to let go of today. Thankfully, Jesus paid mightily for it all, and it's no longer yours to bear.

 **ROMANS 3:21–26**

DAY 24: A 100 Percent Chance of Jesus

On the week leading up to our wedding, the weather outlook was bleak. The forecast predicted thunderstorms and temperatures dropping into the forties—not the rainbows and sunshine you hope for at an outdoor wedding. All those months of planning and preparation were at the mercy of an unforeseen cold front, and just when I was about to succumb to discouragement, my future husband gave me hope in his rehearsal dinner speech with these words: "I don't know if there will be rain tomorrow, but thankfully there's a 100 percent chance of marriage." At those words, our family and friends cheered, and my heart soared. Rain wouldn't change the outcome of the day, because no matter what, we were getting married.

That memory brings to mind three guys from the Old Testament who met another kind of storm. Shadrach, Meshach, and Abednego were sentenced to a fiery furnace at the hand of King Nebuchadnezzar, because they refused to worship anyone but the God of Israel. They were unflinching, even in the face of death, because their future with the Lord was secure. They knew God had enough goodness and power to save them, but even if He didn't, they would remain faithful to Him anyway.

This is the security we have in Christ. God's goodness doesn't sway with our circumstances or the weather. Fiery furnaces, flash flooding, and even soggy wedding dresses won't diminish the security we have found in Jesus. God always has the power and goodness to save us from the threat of our circumstances, but even if He doesn't, He's still good. Our Heavenly Father doesn't withhold goodness from the people who love Him (Ps. 84:11), so we can rest assured that He is working with our best interest in mind at all times.

Are there circumstances you need to entrust to the Lord today? Remain hopeful and at peace even when facing ruined plans or an uncertain future—there's always a 100 percent chance of Jesus.

 **DANIEL 3:8–30**

DAY 25: First Steps

With little to no experience in baking, I decided to make my own wedding cake. Up until that point, my kitchen savvy was limited almost exclusively to break-and-bake cookie dough, so the tiered cake I had in mind was more than a little ambitious. With zero know-how, fancy tools, or starter recipes, I began testing vanilla cakes in the kitchen of my tiny rental house, and a few months later, I was feeding my new husband bites of homemade wedding cake. In retrospect, the cake wasn't much to gush over, but I was so proud. In a way, that cake is where this whole baking adventure began.

All these years (and cakes) later, I'm reminded of Zechariah 4:10 (NLT): *Don't despise these small beginnings, for the Lord rejoices to see the work begin.* Did you catch that? He *rejoices*, celebrating wobbly first steps, failed attempts, and beginner tries. While we're critiquing our prototypes or feeling discouraged about our efforts, He's rejoicing over our beginnings, our bravery, our willingness to step into a new thing.

Wherever you find yourself today—maybe in a new relationship, a new job, or with a new dream in your heart—remember that God is rejoicing in those minutes. There's grace for the flops or things that don't go according to plan, and it's okay if you don't get it all right. Invite God into the process, and be kind to yourself while you figure it all out. Celebrate your new beginnings, and thank God for a future filled with hope and expectation.

 **DEUTERONOMY 28:1-14**

DAY 26: # Making Vows

I was standing at the end of the aisle with my soon-to-be husband when our pastor asked us to recite our vows. There, we made promises to love one another, to value each other's family, and to stand by each other faithfully, no matter the circumstances. It's funny—even then, standing in my white dress with a heart full of optimism and hope for the future, I knew we'd both fail at times. Mistakes, even if only temporary, were most certain, because we were two imperfect humans entering into marriage in an imperfect world.

I'm thankful that when God makes promises, He always keeps them (Hebrews 10:23) His vows stand the test of time and are strong enough to stand even in our fallen world. In Isaiah, God made a promise to His people that stands true for us today: *For the mountains may depart and the hills be removed, but my steadfast love shall not depart from you, and my covenant of peace shall not be removed (54:10)*. His love never fails, and His assurance of grace and compassion resounds true forever and ever. God's heart for you is everlasting and unchanging, forever.

If, somewhere along the way, you've bought into the lie that God's love has somehow been diminished or removed, let me just remind you: every word of God proves true (Prov. 30:5), and He has said that His love is great and permanent. Rest in His kindness and affection, and let it cover you and fill you with hope and gratitude. God has vowed His love to you forever, and nothing, absolutely nothing, can separate you from it.

 **ISAIAH 54:4–10**

DAY 27: When Life Is Unpacked

Brett and I hopped off the plane, gathered our luggage, and made the forty-five-minute car ride to our resort in Mexico. It was day three of our honeymoon, but this leg of the trip I had anticipated for months. I had the spray tan and the new bikinis, and absolutely nothing would ruin what was sure to be a perfect romantic getaway.

That is, until I opened my bag to find . . . men's clothes. No sandals or straw hats or lingerie; no makeup or contact lenses or gauzy white dinner dresses. Just slacks, button-down shirts, and boxer shorts. I had picked up a suitcase at the airport—same bag, same luggage tag, same pink "HEAVY" slip on the handle—but it turned out it wasn't mine. Nothing I could do would transform this disheveled mess of dress socks and shaving cream into my thought-through lineup of honeymoon attire.

Though I was disappointed that my careful plans were thrown out the window, I couldn't help but laugh. We ended up having a lovely time anyway, and I realized that life throws curveballs, ones we never see coming, and we can either roll with the punches or let them knock us out.

Be gentle with yourself and patient in your circumstances. God hasn't abandoned you; instead, He has invited you to trust Him. When life feels weird and uncertain, when you've been let down or disappointed, you can zip up that messy bag of worries and give it to Him. He's promised never to leave us, never to forsake us, and to always be a place of rest for weary travelers. Give your worries, your fears, and your disappointments to Him today, and make an exchange for His peace.

 **MATTHEW 6:25–34**

DAY 28: Resetting

Since our honeymoon, Brett and I have taken a few trips to Mexico just because. It feels good to leave behind our everyday patterns and shed the frazzled versions of ourselves we normally offer one another to reveal someone who is more at rest. We reconnect over tacos and salt-rimmed margaritas, remembering how to laugh and to move playfully, free from agendas, like the two people we were when we first fell in love.

Vacation isn't where real life happens, but it does serve as a nice reset. It's a reminder to love, breathe deeply, and to be gentle with ourselves and one another. I'm grateful for the opportunity to dust off parts of myself that are normally covered in responsibility, and although I wouldn't trade our day-to-day life for anything, we need those minutes of clarity to keep this crazy train going.

How do you reset? What are the things and places, people and activities that awaken parts of yourself to life again? We can't live in a permanent state of vacation, but we can bring some of those things home with us to engage bits of our heart and personality that we normally set to the side. Today, ask God for creative ideas or opportunities, anything that will serve as a reset for your soul. The peace and rest that come from the Lord are better than all the frozen drinks and empanadas you could find in Mexico, so spend time resetting with Him today.

 **MARK 6:30–32**

DAY 29: Black and Blue Margaritas

During the warmer months, margaritas are my grown-up beverage of choice, and this rendition made with fresh berries and honey simple syrup is seriously delicious. The syrup is easy to prepare in advance and will make enough for multiple drinks. For an extra-summery take, I like to add fresh mint or basil leaves to the shaker, which transforms this sweet and refreshing marg into a fragrant and floral one too.

BLACK AND BLUE MARGARITAS

Serves 2

HONEY SIMPLE SYRUP

(Makes 6 Ounces)

½ cup honey

½ cup water

COCKTAILS

½ cup fresh berries (I use a mix of blackberries and blueberries)

4 ounces tequila blanco

2 ounces fresh squeezed lime juice (from about 2 limes)

1½ ounces honey simple syrup

Coarse salt (optional)

TO PREPARE THE HONEY SIMPLE SYRUP

Combine the honey and water in a small saucepan over medium heat. Stir with a whisk until the honey is dissolved and then place the syrup in a small jar or heat-proof container to cool in the fridge. This can be made ahead and kept in the fridge for up to two weeks.

TO PREPARE THE COCKTAILS

Muddle the berries in a tall cocktail shaker until they're broken down and juicy. Add the tequila, lime juice, and honey simple syrup to the shaker and fill it with ice. Shake vigorously for about 20 seconds. Wipe the flesh of the squeezed lime around the rim of two margarita glasses and dip the glass rims in salt, if desired. Fill with ice and strain the chilled mixture into the prepared glasses. Enjoy!

DAY 30: Becoming My Mother

When I was growing up, my mother and I weren't always thick as thieves. She took the role of chauffer and maid, while I played the aloof princess-in-training. As far as I was concerned, she was too strict, too loud, too all-up-in-my-business, and I swore I'd do it better when I had kids of my own someday. Let's all just laugh at that illusion.

As I enter the early phases of what I pray will be many years of parenting, I think about my own children and how I can nurture them to become exceptional humans. I look at my mom, along with so many other beautiful women who have invested in my story, and I think, *How did she make it look so easy?* The honest truth is that I don't have a clue. So until someone fills me in on the plan, here's my strategy.

I will be probably be too strict, too loud, too all-up-in-my-children's-business. I will discipline and ask the hard questions, even when it hurts. There will be fights, apologies, and tears past counting, but I'll do it because I love them, because their future and their spirits and bodies are worth fighting for. In the midst of this impossible job, I will rest in knowing that my children are in God's hands, and I can trust Him in the messy parts that feel too big for me. My mom taught me a lot, but the most valuable thing her life demonstrates to me is this: we can give it all to Him.

The burden, the joy, the questions, and the impossible—it's all safe at the feet of Jesus. Are there relationships or circumstances that you need to offer to Him today? Jesus has paid for the peace and joy that He gives to His people who abide in Him, so bring those cares to Him in prayer and rest there.

 **1 PETER 5:1-11**

DAY 1: Audience of One

My mom is one of the kindest people I know. She's one of those women whom most people love because she consistently treats others with deep kindness and sincerity. There's nothing showy about her, nothing that begs for attention or recognition, but she's always there behind the scenes, quietly caring for, loving, and serving others.

The performer in me wants to be rewarded for my good works. I tend to live for the trophy moments when I get the badge of honor or a gold star next to my name for the good and beautiful things I've accomplished. Although my inclination is to work for the applause, there are several sections of scripture that instruct us to reserve our good works for those secret moments, to do them in private, out of sight from the world. The idea is that we love and serve because it flows from our heart as an act of worship rather than a hunt for recognition. Those minutes when we wear kindness and generosity while doing the dirty work and tough jobs no one else wants are like little deposits of love to God. Ultimately, it doesn't matter if the world sees our service, because it's the hidden treasures that count most in heaven.

We have an audience of one. Gold stars and flashy medals are nice, but treasures in heaven are better. Take a moment to inventory your heart today. If your motive for kindness and love is recognition on earth, you'll never be fully satisfied. Instead, commit your work, your generosity, and your gifts to the Lord. It blesses His heart to see us be the hands and feet He has called us to be, and that's all the reward we could ever hope for.

 **PROVERBS 3:1–4**

DAY 2: Setting Up a Memorial

Some time ago, my mom encouraged me to keep a record of all the baked goods I shared with people—a wedding cake, cookies for a sick friend, cinnamon rolls for a birthday morning, or treats to feed a crew at church. I never wrote it down, because at the time it felt self-serving, as if I was keeping record of all my good deeds. In retrospect, I think what she was suggesting is more like a record of love—a list of opportunities to love God's people and experience the beautiful reward of doing His work here on earth.

There's a story in the Bible about Jacob who had a dream, an experience so vivid and powerful that, upon waking, he set up a pillar in memorial to God's presence in that place. That rock served as a testimony of what God did, so Jacob could always remember and be encouraged by God's work in His life.

We can move through life so quickly that we forget how far we've come. Without a record of those places where God met us, the ways He provided or answered prayers or fulfilled dreams, His presence can go unnoticed and become forgotten. When we intentionally remember God's work in our lives it can serve as a source of encouragement and remind us to partner with Him again and again to love and serve with whatever gifts we have to offer.

Don't miss what God is doing in your life right now. When He shows up, shows out, or loves loud, write it down. Let your past be a testimony to what God has done, knowing that if He's done it before, He can do it again. Today, be encouraged by the work God is doing in your life, and let His love right now be a memorial in your life for years to come.

 **GENESIS 28:10–22**

DAY 3: At Home Wherever

After getting married, I moved to the small town where my husband grew up, and the first few months in my new home were rough. I missed my old friends, my old job, and the luxuries of big-city life. Although I never admitted it, there was a lot of insecurity about who I was and how well I fit into this new community that I was supposed to be calling home, and it took months for me to snap out of that haze.

When I finally opened my heart and mind to my new life, I was overwhelmed by the vibrant community, hope, and possibility that was flourishing all around me. God had brought me into a new season, and although it isn't one I would have ever thought to plan for myself, it was overflowing with incredible blessings.

We all eventually find ourselves in a similar phase: a new hometown, relationship, trial, or even emotional state that we didn't see coming. In those moments of in-between, where the puzzle pieces haven't quite fit together the way we thought they would, God is still there, offering hope, possibility, or blessing wherever we open our hearts to receive it. We're never at risk for losing our happy ending if we rest in the grace of God, the One who works all things together for good (Rom. 8:28).

God doesn't bring us to difficult or new places to make us miserable. There's purpose even in seasons we don't understand, and when we make the decision to lean in to the unknown and choose joy in every circumstance, we will find ourselves ever on the precipice of rich connection and learning and experience. Today, ask God to show you how to rest in every circumstance, and learn to be at home wherever it is you find yourself.

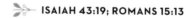 **ISAIAH 43:19; ROMANS 15:13**

DAY 4: Love Next Door

One of my favorite things about life in my small town is how friends, neighbors, and even strangers can come to feel like family. When your life is closely knit together with those of the people around you, wanting the best for them is an absolute no-brainer. Their struggles are your struggles, their joys are your joys, and the triumphs and blessings in their lives will eventually trickle down to affect yours in a positive way too. When one person succeeds in a small town, everyone eventually shares in that reward, and I've found that taking part in their stories by investing passion and love into the things that are important to them almost always feels like a shared victory in the end. This way of living with crazy love and support, even for total strangers, is one of the most heart-filling things I've ever experienced in my life, and if you've felt it too, I bet you'd agree.

Jesus modeled it best when He made the fullness of His inheritance available to us on the cross. Just like that, we were welcomed into His family. Instead of reserving His miracles, love, and glory for a few close friends or family members, Jesus held all He had loosely in order to share more freely with the world around Him.

We have the same opportunity today. Swing open the doors of your heart to love your neighbors wildly in their triumphs and compassionately in their sorrows. Consider if there are people within your circle of influence whom you can come alongside to support or encourage in a special way this week. Look to God for an extra dose of His love to share with the community around you, and He will most certainly equip you with it.

 **1 THESSALONIANS 5:11–15**

DAY 5: Making a Bucket List

A few years ago, my sister and I sat across the counter from one another making our summer bucket lists. My list included things like cleaning out the pantry and going to the beach, while hers was loaded with big accomplishments like becoming a certified scuba diver, training for a half marathon, and learning to sew. In that moment, I was reminded of her bravery, her seemingly unquenchable thirst for new experiences and stories, and I found myself wanting to adopt some of that same adventurous spirit into my goals.

As we get older, many of us tend to stick with the roads most familiar to us, treading the same turns and pathways over and over again. There's nothing wrong with predictability, but people like my sister remind me it's also great to try new things. Although she didn't end up doing *all* the things on her list that summer, she made a whole lot of memories while stepping into the unknown.

What would it look like for you to step into your version of the unknown? Are there desires in your heart, maybe a hobby or career or relationship, that you'd like to see take root in this coming season? Are there hopes and dreams you might have been hesitant to invest in? Share those things with the Lord today, and see if anything sticks. God has great ideas and rich experiences available for His people willing to adventure with Him, so don't be afraid to try. If you align your bucket list with His desires, you'll be in for a wild and beautiful ride.

 **JEREMIAH 33:3**

DAY 6: Sun-Dried Tomato Quiche

Many years ago, my sister and I were enjoying a fancy lunch at a restaurant in Lexington, Kentucky. Reading off the menu, my sister asked the waiter what the "kweesh" of the day was, unsure of how to pronounce the word "quiche." We laughed *hard*, and needless to say, she hasn't heard the end of it since.

This Sun-Dried Tomato Quiche is an incredibly yummy "kweesh" that reminds me of that hilarious meal from years ago. I like to serve this with a simple arugula salad topped with the Simple Shallot Vinaigrette on p. 112 or a small bowl of soup. The pie dough can be made in advance and stored in the fridge for up to a week, or in a pinch you can substitute a store-bought refrigerated deep-dish crust.

....

SUN-DRIED TOMATO QUICHE

Serves 8

CRUST

1³⁄₄ cups all-purpose flour

2 teaspoons granulated sugar

¹⁄₄ teaspoon table salt

5 tablespoons chilled solid
   vegetable shortening, cut into pieces

6 tablespoons chilled unsalted butter,
   cut into pieces

5 tablespoons ice water,
   plus more if needed

1 large egg, beaten

QUICHE

1 tablespoon unsalted butter

¹⁄₂ cup chopped yellow onion
   (about half of 1 medium onion)

2 cloves garlic, minced

2 cups half and half

3 large eggs

¹⁄₂ cup grated Parmesan cheese

1 teaspoon Italian seasoning

¹⁄₂ teaspoon dried basil

³⁄₄ teaspoon kosher salt

¹⁄₂ teaspoon black pepper

¹⁄₂ cup oil-packed sun-dried tomatoes,
   drained and chopped

¹⁄₄ cup feta cheese, crumbled

TO PREPARE THE CRUST

Pulse the flour, sugar, and salt in a food processor to combine. Add the shortening and butter, and pulse until just evenly dispersed, with pea-size clumps throughout. (Or you can mix the dry ingredients by hand and cut in the shortening and butter with a pastry cutter.) Begin adding ice water 2 tablespoons at a time until moist clumps begin to form. Remove the dough from food processor, form it into a flat round disk, and wrap it in plastic wrap. Chill it in the fridge for at least 1 hour.

Use a floured rolling pin to roll the dough out on a floured work surface into a round about 1 inches larger on all sides than a shallow 9-inch tart dish. Roll the dough back onto the rolling pin and the transfer it to the dish, unrolling as you go. Gently work the dough into the edges of the dish and, leaving about 1 inch of dough hanging on all sides, trim off any excess. Fold the dough under itself and gently crimp the edges into the dish, allowing the top of the dough to extend about 3/4 to 1 inch above the lip of the dish. This will help keep the crust tall even after baking. Place the unbaked crust in the freezer to firm up for about 30 minutes prior to baking.

When ready to bake, preheat the oven to 375ºF. To make the egg wash, whisk the egg with a teaspoon of water. Place a crinkled sheet of parchment paper on the bottom of the crust and fill it with pie weights or uncooked dry beans. Bake for about 10 minutes, and then remove the paper and weights. Brush the entire crust with a thin layer of the egg wash, and bake for an additional 15 minutes, or until the bottom of the crust doesn't look too wet and soggy. While the crust is baking, begin to assemble the filling.

TO PREPARE THE QUICHE

In a small frying pan, melt the butter, add the onion, and cook over medium heat, stirring occasionally, until softened and translucent. Add the garlic and cook for an additional minute. Remove the pan from the heat and set it aside.

Whisk together the half and half, eggs, Parmesan, Italian seasoning, basil, salt, and pepper. When the crust is finished baking, spread the cooked onion mixture evenly over the bottom of the crust. Then sprinkle the sundried tomatoes and feta evenly over the onion mixture. Slowly pour the egg mixture over the ingredients in the dish, being careful to not overflow the tart. Bake for about 35 minutes, or until the top is golden and the center is no longer jiggly. Serve warm or later reheat individual slices in the toaster oven.

DAY 7: Common Ground

I met one of my best friends in line at college orientation. It was a total "meet cute"—she was wearing a shirt I owned, and I was wearing a necklace she had. We bonded over our wardrobe, and that marked the beginning of the solidarity that would continue to grow over years of friendship.

Common ground, whether a matching shirt, a favorite team, or a shared experience, is among the many things that help to create bonds, but it's in the deeper unveilings of ourselves—our feelings, beliefs, hopes, and fears—where lasting connections are formed. When we offer the opportunity for others to relate to our joys, our struggles, and our dreams, we make room for more common ground on which to build relationship. Writer C. S. Lewis described friendship as the moment when "companions discover that they have in common some insight or interest or even taste which the others do no share and which, till that moment, each believed to be his own unique treasure." In a nutshell, we find friendship when we find common ground.

Who are the true friends God has placed in your community? Are you sharing in meaningful, authentic, real-life friendship? Don't be afraid to expose your truest self to the people you know you share common ground with. Be vulnerable enough to expose your heart full of curiosities and experiences, knowing that, by doing so, you may be bringing hope and comfort to someone else in different circumstances. If you're unsure where to start, ask God to point out the ground in your life that you can share with others, and use those parts of yourself to encourage and love the world around you.

 **HEBREWS 10:24–25**

DAY 8: Everyone's a Mother

I grew up with a lot of mothers—aunts, teachers, parents of friends, and other women who weren't legally or morally responsible for me, but still took it upon themselves to love me wholeheartedly. These were the women who affirmed and challenged me even into adulthood, extending that same support into the lives of my children. That love—their care and time and physical presence—impacted decades of my life and had a tremendous effect on the outcome of my story.

When shared generously, outside of obligation or hopes of receiving anything in return, love is one of the single most impactful things we can offer to one another, and everyone is qualified to share it. Your opportunity to mother doesn't begin and end with the kids under your roof, and you're not disqualified as a mother if you've never given birth. There's someone out there who needs your prayers, your friendship, and your accountability. They need you to show up at their basketball games, hold their hand when they're hurting, and listen when they just need to process.

As a woman, you are uniquely qualified to mother. Ask God to open the door for beautifully nurturing relationships, and position yourself to love as hard as you can. Your love makes a difference.

 RUTH 1-4

DAY 9: **Our Beliefs**

I spent part of my childhood summers on a lake in Kentucky where we enjoyed sunsets on the "Chicken Cruiser," the pontoon boat affectionately named after our favorite pastime of enjoying Kentucky Fried Chicken on the water. It took an embarrassing number of years for me to realize that buckets of chicken and buttermilk biscuits weren't the official food for pontooners, because the entirety of my experience up until then had been just that.

The Chicken Cruiser is a silly example, but the truth is we all grow up with a host of beliefs that may or may not be true. Thankfully, when it comes to the things we believe about our relationship with God, we've not been left in the dark. Instead, as we grow in our relationship with God, He transforms our heart and mind, revealing beliefs and lifestyles that don't align with His desires. Over time, by abiding in Christ and experiencing His love, our hearts and minds soften and shift into an image that bears the resemblance of Him. The transformation isn't immediate, but by exposing our hearts to His love and truth, the Holy Spirit performs a deep makeover of our soul.

Today, ask God to reveal any places in your life where you've held on to beliefs that are not from Him. If there are areas where you're still choosing thoughts or practices that don't line up with His nature, know there's no shame—only opportunity. Submit your life to the transforming power of God, and allow Him to make you more like Jesus.

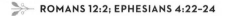 **ROMANS 12:2; EPHESIANS 4:22–24**

DAY 10: Being Real

My friend Devon is one of the nicest people I've ever met. She's sincere, fun, and incredibly easy to talk to, the kind of person who carries so much comfort and ease in her own demeanor that you can't help but relax a bit too. From the get-go, she was so real and open, and that authenticity made me love and trust her quickly—I knew I was getting to know her truest self.

Vulnerability is a tricky thing. So many of us want to expose our hearts, to put ourselves out there with candid bravery, but it's scary. *What if people don't like what they see? What if I don't fit in? What if the real me is too loud, too different, or not enough?* I get it—sometimes it's easier to step away from the risk of relationship than subject yourself to the pain and humiliation of rejection.

Jesus encouraged His followers and friends to be real about who they were, and that vulnerability was always met with love and acceptance. He Himself was never out to be the most popular or well-liked guy in town; instead, He desired true relationships and forged many of them by revealing who He was.

Take a moment for introspection: Are you comfortable with vulnerability? Do you have someone in your life, maybe a friend or an acquaintance, whom you'd like to be more real with? You were created in the image of God, which means there is goodness and beauty inside of you. The world needs people who are authentically themselves in way that honors Jesus. Today, ask God to point out some friends within reach who may be safe people to open up to, and be confident in the real you—God loves who you are, and others will too.

 **1 PETER 3:3-4**

DAY 11: Room in My Heart

When I was pregnant with my second child, there was a part of me that was scared I wouldn't be able to love him as much as I loved the child I already had. Aimee was my first, and I loved her with every ounce of emotion I had to offer. *What if the second was different? Would I be a terrible mom if I didn't love him as much as my daughter? What if I couldn't make room in my heart?*

George came, and everything changed. He looked similar to his sister and felt the same in my arms, but I knew my heart was affected. Somewhere amid the late-night feedings and hours spent in a rocking chair, a little space in my heart was filling. It was a part of me that was his alone, and there he was, filling it as though he had been there all along.

Jesus shared a parable about a shepherd who left his flock of ninety-nine to find the single sheep that had strayed away, and it always reminds me that there's an intentionality in the way that God pursues us. He doesn't just love us with whatever He has left over after caring for the ninety-nine, and He doesn't love us less because we're not just like the others in the flock. Instead, He lovingly draws us to Himself with the desire that we'll, in turn, love Him back.

What do you believe about God's love for you? Do you know what a prize you are? On the flip side, is there someone you can make room in your heart for? You won't run out of love this week, and neither will God. Spend it freely, and make room in your heart for someone new.

 **LUKE 15:1–10**

DAY 12: Rest in the Shade

On the hottest days of the summer, we seek out solace from the heat in the shade of our backyard. With sprinklers, popsicles, or even frozen margaritas in hand, we do what it takes to beat the heat. The warm temperatures, as oppressive as they can be, make those brief moments of refreshment from a gentle breeze, an icy beverage, or a quick plunge in a cold pool that much sweeter.

Song of Solomon describes God's love as a source of solace and refreshment: *As an apple tree among the trees of the forest, so is my beloved among the young men.* He sustains us, providing nourishment for our heart and relief from the elements of the world. This sustenance is not just physical either—it's emotional and spiritual too. When our souls are heavy, when our spirits feel dry and weak, or when our hearts have been beaten down and exhausted by the elements of this fallen world, He is our shade and our portion. He surrounds and revives us with His love.

Be encouraged in this moment: your Savior is an ever-present apple tree for your wanting heart. If there are pieces of your inner self that need refreshment this morning, God is able and willing to restore you with His love. He's privy to the needs of your heart, and He desires to meet them in both extravagant and simple ways. Rest in His shade today, and be revived by the sweetness of Jesus.

 **SONG OF SOLOMON 2:3-5**

DAY 13: Strawberry Shortcakes

Mimi, my grandmother, used to make chicken biscuits and gravy when I was a kid, and any leftover biscuits were topped with fresh whipped cream and macerated berries for dessert. Over the years, I've played with various recipes for strawberry shortcake, but I'm partial to this one. The shortcakes are tender and come together in the time it will take you to macerate a bowl of fresh strawberries. We like to serve these with whipped cream, but you could opt for ice cream, nondairy whipped topping, or even a pastry cream if you'd prefer. When beautiful summer berries start popping up at your local market, this will be your favorite bite of summer.

....

STRAWBERRY SHORTCAKES

Serves 10

SHORTCAKES

2 cups all-purpose flour

2 tablespoons granulated sugar

1½ tablespoons baking powder

⅛ teaspoon table salt

½ cup chilled unsalted butter

1 cup whipping cream

Demerara or sanding sugar
   for sprinkling (optional)

STRAWBERRIES

2 pounds strawberries, stemmed,
   and cut into ½-inch pieces

¼ cup granulated sugar

Pinch of table salt

WHIPPED CREAM

1¼ cups heavy whipping cream

¼ cup granulated sugar

1 teaspoon vanilla extract

TO PREPARE THE SHORTCAKES

Preheat the oven to 425ºF. Line a baking sheet with parchment paper.

Whisk together the flour, sugar, baking powder, and salt in a medium-size bowl. Using a pastry cutter or the backs of two forks, cut the butter into the dry ingredients until well combined, with pea-size clumps uniformly throughout. Add the cream, stirring until a shaggy dough is formed. Use an ice cream scoop or a large spoon to portion out $\frac{1}{4}$-cup mounds of dough onto the baking sheet. Sprinkle a little demerara sugar on top, if desired. Bake for about 13 minutes, or until the shortcakes are golden and cooked throughout. Allow them to cool on a wire rack.

TO PREPARE THE STRAWBERRIES

Use a potato masher or the backs of two forks to mash up about half of the strawberries. Toss in the remaining strawberries, the sugar, and a pinch of salt, and stir. Set aside to allow the berries to macerate (let the juices break down), about 10 minutes.

TO PREPARE THE WHIPPED CREAM

Pour the whipping cream into a large bowl or the bowl of a stand mixer (if using a stand mixer, use the whisk attachment). On medium speed, whip the cream until it foams and thickens slightly. Slowly add the sugar and vanilla and then continue whipping on medium speed until the mixture thickens to a cloudlike consistency. Set aside.

TO ASSEMBLE THE SHORTCAKES

Slice each shortcake in half horizontally and remove the tops. Spoon a generous dollop of whipped cream and a large spoonful of strawberries on each bottom. Replace the tops and enjoy immediately!

DAY 14: Use It or Lose It

After my second child was born, I hit the gym hard on a mission to get back into my old blue jeans. For a while, I was dedicated to the work, and every evidence of my effort made me incredibly proud of the progress. But over time, I started skipping my workouts, indulging in an extra glass of wine or a second cookie before bed, and my results faded. My jeans got tighter, I lost some of those muscles, and within a few months I was back at square one.

The phrase "Use it or lose it" comes to mind here, and it's a truth that I believe extends into other disciplines of our lives as well. We acquire knowledge, intimacy in relationships, and even hobbies or skills that, without the continued attention of time and participation, won't remain as strong as they once were. Just because we could do a back flip or cartwheel or recite a bunch of verses years ago doesn't mean we've still got it today, but by regularly engaging those mental, spiritual, and physical muscles, we are more prepared to flex when our strength is required.

Are there things in your life, maybe a relationship, a spiritual discipline, or a skill you worked hard to acquire, that could benefit from a little TLC? Don't wait for a rainy day to begin sowing good seeds where they're needed. Begin today with a time of prayer, a phone call, or a few minutes of practice. Ask God to show you some parts of your spirit that He wants to begin exercising, and allow Him to strengthen you, even now, in preparation for the days to come.

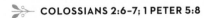 **COLOSSIANS 2:6–7; 1 PETER 5:8**

DAY 15: Confronting Our Peas

As a kid, I hated peas. I spit them in my napkin, hid them under the rim of my bowl, and spread the little spheres around my plate until it appeared as if I'd attempted to consume them. There was something about the flavor or texture that I couldn't stomach, so instead of eating them I just pretended they didn't exist.

Some of that avoidance has stayed with me into adulthood, except now it's the parts of reality that are hard for me to confront, things like injustice, crisis, and tragedy, which feel too big to even begin to deal with. Rather than address those needs, I've become tempted to look the other way, to shove them under my plate and pretend they don't exist. Quite often, the fear that I'll cause more harm than good is paralyzing, and rather than move on behalf of the people without a voice, I pause, filled with my own with anxiety: *How can I even make a difference?*

Jesus never hesitated to address the injustice that was right in front of him. He touched lepers and defended prostitutes and turned over tables in the temple. He met the hurting and broken with love, every time, and spoke on behalf of the people who had no voice. Never once do we see Him looking the other way or leaving the problem for someone else to manage. He offered His hands for healing and His heart for love, because that kind of provision is within His very nature. It's who He is, and it's who He called us to be.

I'm still learning what it looks like to confront the difficult parts of the world, and maybe you are too. Most of us haven't even begun to scratch the surface of our privilege and responsibility to meet the needs of a fallen and broken humanity, but I know it's supposed to look an awful lot like Jesus. So, today, instead of avoiding the things that seem uncomfortable to deal with, ask for an extra serving of grace to love and fight and serve as Jesus did.

 **MATTHEW 25:37–40**

DAY 16: Mustard Seeds

Sometimes I'm astounded by the evidence of faith in the Bible. When I try to imagine myself having the faith to take on giants or build an ark or wipe mud on a blind man's eyes, it's almost laughable. God says a mustard seed of faith is enough and nothing is impossible with Him, but do we believe it when clouds darken the light and big mountains stand in our way? Do we have faith when our circumstances are outside the realm of human control and God is, quite literally, our only hope?

I'll be honest—that kind of faith can feel difficult to access some days, but I want to. I think it's okay to be vulnerable with God and expose where our heart is: *God, I don't know if I have faith for this, but I want to. Help my unbelief.* On our own, we may not have the faith and hope necessary to make it out of this world unscathed, but Christ in us has plenty to go around. We can trust that He is sufficient for all the needs we have today, tomorrow, and forever.

Are you facing a circumstance that is stretching your faith? Is there some place in your life that is lacking hope? God has said, "Come to me." He has the faith for everything you'll face today, so don't doubt your mustard seeds. Give them to Him.

 **LUKE 17:5-6**

DAY 17: Peeking Behind the Curtain

I grew up frequenting a local Japanese restaurant that became like a second home to my family. We ate at the hibachi table weekly, and I was fascinated by the show of it all: the fire, the onion volcanoes, and the clang of utensils on the stainless-steel cooktop. At other restaurants, we didn't get a look at how our food was prepared, but the hibachi table was like a peek behind the curtain, a place where we were all invited to participate in the spectacle of our meal.

Unlike at a hibachi table, in life we rarely have an idea what's going on behind the scenes and tend to get caught up in the here and now. Although it's easy to become overwhelmed by the unknown and begin to hope that God will work things out in a manner that suits our own understanding and preferences, He has asked us to trust Him. Thankfully, we can rest in the promises of God and relinquish control into His loving hands, knowing He can and will work out the details of our everyday lives for His glory and our benefit.

Today, are there areas of uncertainty or circumstances that you've been struggling to control in your everyday life? You don't have to see it all laid out on the table to be afforded the opportunity to rest in God. You can trust that He is only doing good things behind the curtain, so rest at His table and know that He will be faithful to serve you good and wonderful things.

 **PSALM 145:13-21**

DAY 18: Our Helper

On Saturday mornings, my kids like to help with whatever I'm preparing in the kitchen. They're great at taste testing and at stealing chocolate chips and swipes of frosting when you're not looking, but they're not so great at productively *helping*, so to speak. I let them join me at the counter anyway, because I know welcoming them into the kitchen is an opportunity for connection, and, at the end of the day, I deeply desire for our relationship to grow.

Before Jesus died, He told everyone He was sending a Helper. The Holy Spirit would tag in and become the unfailing source of truth, a constant help to guide and lead God's people while they were here on earth. Let's not miss the glory of this reality: we have access to the God of the universe, the Authority of Heaven, because we've been given Himself as a Helper who lives *inside of us*. He never leaves, never rests, never ceases the whispers and proddings of our heart.

Talk to Him today, and thank the Holy Spirit for His helping presence in your life. Ask God for a fresh infilling of the Holy Spirit and an increased awareness of His working in your heart. Spend some time this week reading about the power that is available to you through Him, and let that gift, the incredible offering of God in you, be a blessing to your heart.

 **JOHN 16:7–15**

DAY 19: On Our Qualifications

Back in high school, I started playing tennis just for the cute outfits. Yes, it's totally embarrassing to reveal this truth to you, but if pleated skirts and coordinating visors could have won my matches, I'd be right up there with Serena Williams today. I looked every bit the part, but it only took a couple of lessons for me to learn that nothing about my apparel would qualify me for a win on the court.

Our appearance doesn't carry much weight on the tennis court, and, thankfully, it doesn't in God's kingdom either. Our looks, our background, and our past or present difficulties do not disqualify us from the Christian life, and our ability for impact isn't limited by our gender, our eloquence, or our level of education. Our qualification to walk as powerful, godly women begins and ends in Christ, the One who offers us eternal life, freedom from sin, and authority from heaven. The world's opinions and stereotypes can't hold a candle to the glory of His word, and if He has declared us worthy of a calling, then that is exactly what we are.

The Bible says that apart from Him, we can do nothing (John 15:5). In fact, the greatest qualifier in our lives is that the same power that raised Jesus from the grave lives *in us* (Rom. 8:11). It is Christ in us that qualifies us to achieve every dream, every calling, every word spoken over our lives, and we have direct access to that power even today.

Are there paths God has called you to walk that feel big or out of reach? Be emboldened to step into that calling with the confidence that, if He commanded you to go there, He will surely equip you for the journey. Jesus is the only qualifier that counts, so rest in Him today.

 **2 CORINTHIANS 3:1-6**

DAY 20: Smash Burgers and Baked Truffle Fries

Cookies and milk. Popcorn and Diet Coke. Tacos and margaritas. Some foods just taste better together, don't you think?

Cue these Burgers and Fries. Few foods satiate my carnal cravings for greasy, salty, comfort food like a good burger with fries, and the following recipe is my absolute favorite rendition to make at home. Here, simple smashed burger patties are lightly seasoned and cooked diner-style in a skillet to be served alongside a mound of Parmesan truffle fries. There's no grill, no fryer, and little prep time—I call that a winning combination.

....

SMASH BURGERS AND BAKED TRUFFLE FRIES

Serves 6

BURGERS

1½ pounds ground chuck (80/20)

1½ teaspoons kosher salt

1 teaspoon black pepper

½ teaspoon onion powder

½ teaspoon garlic powder

2 tablespoons canola or
    vegetable oil, divided

6 slices cheese of your choice
    (I always pick melty American)

6 potato buns

Toppings: lettuce, tomatoes, ketchup,
    mustard, mayonnaise, or any others
    as desired

FRIES

1 (28-ounce) bag frozen shoestring
    French fries

3 tablespoons white truffle oil

1 teaspoon minced garlic

¼ cup chopped Italian flat-leaf parsley

½ cup finely shredded Parmesan cheese

1 teaspoon coarse kosher salt

¼ teaspoon black pepper

TO PREPARE THE FRIES

Heat the oven to the temperature specified on the package and cook the fries, flipping occasionally, until crisp. In the meantime, combine the truffle oil and garlic in a large bowl. When the fries are crisp, add them to the bowl and toss with metal tongs to coat them evenly with the oil. Add half of the parsley, half of the cheese, and all the salt and pepper and give the fries another quick toss. Plate the fries on a large platter and top with the remaining parsley, cheese, and any extra salt and pepper you may want to add.

TO PREPARE THE BURGERS

Allow the beef to rest at room temperature for about 30 minutes prior to cooking. Portion it into 6 (4-ounce) balls, using your hands to lightly pack and form them into small, puck-shaped disks. Combine the salt, pepper, onion powder, and garlic powder in a small dish and generously season all sides of the patties according to your preferences. (You might not use all the mixture.) Heat a large heavy-bottomed skillet (I prefer cast-iron) on high for at least 5 minutes to get the pan extra hot. Lightly grease the pan with cooking spray or 2 teaspoons of vegetable oil.

Add half of the patties to the skillet and use a large metal spatula to press down on the patties until they're just over ¼-inch thick. Cook on the first side for 2 minutes, or until the edges have browned—this will vary depending on how hot your pan is. Flip the burgers, pressing down gently to keep the patties just over ¼-inch thick, and add the cheese, if desired. Cook for an additional minute for medium-rare burgers, longer as needed. Remove the patties from the skillet to a plate and repeat with the remaining oil and burger patties. When finished cooking, pour off any excess grease and quickly pop the buns on the hot skillet, insides facing down, just until toasted, about 30 seconds apiece. Dress the burgers and serve with the fries.

DAY 21: Sweet Like Honey

When my parents moved out of their home of twenty-one years, I wound up with corrugated boxes full of memories from my childhood. We're talking books, blankets, photo albums, and no less than 150 Beanie Babies. Over the next few weeks, I laughed and cried as I uncovered old treasures, silly drawings, and stacks of photos from my childhood.

From one box, old letters from family and friends overflowed onto my living-room floor, and I uncovered a journal with a note attached from my third-grade teacher: "You are a terrific writer, Katie! Never stop!" It wasn't the only time she encouraged me to write; for years, when dreams of blogs and cookbooks and children's books crept into my imagination, I remembered her calling out that skill, all those years ago, telling me I could do it. Her encouragement had stuck with me, and those words bolstered my confidence, giving me bravery to pursue dreams that seemed impossible (like this book!).

The words you say to people matter. I've experienced firsthand the power of encouragement and have seen how transformative a single kind word can prove to be. The Bible says that death and life are in the power of the tongue (Prov. 18:21), and that power is ours to use, for better or for worse. As believers, we can change the way people see themselves by calling out the good and declaring God's truth over their lives, and because God's truth has power, those words never go out without effect.

The encouragement from my teacher made me brave and honest and willing to share. She told me I had something valuable to say, so I said it. What about you? Have you experienced the life-changing goodness of a kind word from someone? Likewise, is there anyone you might have the opportunity to encourage today? The Bible says, "Kind words are like honey . . . healing to the body" (Prov. 16:24, NIRV), so use yours today with intention to sweeten the world around you.

 **EPHESIANS 4:29**

DAY 22: Redeeming the Hard Parts

For the better part of a year, I had driven Aimee to weekly dance classes, and it was finally the big day. She had the tights, the shoes, and the costume, and the girl knew every step by heart. Grandparents and even great-grandparents traveled into town for the recital, but when the curtain drew back, there stood Aimee: arms crossed and unmoving, with big tears streaming down her face. While her friends danced around her, she refused to take a single step.

The next year's recital went without a hitch, and the one after that did too. I remember smiling and cheering through those shows, but they're otherwise a blur. The funny thing is, out of all the recitals, the one that remains most memorable and imprinted in my mind is the year she didn't even dance, and somehow those two torturous minutes have become an opportunity for reminiscing and laughter for Aimee and me. Although she was so nervous at the time, it's a sweet memory that we get to connect over, both of us proud of how far she's come.

I think sometimes we observe our own personal failures in the wrong light. When our big moment in life came, with drawn curtains and bright lights, some of us were caught with our arms crossed and tears streaming down our faces. Maybe you botched a presentation, were passed over for the promotion, or got your heart broken. Maybe you got caught doing or saying something you now regret. Although those moments are painful and scary when they're happening, I really believe God wants to use them for our good—as a learning opportunity, as a platform from which you'll speak in the future, or as a reminder that occasionally a bit of humility is in order. God doesn't waste parts of our lives, not even the hard ones, because He has purpose for every single bit of it.

Have there been moments or seasons of life that felt heavy or painful? Ask God to point out purpose or to expose your heart to ways He wants to use that moment for His glory and your good. What the enemy may have intended for your harm, God can use for your good. Welcome Him into your past and present, and allow Him to redeem the parts you don't understand.

 **GENESIS 50:20**

DAY 23: Little Big Dreams

From early on, I had dreams of raising a family. While other friends were applying for graduate school, planning careers, and traveling the world, I had visions of front-porch swings, brown-headed babies, and a dining-room table filled with faces I loved. Deep down, though, there was a part of me that wondered if I should be reaching farther. My ambitions appeared simple in comparison to the ones I saw playing out around me, and I often felt as though my dreams just weren't big enough.

But now, as I watch my hopes unfold within the ordinary backdrop of my own home, around a table that is somehow busier and louder than I ever could have imagined, I see that everyday ambitions can be marvelous and brave in their own way. My role as a mother doesn't come with fancy titles or red carpets, but it is still important, holy work. It might have taken some time, but I'm finally learning to settle into the role God has me in, right here, right now.

Every work is good work if it's what God has called you to. It doesn't matter if your dreams come with worldwide influence or just a small band of followers in the kitchen of your own home; they are still your dreams to carry out, and it takes guts to wake up and chase after them, taking on the challenges and delights of that work day in and day out.

What is God saying about your ambitions in your heart? Have you discerned what He's calling you to in this season of life? Turn down the noise of the world or any pressure to shape your story with the cookie-cutter molds you see around you, and, instead, listen in for the assignment He's commanded to you. God's vision for your life is so much bigger than your own ambitions, and He is delighted when you are brave enough to chase after them with all you've got.

 **1 CORINTHIANS 15:58**

DAY 24: "X" Marks the Spot

After months of overcommitting at work, I was burned out. My website was a success. I was developing partnerships, earning a living, and my work calendar was full to overflowing, but it had come at the cost of my own exhaustion. My struggle for more had left me uninspired, resentful, and completely dissatisfied, and by the end of the year I was ready to call it quits.

We'll all find ourselves, at some point, carrying treasure maps that lead absolutely nowhere. When the efforts of our lives are spent on the hunt for things that won't satisfy, we'll forever have our sails up, at the mercy of the wind of our own stamina and ambitions. If the X on our map only leads us to more money, more applause, or more self-sufficiency, we're searching for a bounty that won't last.

Jesus told us to store up treasures in heaven. There will always be small rewards and shiny things here on earth, but for us, as believers, the X on our map should always lead to Him. The wonderful thing about searching for Jesus is that we barely have to dig below the surface to uncover the gold: layer upon layer of beauty and love and glory that is ours to unpack and enjoy forever and ever. As I continue to learn this lesson, it's bringing the joy back to my work and other areas of my life that have lacked balance, and, thankfully, that contentment is available to you too. Today, find your gold in the Rock of Christ: the only treasure that will eternally satisfy.

 **LUKE 12:13–21**

DAY 25: Waiting for Sunrises

My parents live in a home that's situated on a curve of a lake in central Alabama. The back porch faces east, and when I'm visiting, I like to I take my coffee with a side of sunrise and watch as the earth awakens.

At my own home, I rarely catch a sunrise, and trust me—this is telling about other areas of my life too. The world has a way of distracting us from the beauty and promises that are contained within each day, and without a pause, a minute of stillness to catch the wonder as it's unfolding, it will pass us by without any thought of the One who created it. Our lives are covered with evidence of God's goodness, but if we race through our days, we'll miss every one of them: the sunrises and the songs, the places of healing and forgiveness, and the sweet little gestures that are nothings to most people but mean the world to you. God is intentional and grand and glorious every single day, and if we wait for a show of His grace, we won't miss it.

Wherever you find yourself today, don't miss God. Set aside the distractions and tasks that keep your head down, and look up. Where is there evidence of God's glory within your home, in your relationships, and beyond? Thank Him in advance for a revelation of His beauty, and then open your eyes to a creation that points to Him.

 JOB 37

The Reward of Following Jesus

When I was growing up, my family spent one day each summer picking blueberries on the side of a hill just a short drive from our home. The sun was relentless, and the bugs were too, but the promise of fresh berries drew us into the dirt anyway. We picked for hours, filling our buckets and bellies with the sweet rewards of our labor, and in the days that followed we'd nibble on the fruit, freezing some for later and mashing the rest into a bubbling pot of jam that we'd preserve for the months that followed.

I don't recall looking forward to the anthills or the oppressive heat. There was always the threat of stained fingers and chiggers, sunburned shoulders and sweat stains, but in the case of blueberries, our prize was worth the risk. The best prizes are like that—we treasure them most when we invest ourselves in significant ways.

Today, I want to remind you that the reward of following Jesus is always worth the risk. So often, fear and doubt distract us into making decisions dictated by what-ifs instead of what God has promised. As believers, we can enter into risk with confidence knowing that, if God has called us there, He will not leave us to wander it alone. The reward of following Jesus, even into uncomfortable territories of the unknown, is always better than forging a path of our own.

Are there places or things God has called you to that require a little risk? Are there fears or hesitations that you can replace with faith? Someone recently reminded me that faith doesn't ignore the facts, it just overrides them with truth, and the truth here is that the reward of following Jesus outweighs any risk you might encounter today. Ask Jesus where He wants to go in the coming days, and step into that territory with confidence.

 **ISAIAH 43:1–13**

DAY 27: Blueberry Muffins

George is my muffin man. I can convince him to eat just about any variety, but he especially loves anything with chocolate or fruit. I make these Blueberry Muffins for him in the summer to use up any berries we've picked, and they've become a favorite due to their tender texture and lightly sweetened flavor. Although they're best straight from the oven, the maple syrup keeps them moist for days, and you can regain any crisp edges by rewarming them in the oven. Try subbing your own favorite varieties of fruit, fresh or frozen, but be sure to keep any fruit bits small.

....

BLUEBERRY MUFFINS

Makes 1 dozen

1/3 cup milk

1/4 cup canola or vegetable oil

6 tablespoons melted unsalted butter

1 cup maple syrup

1 teaspoon vanilla extract

1 large egg

2 cups all-purpose flour

2 1/2 teaspoons baking powder

3/4 teaspoon table salt

1 cup fresh or frozen blueberries

1 tablespoon granulated sugar

Preheat the oven to 400°F. Put paper liners in a 12-cup standard muffin tin.

In a large bowl, whisk together the milk, oil, butter, maple syrup, vanilla, and egg until smooth. Add the flour, baking powder, and salt, and stir just until barely combined. Fold in the berries. Divide the batter evenly among the 12 cups; mine usually end up about three-quarters full. Sprinkle a bit of the sugar over each portion of batter. Bake for about 18 minutes, or until a toothpick inserted comes out clean. Allow them to cool briefly before consuming!

Variation: For Lemon Blueberry Muffins, add 1 1/2 tablespoons lemon zest and 2 tablespoons lemon juice to the liquid ingredients.

DAY 28: Quilted Treasures

A few years ago, my mother and grandma taught me how to quilt, and it's quickly become one of my favorite hobbies. I love how each quilt tells its own unique story of when we made it, who we made it for, and the hours of love we poured into it. Best of all, the end product of those efforts is a keepsake that we can save and treasure for years to come.

Just as the squares of each quilt are intentionally crafted, I'd like to live a life that is intentionally filled with words and thoughts and actions that will last. We were created for impact, for relationship, and to be the transforming love of Jesus here on earth, and when we set our hearts on using our time for those purposes, we'll forever find ourselves sewing into the beautiful finished work God has in store for us. By aligning our efforts with God's heart, we can begin living a life that has kingdom impact and eternal reward.

Take inventory of the fruit in your life. Are you engaging in activities and relationships that have lasting impact? Where is there evidence of God's work in your life? Don't be discouraged if you're not satisfied with what you find—just press in for more. Talk to God about how you can advance His agenda this week, and spend your time, energy, and love on treasures that will make it to heaven.

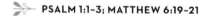 **PSALM 1:1–3; MATTHEW 6:19–21**

DAY 29: Wearing All the Hats

Sometimes it feels as though the various roles women take on carry their own assumed limitations, and we begin to believe that our lives as daughters, wives, mothers, and friends must look one specific way. Let's just demystify a few things—being female doesn't prevent us from being strong or bold or independent. Being a mother doesn't exempt us from pursuing career opportunities or dreaming dreams that serve only ourselves. Being married doesn't limit us to a dull future. Being a Christian doesn't mean the end of fun and adventure.

This life is not either/or, and instead is made up of a variety of beautiful things that can be true even when they seem in opposition. As women of God, we are empowered to embrace every single version of ourselves that God has called us to, and there is grace to navigate that balance as we step into new roles. Yes, there will be seasons of our lives where one of those hats we wear may require most of what we're able to give at that time, but if we're in a place where we can wear multiple hats at one time, who's to say we shouldn't?

Who does God say you are? What are the dreams He's placed inside your heart? Today, know that you are not limited by the world's standards, because you stand as a child of a limitless God. Let Him call out who He's made you to be, and know His word enables you to wear any number of hats with confidence.

 **ROMANS 8:31-39**

DAY 30: Free from Perfect

A few years ago, Brett told me I wasn't allowed to make frosted sugar cookies anymore. Although I loved baking (and eating!) cutout cookies, it was the icing I couldn't handle—the intricately piped lines that went askew and the pools of glaze that would spill and smudge off the sides. Each time I attempted them, I became so frustrated by the imperfections, by my inability to get everything just so, that I was unable to enjoy what was supposed to be a sweet and delightful treat, and Brett kindly suggested I take a break for the sake of my sanity.

Perfectionism hampers us from experiencing the world, for fear that our true selves will somehow not be enough. Within perfectionism, there's no freedom for mistakes or minor slip-ups, because the pride in our heart has tethered our worth to our ability to perform. The truth is, we've all fallen short of perfection (Rom. 3:23), and God, in His goodness, has provided grace for every defect and deficiency He knew we'd bring to the table. He's seen our imperfections, and you know what? He's okay with them. After all, what use would a Savior be if we needed no saving? Jesus came to be the perfection we could never be, embracing our flaws and setbacks with love, because the atonement of His blood is more than enough.

Sister, take your eyes off yourself. Your worth is not tied to your getting it all right every time—it's tied to the perfection of Jesus, who lives in you. Are there places where perfectionism has hindered you from resting in the freedom and grace that Jesus purchased with His life? Ask God to instead fix your eyes on Him, unhindered by the need to do better, so that you may run freely toward a life that looks like Jesus's.

 **HEBREWS 10:14**

DAY 31: On Taking No for an Answer

My senior year of college was filled with lots of noes: from graduate schools, from summer internships, and even from the guy I thought I'd marry. I don't know many people who take rejection well, but I learned that year that I'm certainly not one of them. My identity was so wrapped up in my future, in some Norman Rockwell version of what I thought life would be like, that when it all fell apart, I did too.

It's easy to forget that Jesus felt the weight and loneliness of rejection while He was here on earth too. There He was, God in human form, with arms full of hope and promise and love, and the world rejected Him. First Peter 2:4 says He was honored by God but rejected by all people, and it should comfort you to know that, on days when that's your story too, you're not alone. Even when friends turn their back, your heart is broken, or your future falls apart one rejection letter at a time, God has promised to always be there. Jesus bore the weight of the rejection owed to us, so that God in heaven would forever receive us with open arms proclaiming, "YES!"

Are there areas of your life where the pain of rejection still stings? Let God tend to those wounds with His unfailing love, and remember that He is the One who will never turn His back on you. Even when the world shouts "No," His love for you is always "Yes."

 **PSALM 27:10; ISAIAH 53:3; JOHN 15:18**

DAY 1: Buoyancy

Shortly after graduating from college, I went through a season marked by loneliness and utter exhaustion. My relationships suffered, work was difficult, and on some days I had a hard time even getting off my couch. During that time, I lost a lot of weight and made some bad choices, and for about a year every day felt like another thunderstorm. Every new setback just reinforced my belief that when it rains, it pours.

Although I'd never suggest you should hide from your feelings or turn a blind eye to difficult circumstances, I do believe that, even in the face of heartache and injustice and uncertainty, we can remain rooted in the joy of the Lord. Abiding in faith with a good Father who is our joy and strength does not make us naive, but instead connects us to a life source of all that we need to remain buoyant when turbulent waters come. When we are hopeless, He *is* our hope. When we are weak, He *is* our strength.

Are you walking through any circumstances that feel desperate or without hope? Have you found yourself in a place that feels more sorrowful than joyful? Remain in Him. Allow your circumstances to point you to the safety and peace found in the arms of your good Savior, and look to His word for encouragement. He is sufficient to meet your needs and strong enough to be your steady ground, even in uncertainty. Surrender those circumstances to Him today, and remain buoyed to the rest found in Him.

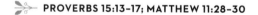 **PROVERBS 15:13–17; MATTHEW 11:28–30**

DAY 2: Not Afraid of a Little Mess

Fairly regularly, my kids will saddle up to the counter and help me in the kitchen. They snap the ends off green beans, fill measuring cups with shredded cheese, and throw pats of cold butter into bowls of flour and salt. It's always a competition between my two older ones: who gets to add the most ingredients, who can sneak away the most chocolate chips, and who gets to lick the bowl clean. In most cases, it takes no more than five minutes for there to be syrup on the counter, eggshells on the floor, and a light dusting of sugar, well . . . everywhere. Kids in the kitchen are messy and often exhausting, and while I enjoy that time, their clumsy hands make for anything but a peaceful experience.

We adults are kinda messy too. Instead of chubby fingers and fumbling motor skills, we bring emotional baggage and bad habits. We carry things like negativity, fear, and defensiveness in a way that makes them feel as though they're a part of who we are. We bring our past experiences and pain, often allowing them to cloud over all of the good. Adults each make a mess in their own unique way, but unlike the messes kids make, there's rarely someone to clean up after us.

Aren't you thankful that God isn't afraid of a little mess? Where there's a bitter heart, He sees wounds that He can heal. Where there's negativity, He sees a child who hasn't yet experienced hope in Him. When we veneer our hearts with fear and pride and stubbornness, He chips away at it with His love. He sent His Son to save us from our sin because nothing is too messy for Him—He's in the business of making old things new, unclean things pure, and broken things whole.

God doesn't shy away from a mess, and He'll never turn His back on you. If you find yourself burdened by a heavy heart, mind, or attitude, go to Him today. Watch Him make something beautiful from your mess.

 ISAIAH 61

DAY 3: Cookies-and-Cream Ice Cream Sandwiches

Cookies-and-Cream Ice Cream Sandwiches are one of my favorite show-off desserts. I think everyone secretly loves ice cream sandwiches, and if you show up bringing ones with homemade ice cream and chocolate chip cookies, you're bound to feel like a rock star.

For a simplified take on this recipe, you can opt for store-bought ice cream instead of homemade, but rest assured, no-churn ice cream is surprisingly easy to make. For a simple vanilla filling, you can leave out the chocolate cookie crumbs, or feel free to toss in another topping of your choice—maybe sprinkles, mini chocolate chips, or mini candies.

....

COOKIES-AND-CREAM ICE CREAM SANDWICHES

Makes 10 to 12 sandwiches

ICE CREAM

2 cups heavy whipping cream

1 teaspoon vanilla extract

1 (14-ounce) can sweetened condensed milk

18 chocolate sandwich cookies (like Oreos), chopped

COOKIES

1/2 cup unsalted butter, at room temperature

1/2 cup packed brown sugar

1/3 cup granulated sugar

1 large egg

1 teaspoon vanilla extract

1 1/4 cups all-purpose flour

1/2 teaspoon baking soda

3/4 teaspoon table salt

3/4 cup (3 1/2 ounces) finely chopped semisweet or bittersweet chocolate

TO PREPARE THE ICE CREAM

In a large bowl or the bowl of a stand mixer, whip the cream on medium-high speed until slightly thickened and fluffy. Add the vanilla extract and continue beating until stiff peaks form. Fold in the sweetened condensed milk and cookie crumbs and spoon the mixture into a freezer-safe container (I like to use a loaf pan). Cover it with aluminum foil and allow it to freeze until it reaches a scoopable consistency, about 6 hours.

TO PREPARE THE COOKIES

Preheat the oven to 350°F. Line two baking sheets with parchment paper or use silicone baking sheets.

Cream the butter, brown sugar, and granulated sugar with a mixer on medium speed until light and fluffy, about 1 minute. Add the egg and vanilla and mix to incorporate. Add the flour, baking soda, and salt, and stir on low just until combined. Fold in the chopped chocolate. If the cookie dough looks shiny and greasy, or if you know you used butter that was too soft, allow the dough to chill in the fridge briefly, about 20 minutes. Roll the dough into 1½-tablespoon-size balls and place them on the baking sheets about 2 inches apart. Bake for about 10 minutes, or until the outer rims of the cookies are set and starting to bronze and the insides of the cookies still look slightly underdone. Allow the cookies to cool completely (you can speed this process up in the freezer!).

TO PREPARE THE SANDWICHES

Spread out half of the cookies on a work surface, bottom side up. Place approximately ⅓ cup of ice cream on each cookie, flattening slightly. Top with the remaining cookies, bottom side down, and press gently. Eat immediately or freeze. You can store these in the freezer wrapped individually in aluminum foil for up to two weeks.

DAY 4: Good Things Ahead

When I was a little girl, my nana drove a red Cadillac. She'd fold the roof down, and we'd ride Kentucky backroads as though they were ours alone. Those rides are a blurred memory of windblown hair and Bonnie Raitt, but the feelings attached to them—the freedom, the joy, and the camaraderie we shared—are so vivid that I can revisit them, even now, as if they happened yesterday.

I notice that, as I get older, I often trade my opportunities for vulnerable encounters for the chance to rush on to something new. Some days, my hours and weeks run together, and at the end of them I have little to show for it: no memories of wild, wind-blown hair and blaring car radios, just burning up miles on a road to absolutely nowhere.

Sister, don't race through this season and miss the moment while you're living it. God has good things up ahead, adventure and miracles and a million little pit stops where you'll fill up on His goodness. Roll the windows down, feel His goodness, and truly absorb the world around you: the faces, the sounds and smells, and the details you'll revisit for years to come. God's still writing terrific things in your story, so today open your eyes to the road you're traveling, and take it all in. He's promised good things just up ahead.

 JAMES 1:17

DAY 5: Jesus, Take the Wheel

I had this idyllic image of what it would look like to take a road trip with my kids. In my head, there would be backseat dance parties, a few naps, and silly photos next to roadside welcome signs for every state border we crossed. I was naive to think we were above road rage, bickering, and boredom, but the initial eight hours of our first long ride, with its complaining and car sickness and leg cramps, still took me by surprise. By the time we arrived, I was exhausted in every sense of the word and immediately began dreading the ride back.

On long car rides and in life, it's important that we fix our eyes on the destination. When we find ourselves on detours or bumpy roads, stuck in the occasional traffic jam, or saddled with a backseat pessimist, it's helpful to remember why we're making the journey in the first place. Where are we going? Why are we going there? What is promised at the destination?

God doesn't send us anywhere without equipping us for the ride. Even on days that aren't easy, He has promised His presence and if we rest in that offering, the gift of His ever-present help, He will bear the brunt of that weight. We will wear ourselves out trying to complete the journey on our own, but if we wait for Him, we will see the goodness and outcomes He desires in our lives and in the world (Ps. 27:13-14).

Are there places the Lord is nudging you to go with Him? You can remain confident in His ability to direct you to a good destination. Fix your eyes on His promises and the call He's placed in your heart, and remember, you're just the passenger—Jesus has the wheel.

 **PROVERBS 4:25-27**

DAY 6: Praising God Exactly Where We Are

We spend a lot of time waiting for the next big thing—a job promotion, a relationship, a baby, a school, a bank balance, or the perfect body. Some of us will spend our lives forever in a hustle, scoping out the next big milestone and being entirely spent in the process. If our ability to be content rests solely in our ability to get to the next big thing, truly, we will wear ourselves out.

Although there's loads to celebrate in those big life milestones, God has all sorts of beauty prepared in the mundane moments of our everyday life. I propose we make a little more room for grace and slow down long enough to enjoy being exactly where we are. I'm not saying that we set aside hard work or that we forget about our dreams, but I do want to be more intentional about being joyful in the here and now. My gut tells me that the best parts of our stories will be a culmination of all those unremarkable moments. We can choose to create beauty and color and joy in the everyday, or we can pass them over on the hunt for something more grand.

Praise God for the mundane: the sound of babies talking over a monitor, the taste of ice cream cones on summer days, and chilled glasses of wine shared with a friend. Praise Him for the opportunity to love people we meet in the grocery store or while we're pumping gas. Praise Him for the little life offerings that culminate in huge seasons of love. Sister, your life is not small—celebrate every moment of it.

 PSALM 16

DAY 7: Planting for the Harvest

During our first few weeks as newlyweds, Brett planted me an above-ground garden filled with herbs, tomatoes, and a few other vegetables. I didn't know the first thing about gardening, so I let him pick out seeds to plant in our little squares of dirt. When summer rolled around, I was surprised to find tiny orange peppers growing abundantly on one of the plants—habaneros. Turns out, Brett didn't know habaneros are intensely spicy, and we were left with produce that we didn't know how to use. I learned in a very practical way that summer that we shouldn't be planting things we don't want to harvest.

Although we haven't repeated that mistake in our garden lately, I still find myself continuing that practice in more personal ways. I sow unpleasant habits in my marriage, things like selfishness, pride, bitterness, and impatience, and am somehow surprised when the harvest in our relationship isn't always love. Other times, I fail to sow time, care, or kindness into friendships, and sure enough, they fail to grow. I say I want better self-image, to truly love this body I'm in, but then I poke and pull and cast sideways glances in the mirror, sowing seeds of disdain instead of ones of confidence.

What are you looking to grow in your life? If we desire a harvest of love in our relationships, peace in our home, excellence in our workplace, or respect from our children, we've got to start planting those things in the present. Take some time to reflect on the things that you're harvesting in your life right now. Are there some things popping up that you really don't have room for? Behaviors, thoughts, or relationship patterns that have just got to go? Ask God what He wants to plant in your life, and don't be afraid to get in the dirt. Planting good seeds is always worth the effort.

 **GALATIANS 6:7–10**

DAY 8: Buttery Love Notes

Early on, baking was my hobby, a respite from the tedious drone of everyday life: wake up, go to work, come home, repeat. In the kitchen, there was always something new to learn or explore, and I took pleasure in conquering foreign territory. Over time, that hobby melted into the nooks and crannies of my life, pouring edges into the mold of who I am. It became something that nourished me in intangible ways, quenching my thirst to create and offering me the chance to love the people in my world in sweet and delicious ways: a peanut butter pie for a friend, a birthday cake for my child, or a chocolate dessert for my husband. Each pie or pastry contained within it an offering of affection, like a buttery little love note to the people who mattered.

Baking may not be your thing. Maybe you're more of a painter or a scientist, or perhaps you're the girl who builds kites or plants gardens or strums melodies on a vintage guitar. Words or numbers may mean more to you than flour and sugar, but the point is, whatever your gifts are, you should use them! There is more fulfillment and honor and fun to be found when we use our passion and talent for the benefit of the world around us, so don't just keep all that love to yourself—share it!

Today, let me be the one, maybe even the first, to encourage you to share freely and abundantly the things that give you joy. And please know that if you haven't found your "thing" yet, I can assure you that there is room in the kitchen. There is space to create, to fail, and to try again, particularly when it serves as an offering of love to the people around you. Ask God if there's someone you can love this week by sharing your gifts.

 **1 THESSALONIANS 3:11-13**

DAY 9: Stepping into a New Thing

When Brett and I were dating, we traveled to the beach to spend a weekend with some of his oldest friends. Their summer routine of deep sea fishing, crabbing, and shrimp boils was far outside of my comfort zone, and I had the seasickness to prove it. Although I went into the weekend with a fair share of uncertainty (*Will they like me? Will I fit in? Will I be able to keep my sea legs?*), I found my courage was met with kindness, and I ended up making a few new friends and memories.

It takes courage to step into a new thing. Many of us have the tendency to avoid the unknown, because we feel safe in the comfort of our norms. Whether we like it or not, our lives as believers is anything but safe, and we all, at some point, will be faced with perilous, uncertain, or downright absurd circumstances that require every ounce of faith we've got. Thankfully, whether we're building an ark, filling our slingshot with stones, or casting out the net to the other side of the boat, God has promised to reward our obedience and willingness to try something new with His presence. We're never alone, and He always remains faithful.

How is God stretching your faith today? Has He asked you to step into something new or unfamiliar? There will always be barriers attempting to prevent you from following God, but you can trust that He will prepare you for whatever is in store. God is always victorious, and He has offered the faithful His presence, so you can trust Him in the unknown today.

 LUKE 5:1-11

DAY 10: Two-Bite Crab Cakes with Lemon Dill Aioli

I've always believed that every party needs a cake, but in the summer my favorite parties come with *crab* cakes. These petite bites of salt and sea are shockingly simple to prepare and make for a yummy summer dinner or appetizer option.

Preparing seafood may be intimidating but these Two-Bite Crab Cakes are a one-bowl dish that can be prepped in advance with very little effort. The Lemon Dill Aioli here is absolutely nonnegotiable. Tartar sauce is good, yes, but the homemade aioli just takes this dish to the next level.

....

TWO-BITE CRAB CAKES WITH LEMON DILL AIOLI

Makes 12 small cakes

AIOLI

1/2 cup mayonnaise

1 clove garlic, minced

3/4 teaspoon lemon zest

2 tablespoons lemon juice

2 teaspoons chopped fresh dill

1 teaspoon chopped fresh parsley

1 teaspoon granulated sugar

1/4 teaspoon seasoning salt

1/4 teaspoon black pepper

CRAB CAKES

2 large eggs

3 tablespoons mayonnaise

1 teaspoon stone-ground mustard

2 teaspoons Worcestershire sauce

1 teaspoon Old Bay Seasoning

1/2 teaspoon seasoning salt

1/4 teaspoon black pepper

1 1/2 tablespoons finely chopped
    fresh parsley

1/3 cup finely chopped celery

1 pound lump crab meat, with large pieces
    broken up slightly

1/3 cup bread crumbs

Lemon wedges, for serving

TO PREPARE THE AIOLI

Stir to combine all the ingredients in a small bowl and set it in the fridge while you prep the crab cakes, up to three days in advance.

TO PREPARE THE CRAB CAKES

In a large bowl, whisk together the eggs, mayonnaise, mustard, Worcestershire, Old Bay, seasoning salt, pepper, and parsley. Stir in the celery, and then fold in the crab meat and bread crumbs. Don't overwork the mixture once you've added the crab and bread crumbs—this can make the cakes tough. Use a cookie scoop or a large spoon to scoop out 3-tablespoon-size mounds of crab-cake mixture onto a cookie sheet. Using your hands, round the mounds into balls and then flatten slightly until they're just over 1 inch thick. Space the cakes out on the cookie sheet, cover the pan, and then place in the fridge for at least 1 hour or overnight to set up.

When ready to cook, preheat the oven to 350°F. Heat a heavy-bottomed pan on medium-low. Grease it lightly with cooking spray, add half of the cakes, and cook for about 3 minutes. Once golden brown on the first side, carefully flip over and cook the second side for 3 minutes. If you notice the crab cakes getting dark too fast, turn the heat down slightly and cook them slower. Once golden on both sides, remove the cakes from the pan, and repeat with the remaining cakes. If the crab cakes still look slightly wet around the sides, place them in a single layer on a sheet pan and bake them for 4 to 5 minutes, or until they no longer appear wet. Serve with lemon wedges and the aioli for dipping. You can drizzle the aioli on the serving plate and place the cakes directly on top, serve the aioli on the side, or spoon a dollop of sauce directly on each cake. Enjoy!

DAY 11: Redeveloping Snapshots

Many of my memories occur in snapshots. I rarely remember full conversations or extensive details about the scenery, but quite often smaller details will stick out in my mind: the chill in the air, the laughter in a friend's voice, the echo of a single word said in passing. Although I relish those brief moments of recollection when it comes to happy memories, in more painful moments I'm grateful to be left with just a few faded seconds from an old wound.

I know God is in the business of cleaning up old offenses, and I like to think those fleeting memories are a sign of His grace. He doesn't want us to keep picking at our festering wounds, but instead longs to restore our hearts and heal our wounds (Jer. 30:17). Now when I see an open door for a painful thing from the past to sneak in, I ask God to take care of it. I pray for forgiveness, for a release from shame, for a renewing of my mind, or for a fresh covering of His peace. Instead of carrying that burden on my own, I ask God to move into the places where it hurts.

We can use our hurtful moments from the past as a tool for learning. We can grow, shift course, or love others better as a result of our pain. Today, ask God to heal you from the ugly words, thoughts, and actions that were committed against you. He won't leave your wounds untended when He's already paid for your wholeness.

 **EZEKIEL 36:22–32**

DAY 12: The Best Part

There was a time when I baked for the challenge of it all. I loved the process of honing a new skill, of being able to mix and fold and pipe until I created something I was proud of. But over time, I found that the best part of baking was more than just producing a tray of perfect cookies or a pretty cake; it was the people I shared those foods with. It was the little eyes that peered over the top of the counter, eager for a nibble of something sweet. It was the best friends who shared laughter and stories over pans of brownies. It was the husband and parents and neighbors who received those bites of food as an offering of love. More than the flavors or the feeling of success, I fell in love with the community and took comfort in the solidarity that I found when sharing my gifts with those I love.

Community at the table can be a worshipful experience, and at the very least it's a great way to remain connected. Whether it's cooking, baking, setting an inviting tablescape, or just offering good conversation, God has equipped you with beautiful, fulfilling gifts that are yours to share. Once you start offering those gifts to the world around you, you'll find that the best part is the people you'll bless with those gifts. If you're unsure where to begin, look no further than Jesus; He participated in deep, life-giving intimacy around the table, and I really believe that space is a venue welcome to us all, even now.

Today, ask God to point out someone in your life who would benefit from a shared meal. Is it a neighbor? A child? Maybe even someone you don't know well yet? There's no need to wait for a special occasion, a clean house, or a wide-open schedule, because the best part of community is rarely the place or the setting; it's the people you'll share the meal with. Invite Jesus along next time you break bread, and keep your eyes open for people you can bless with gifts He's equipped you with.

 **ACTS 2:42–47**

DAY 13: Better Flavors

My daughter has recently become obsessed with my coffee drinking. She sniffs at my French press, peers into my mug, and swirls the liquid with a spoon. Even at the store, she points out the bottles of coffee creamer, begging for the ones labeled with chocolate bars and peppermint sticks. To satisfy her interest, I recently poured a smidge of hazelnut coffee creamer into her milk just so she could get a taste of what Mama was enjoying every morning. Game over. She was enamored, and now she requests coffee creamer in her milk 100 percent of the time, because plain milk, to a six-year-old, is just kinda, well, plain.

Life with Jesus is sort of like that too. Before we come to know God, life may seem sufficient as is, but when we truly encounter God for the first time, get a taste of His love, and experience the freedom of His grace, our whole world opens up. Things that were previously a part of our everyday norms no longer fill us as they used to, because life flavored with Jesus is always going to be sweeter than plain old life on its own. (*Sidenote: I know those of you who enjoy your coffee black are reading this and shaking your head, "Nope." I hear you. Just go with the analogy.*)

As followers of God, we are sweetened with the love of Christ, dripping with His joy and kindness. Once we've experienced His love in a deep way, we're rarely the same. Today, love people in a way that reflects the grace of God at work in your life. Bring the sweetness of Jesus with you wherever you go, and let that be what flavors your work, relationships, and daily activities.

 **MATTHEW 5:13–16; EPHESIANS 4:17–32**

DAY 14: Inescapable Hope

I took offense at something a friend did the other day, and for a couple of hours I tricked myself into believing I was entitled to my complaints. After some time, the reality of my own selfishness sunk in, and I was totally convicted with the gut knowledge that I was wrong.

You'd think after a few decades of life, three kids, and reading innumerable books on inner growth, I'd somehow manage to take the high road in my relationships, but dealing with our own sinfulness is something that we never grow out of. All too often, I find selfishness simmering below the surface of my cool and content façade, bubbling up with pride, mental accusations, and the feeling that I somehow got the short end of the stick. *What about what I want? What about my own needs? What about ME?* The inescapable truth about selfishness is that it's inescapable—we'll never fully shed the layers of humanity, never lie to ourselves enough, never share enough fake smiles and verbal assurances to evade the narcissism that hides in the corners of our hearts.

The only way to find light at the end of those bitter tunnels is to move toward God. In Christ, we are liberated from the sneaky hold of those feelings, because He offers the Holy Spirit, who will walk us through them with grace. We can receive forgiveness when we have made it all about ourselves and offer grace to others who are figuring it out too. Although being a believer doesn't mean we're perfect, it does mean we have hope for a beautiful life outside of ourselves. Today, remember you have a new reality that comes with loads of grace from Christ, and allow God to fill you with it wherever your circumstances may bring you.

 **2 CORINTHIANS 2:5-11**

DAY 15: No Need for Training Wheels

We're currently teaching Aimee to ride a bike. She struggles with the lack of control and uneasiness of balancing, and I really feel for her; for me, riding anything with wheels for the first time feels about as natural as wearing a snorkel. (Honestly, if God wanted us to breathe under water, we would have gills. Am I right, or am I right?)

All Aimee can see is the hard pavement beneath her. She's completely forgotten that her dad is right behind her, steadying the bike with one hand and ready to catch her if she falls. To her, it doesn't matter that he's guiding her bike right near the edge of the grass so that any fall will be met with a soft place to land, because she's paralyzed by the fear that she might get hurt.

How often is this us in life? We wobble and race through our circumstances, so focused on our insufficiencies, fears, and uncertainties that we forget who is supporting us. Fear has a way of capturing so much of our attention that we forget to look up and notice the soft grass God has surrounded us with.

In the Psalms, it says God is a shepherd who meets all our needs. He leads us beside still waters and provides green pastures for us to rest in. He restores us from the inside out and leads us only down righteous paths. Even when we walk through dark times, we have no need for fear, because He is with us every step of the way. He gently corrects us, He provides for us even when others are against us, and the proverbial cup of our lives is constantly overflowing because of His goodness and mercy in our lives. Sister, this good, good Shepherd is for you. He has your back, and if you head toward His voice, you're going to find yourself on a sure path.

Do you find yourself being afraid to trust God? You can have faith that His direction is good and His provision is constant. Ask Him where He wants to go today, and get excited about the ride.

 PSALM 23

New Worlds

When I moved to the deep South, I discovered a new world of food I never knew existed: fried okra, cheesy grits, lady peas, and peaches unlike anything I'd ever had in my life. I was content with the foods I had enjoyed up until that point in my life, but discovering there was more beyond my own experience made meals more exciting. It whet my appetite to discover more, to expand my knowledge, and to taste things I'd yet to try.

Life with Jesus is similar. Just when you think you've packed Him neatly into the confines of your understanding, He explodes with new facets of His character, love, and personality. He peels back the layers of His heart for you and draws you deeper into relationship, faith, and understanding. A Christian's life is never dull, because there are always new ways to grow into something that looks more like Him. Our understanding of this world is so limited, and the sooner we realize God has more for us right here, right now, the sooner we get to taste all of the goodness He has in store.

Don't settle for a bland experience with Jesus. There is so much flavor and blessing just beyond the confines of wherever you've put Him. Ask for more, and absorb every bit of goodness you find along the way, because God will never stop nourishing you in beautiful, exciting ways.

 **EPHESIANS 3:14-19**

DAY 17: Peach, Tomato, and Lady Pea Salad

Lady peas are a Southern treasure, and if you've ever had those yummy little cream peas, you know. Here, lady peas lend their terrific texture, flavor, and pale color to a tomato and peach salad that makes a tasty addition to summer menus. If you have a hard time finding lady peas, feel free to substitute cooked purple hull peas, black-eyed peas, or even edamame! Cooking time may vary with other varieties of peas, but you'll still wind up with a refreshing option for your summer suppers.

....

PEACH, TOMATO, AND LADY PEA SALAD

Serves 3 to 4 as a side

VINAIGRETTE

1½ teaspoons lemon zest

3 tablespoons lemon juice

1 teaspoon minced garlic

1 tablespoon honey

¾ teaspoon kosher salt

¼ teaspoon black pepper

3 tablespoons extra-virgin olive oil

SALAD

2 cups diced peaches (peeled or
   unpeeled, your preference)

2 cups cherry or grape tomatoes, or
   cut-up (bite-size) heirloom tomatoes

¼ cup finely chopped red onion

1 cup fresh lady peas
   (or cooked purple hull peas, black-eyed
   peas, or edamame)

2 teaspoons chopped fresh basil

2 teaspoons chopped fresh mint

In a large bowl, whisk together the lemon zest, lemon juice, garlic, honey, salt, and pepper. While continuing to whisk, slowly drizzle in the olive oil. To that same bowl, add the peaches, tomatoes, red onion, lady peas, basil, and mint. Toss together to combine. Allow the salad to marinate at least 10 minutes before serving. After marinating, add additional salt, pepper, or lemon juice to taste.

DAY 18: Making Friends

When I was growing up, my mom used to tell me, "You gotta be a friend to make a friend." I remembered those words on first days of school, throughout college, and on into adulthood. There were moments when the only reason I got out of my chair or stuck out a hand for an introduction was because I could hear Mom in the back of my mind urging me to take the initiative. Even now, in seasons of loneliness, I have to remind myself to do the work of putting myself out there, because, after all, I can't be the only one needing a friend, right?

Feelings of insecurity can prevent us from authentically engaging, as we buy into the lie that tells us we have nothing to offer, that we're excluded because of who we are, or that no one can relate to us. Ultimately, we were created for relationship, and accessing deep intimacy, both with humans and with God, requires our intentionality and vulnerability.

On this side of heaven, putting yourself out there does come with a risk, but fortunately, when it comes to our relationship with God, He's always doing the legwork to bring us closer to Him. The Bible says God seeks, knocks, and is calling out for relationship with us, and our job is simply to say yes. We participate by nurturing that relationship and loving Him back.

Today, be the friend. Be the phone call, the coffee date, the friendly hello, whatever. Take risks, put yourself out there, and don't forget to extend kindness to the people who might be initiating relationship with you as well. Remember that, with God, it's simple: just answer His call for relationship with a yes. You'll never have another friend like Him.

 **JAMES 4:8; REVELATION 3:20**

DAY 19: Blazing God's Trail

There have been countless times in my life where my desire to achieve and be some kind of a self-made superwoman drove me to blow through my days, ever in search of that next box to check off. I may have appeared ambitious or accomplished, but the pace I kept was fueled solely by my human efforts rather than purpose and direction from God. It's no surprise that many of my plans often failed or buried me in exhaustion, leaving me to wonder where God was in the midst of my disappointment; after all, I never stopped to invite Him along in the first place.

Some of us are at risk of pursuing every opportunity without asking God if it's from Him. We hustle and strive with the expectation that if we earn our successes with enough blood, sweat, and tears, He'll decide to come alongside us and bless it. *God, I worked so hard. Where is the anointing? Why is this so difficult? How could you let this fail?*

There are tons of stories throughout the Bible in which God's people ignore His instructions to do things their own way. Instead of asking God where He wants to go, they blaze their own trail and usually find themselves stuck in some kind of a wilderness. But as often as we see examples of God's people trying to do it their own way, we're offered instances of unassuming people fighting uphill battles with ease and victory because God was on their team. Often, what they lacked in numbers or size or resources they made up for with bold faith that empowered them to set after what God called them to do.

Rather than relying on your own strength, ideas, or plans, ask God where He wants to go this week. When He's invited along, He always brings the anointing and grace to achieve whatever He has in mind. Today, instead of blazing a trail of your own, ask God which one He's already prepared for you.

 **NUMBERS 14**

DAY 20: Not Mine to Judge

I've spent a major part of my adulthood hating my body to some degree. I've pinched and jiggled and looked longingly at old photos, wondering what it would take to lose an inch here or there, to get back to "what I once was." I wanted to love myself, but my unrealistic preoccupation with perfection and a general sense of shame about who I was kept me zeroed in on all the things I didn't like about myself. Hear me, sister: I understood this was warped thinking. I knew I should celebrate my body, marvel at the miracles it achieved, and truly I tried, but somehow I just couldn't.

I wonder how God feels when He sees me poking at His creation, this body that He imagined and formed and made to work from the inside out. He intentionally designed my body, right down to my skin tone and elbows and every shade of hazel my eyes have ever been, yet I have the audacity to despise it? To wish I had better? To dismiss His handiwork that He declared was good?

I want to spend less time wishing I looked different and more time celebrating God's creation. Everything our God has made is good and, ultimately, is His to use for His purposes and glory. When I look at myself, I want to see fewer imperfections and more of the face of Jesus. If this is you too today, let's pray:

"Father, thank you for making me in your image. I praise you because I am fearfully and wonderfully made! Change my eyes to see myself, others, and the world as you see them. Your creation is magnificent, and I'm grateful to be a part of it. Amen."

 PSALM 139

DAY 21: God Confidence

Long before I started this book or even began my website, the biggest dream in my heart was to be a writer. Honestly, it felt audacious. *Did I have anything valuable to say? Did the world need another book, particularly one written by me?* I was doubtful. I eventually began the pursuit anyway, and it became evident that this wasn't a selfish desire—it was one God had given me.

You could chalk it up to a lack of self-confidence, but the truth is, what I really lacked was God confidence. I put so much focus on myself and my own abilities that I completely discounted *His* ability to work things out for my good. Becoming a writer was always a dream planted by Him, and because I couldn't see how I could achieve that goal on my own, I forgot to press in for His plans and vision.

In a story in Genesis the Lord promises Abraham and Sarah a baby. She was ninety at the time and responded the way most of us probably would have: she laughed. In her heart, she probably knew the Lord was capable of anything, but she was so distracted by the facts that she lost sight of who was making the promise.

Are there areas of your life where you've become distracted by the facts? If we really believe God is as good and powerful as we say He is, we can trust Him with the details of our story. Today, instead of looking for more confidence in yourself or in the world, remember whose team you're on and place your confidence in His goodness.

 **GENESIS 18:9–15; 21:1–7**

DAY 22: Key Ingredients

Most of my favorite recipes start with butter: chocolate chip cookies, caramelized onions, garlicky noodles, and so on. There are other favorites too, things like salt, lemons, and sugar, and those key ingredients have become cornerstones in the foundation of many of my best meals.

The Bible has key ingredients too. All throughout scripture, there are common themes of love, thankfulness, prayer, and faith that pop up chapter after chapter, and something about that repetition throughout His Word tells me God doesn't want us to miss it. The reiteration is like a neon sign from heaven saying, "Hey! You're gonna want to pay attention here!" The nineteenth-century preacher Charles Spurgeon once wrote, "We may be certain that whatever God made prominent in His Word, He intended to be conspicuous in our lives," meaning, if God wrote a lot about it, it should be reflected in our day-to-day, even now.

When reading your Bible this week, look for the common threads. What stands out to you? What are the neon signs God is hoping you'll notice? How are those truths applicable to your life today? The Bible has the same power to speak into your life today that it did when it was written, so let those words sink in and become the key ingredients of your life.

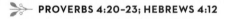 **PROVERBS 4:20–23; HEBREWS 4:12**

DAY 23: Fun Revival

I need a fun revival—a fresh taste of what it means to laugh and play and find joy in frivolous things. The days before kids were different, with their late nights and silliness and freedom, but at some point I allowed the responsibility of adulthood and parenting to strangle some of my playfulness and ease. I embraced checklists instead of rest, structure instead of spontaneity, and now, years into this lifestyle of rules and accountability, I wonder: *How do I get back some of that fun?*

Can we just take it easy on ourselves? We don't have to do it all to be every-thing God wants us to be. We don't have to have it all together or check off all the boxes to call our lives a raging, joyful success. In fact, I think by doing less, by allowing God to narrate our lives, we might find those pieces of ourselves that we lost to the weight of this world.

Take a moment to think about which pieces of your life you'd like to start re-vitalizing. Is there something that brings you joy that you could include more of in the coming days? What would it look like for you to feel like your younger self again? Whatever it is you've misplaced en route to adulthood, ask God to show you how to find it again. He's the God of revival, and He desires to see the very best parts of you come alive for Him.

 **ECCLESIASTES 3:9-15; 5:18-20**

DAY 24: Honey Lime Fruit Salad

I'm ordinarily indifferent toward fruit salad, but there is nothing average about this one. Here, fresh lime and honey transform simple fruit into a flavorful mixture that makes summer's ripe offerings really shine. You can substitute any of your favorite fruits here (think apples! pineapple! blackberries! orange slices!) or even opt for lemon juice and zest in place of the lime. If you're preparing this Honey Lime Fruit Salad ahead of time, be sure to avoid bananas, raspberries, or any other fruit that will easily break down.

....

HONEY LIME FRUIT SALAD

Serves 4 to 6 as a side

¼ cup lime juice

2 teaspoons lime zest

¼ cup honey

2 cups cut-up melon, in 1-inch pieces

2 cups cut-up hulled strawberries, in 1-inch pieces

1 cup blueberries

1 cup grapes, halved

In a medium-size bowl, combine the lime juice, lime zest, and honey, and whisk together until the honey has dissolved. Add the fruit and toss to combine. Refrigerate until ready to serve, and toss just before serving.

DAY 25: The Comfort of Discomfort

Have you seen that meme that says, "Welcome to adulthood. You have a favorite spatula now"? I can relate. I have a favorite sponge for cleaning dishes, a favorite coffee cup, and even a favorite brand of butter. For most of us, adulthood is filled with habits and patterns that indicate we are set in our ways, and who could blame us? It feels good to be within the safe confines of our comfort zone.

A few years ago, my close-knit small group grew to include a few women who were different from me. Suddenly, I was involved in conversations exploring needs and crises that were far outside my scope of practice, and frankly it was uncomfortable. I knew God was presenting an opportunity to learn and love and grow, but deep down I was terrified.

The life of a Christian is anything but comfortable or routine, but it always promises the security of a Heavenly Father. If you're following Jesus, you can trust that you're being led by the Good Shepherd—one who has your interests at heart and will never lead you astray. Even in terrain that feels awkward or treacherous, we can put our faith in the God who has promised to never leave or forsake us. He always leads us down the right path and offers His rest along the way.

Ask Jesus where He wants to go in this season of your life. He won't lead you anywhere that He hasn't already equipped you with the grace for. Today, ask Him to open your heart to new people or opportunities that are outside your comfort zone, knowing you can trust Him wherever He takes you, even if it's uncomfortable.

 **ISAIAH 41:1–20**

DAY 26: The Wilderness of Waiting

In Exodus, God had already fulfilled His promise to deliver the Israelites from the hand of the Egyptians. With the help of Moses, they'd made their way out of Egypt, but when Pharaoh began pursuing them, it appeared their time had run out. In that moment, they wanted to fight back or run away, but Moses's commandment from the Lord was simple: just wait.

Like the Israelites, I'm no good at waiting. It feels unproductive, like a waste of valuable hours I could be using to create a battle plan. I'll often pray for wisdom and resources, open doors and ways out, but if an immediate answer doesn't come, I don't hesitate to take matters into my own hands. Surely, I'm not alone here, right?

The truth is, we're not always meant to take on the giants in our story. Sometimes God calls us to gather some stones and fight, but other times He just asks us to stand, to rest, and wait for His deliverance. Although it's tempting to grumble about our circumstances or retreat to the pain of our former life, when God asks us to wait, He will always make a way.

Are there areas of your life that feel like a wilderness of waiting? Has God asked you to wait when all logic has made you want to take control of the situation? You can trust Him in the waiting, because if He called you to the wilderness, He will absolutely make a way. Your job is simple: to stand firm in the power of His love.

 EXODUS 14

DAY 27: Quick Fixes

A few years ago, I started preparing fresh sandwich loaves regularly for my family. Once you have a great recipe, baking bread is surprisingly simple, and the rewarding, intoxicating scent of thick slices slathered in salted butter is beyond worth the effort. Sure, it requires rise time, proper ingredients, and some attention, but as with many things, even the smallest efforts can yield generous returns. (See my favorite bread recipe, Mom's Homemade Bread, p. 83.)

In life, I'm not always patient enough for the good rewards. Quick fixes and instant gratification suit personalities like mine who want it all and want it done yesterday. But as a result, there have been many instances where I've missed out on simple sources of goodness because I lacked the determination and intentionality to see things through to the end. There are so many gifts in this life—blessings and breakthroughs, revelations, and relationships—but, more often than not, persistence is required to obtain them. They mandate effort or prayer or waiting, absolutely none of which are shortcuts.

Shortcuts don't work with bread, and they rarely do in life either. I'm learning that the most satisfying rewards, the ones that deeply nourish with overwhelming goodness, go best with intentionality.

So what are the things you're going after? Where in your home, your workplace, or your relationship with God are you seeking out more? Spend some time in prayer today, and ask God to show you areas where some intentionality, patience, or bits of daily effort will make room for growth. I really believe God honors our small efforts in big ways, so don't settle for the quick fix—hang in there for the real thing.

 **PSALM 145:15–16**

DAY 28: My Strength

On days when my flesh is weak and I'm unable to thrive by means of my own strength, I find it comforting to remember that Christ remains abundantly able, an ever-present source of life and power. Even when the world is dark with brokenness, devoid of hope and possibility, in Christ we are connected to a joy that is stronger than the weight of sin. So today, in whatever impossible situation you find yourself in, let me remind you where your strength comes from:

They broke my heart.
The joy of the Lord is my strength.
I'm just not qualified.
The joy of the Lord is my strength.
I'm not sure I can recover from this.
The joy of the Lord is my strength.
There's no one in my corner.
The joy of the Lord is my strength.
It's just too much for one person to make a difference.
The joy of the Lord is my strength.
I don't know if I can keep going.
The joy of the Lord is my strength.
But I'm doing this all alone.
The joy of the Lord is my strength.

If you're in a wilderness of difficulty, loneliness, or despair, run to Him and be filled with joy. There is peace and love that is available for you in His presence (Ps. 16:11), so if you are tired, empty, or unable to go on, find rest in this truth: the joy of the Lord is your strength (Neh. 8:10).

 **PROVERBS 18:10**

DAY 29: Flavor du Jour

When I was younger, my parents and I spent summer evenings at an ice cream stand just down the street from our home. Every day, they offered a new soft-serve flavor, and it was always the best one to order—black raspberry, orange creamsicle, peanut butter, or pistachio—all swirled high on top of a fresh sugar cone. Sure, there were sundaes or twisted cups of chocolate or vanilla, but the real treasure was always the flavor du jour.

Some of us settle into a predictable existence, because we like the comfort of what we know, but as believers we have been invited to participate in what God is doing in and through our lives right now. His work in this moment, His flavor of the day, is always the very best decision for our lives, because He's promised purpose, progress, and fulfillment for all those who partner with Him. When we collaborate with God, there is always the promise of fruit, growth, and reward.

Ask God what He wants to do in your life today, even right now. What's the flavor du jour? He offers new mercies every morning to meet your needs as you pursue His purposes. Listen closely for your opportunity to invest in the blessing of God's work and partner with Him today.

 **1 CORINTHIANS 3:5–9**

DAY 30: An Ordinary Wonderful

There is no end to the number of things you can do with a rotisserie chicken (see tomorrow for just one!). Has someone made a cookbook out of that yet? If not, sign me up. I love those simple staples that can be used in any number of ways, making an ordinary thing into something wonderfully delicious.

I want you to know that this is just like what God has in store for you. He has the capacity to use all your ordinary parts to lead, to heal, to break down walls, and to rebuild in His name. God takes your gifts, your dreams, and even the parts of you that are presently undiscovered and transforms them into tools for His use. He's not looking for mighty people to do mighty things—He's looking for willing, obedient hearts that desire to work for His kingdom and glory.

Take the pressure off yourself. God doesn't need your perfection in order to accomplish His will, but it pleases Him to no end when His people show up ready to play on His team. If you have no idea where to start, just surrender your life in prayer to Him now. Tell Him your heart and hands and feet are available for His purposes. He'll show you where to begin and make something magnificent of everything you offer to Him.

 JOSHUA 6

DAY 1: Lemon Chicken Salad

Southerners are serious about their chicken salad. For this rendition, I've skipped some of the usual suspects—nuts, grapes, and relish—to make room for the bright flavors of savory herbs and lemon zest. The end product is a delightful pulled chicken salad that tastes great on a sandwich, bed of lettuce, or even on its own.

LEMON CHICKEN SALAD

Makes 2½ cups

6 tablespoons good-quality mayonnaise

1 tablespoon lemon juice

1 teaspoon lemon zest

½ teaspoon minced garlic

½ teaspoon dried thyme

¼ teaspoon dried rosemary

¾ teaspoon kosher salt

½ teaspoon black pepper

3 cups cooked and pulled chicken

In a medium-size bowl, stir to combine the mayonnaise, lemon juice, zest, garlic, thyme, rosemary, salt, and pepper. Add the chicken and stir together. Taste and add additional salt and pepper as desired or additional mayo or lemon juice for extra moisture. Store in a sealed container in the fridge for up to one week.

DAY 2: Surprise!

The doctor held up our brand-new baby and shocked us all: "It's a . . . boy?"

We spent months preparing for life with another daughter. After multiple ultrasounds, we had a gender-reveal party, complete with pink confetti and balloons. All signs pointed to "girl," until Charlie came on the scene: a happy, blond-haired, blue-eyed baby boy who was anything but a girl. Even his name, Charles, means "man." *(Sidenote: I know that right now there's a pregnant woman reading this who is panic-texting her doctor to schedule another ultrasound, but, please, don't worry. I'm told this happens very, very rarely.)*

The point is, life surprises us. There are moments we expect, ones we dream about and plan for and map out years in advance, but there are also others that will blindside us like a curveball to the face. But here's what I am sure of: God is sovereign no matter what life throws at you. He's sovereign when your relationship falls apart, He's sovereign in your disappointments, and He's sovereign when your plans don't work the way you expected. He's not surprised by anything, so we can rely for Him for our sure and steady ground when everything else is quaking.

Regardless of what life scenario is throwing you for a loop today, you can give it to God. Hand over the reins of control and grasp onto the rest that is promised to us in Christ. Whether it is a happy surprise, a painful disappointment, or a devastating setback, God is sovereign over it all.

 ISAIAH 45

DAY 3: Meet the Need in Front of You

I didn't realize how attached I had become to the idea of a daughter until our "daughter" turned out to be a son. When the doctor announced it was a boy, our first reaction was, "*Twins?*" Surely, the daughter we had spent months praying for and imagining life with was somewhere in there, and this new baby boy, the one we must have missed in all the ultrasounds and heartbeat scans, was just the happiest little addition, right?

Well, you know the story. There wasn't a girl in there, and once the adrenaline wore off, the reality sank in: I wasn't bringing my daughter home. I spent the next two days in the hospital getting to know my baby boy, and on the inside there was a tiny part of me I was ashamed of, a part that felt selfish and bitter and nearsighted, because I was struggling to disconnect myself from the future I had thought was mine. I knew when I got home there would be a nursery to pack up full of pink clothes and baby dolls, homemade quilts and hair ribbons, and with it I'd have to put away some of those dreams I had imagined too.

I got home to find that my parents had gone shopping for boy items. They were washed and neatly folded on the changing table, a little act of love that saved me. They knew they couldn't help me process the circumstances, but instead of judging my heart, of telling me how I should feel or how to best move on, they simply came alongside of me to help in the way that they could.

Sometimes, we just have to meet the need in front of us. We won't always fix it, but our small offerings of grace, free of advice or judgment or solutions, can be a lifeline to the people we love. Today, consider if there is someone within your circle who needs to experience the love of God. You won't be able to unpack all of their burdens, but you can help tote the load. Be the hands and feet and meet them with God's love wherever they are today.

 **GALATIANS 6:2**

DAY 4: Changing Names

Before we knew Charlie was a boy, we had a beautiful girl's name picked out. Pink onesies, frilly blankets, and even a handmade sign on the nursery wall were assigned to the baby girl we had named. Ultimately, it didn't matter who we thought the baby was, because God had other plans in mind.

All throughout the Bible are instances where God changes the name of His people to call forth their destiny. Back then, names were intentional, signifying truths about individuals' heritage and purpose, so when God changed a name, He was literally changing the outcome of a person's story. Abram becomes Abraham, the father of a nation, and Sarai becomes Sarah, His princess (Gen. 17). Instead of "supplanter," Jacob's name becomes "Israel," meaning "triumphant with God" (Gen. 32), and even Simon, the one who denied Jesus on the eve of His death, became Peter, the very rock on which Christ would build His church (John 1:42). Despite their sin, unbelief, or obvious shortcomings, God spoke purpose with their name and ultimately decided who they would become.

The same is true for you too. Your identity is not the sum of your past, your efforts, or who the enemy has tried to whisper you are—you are who the Father says you are. God has the final say on your destiny, because He is the One who calls it forth. This week, instead of listening to the opinions of others or the things you say about yourself, begin asking Him who He says you are. He has a calling and purpose for your life, and His opinion is the only one that counts.

 **1 PETER 2:9–10**

DAY 5: **Masterpiece**

One of my dear friends is a photographer. She has the gift of capturing people in a way that makes them feel truly seen. Even in photo sessions where my kids are screaming, I'm sweating like an animal, and everyone involved is close to tears, she produces photos in which I look like I love my life and family as much as I truly do. Those pictures capture the intangible beauty of her subjects and produce something that feels raw and authentic.

I think God loves to see our truest selves. He's not looking for a show of fake smiles or buttoned-up coordinating outfits, because He's in it for the moments when we trust Him with our hearts and vulnerability. He knows our inner workings—our beliefs, our fears, our scars, our passions—and is honored when we let Him capture us just as we are.

The beautiful thing about relationship with Jesus is that we don't need fancy prayers or a cleaned-up façade to come face-to-face with our Creator—we just need to trust that He'll create something beautiful from whatever we show up with. Today, spend some time in prayer and share the words of your heart and mind with the Lord. Offer Him your thoughts, ask your questions, and tell Him what He is to you. Bring your truest self to the feet of Jesus, and let Him make a masterpiece of you.

 JOHN 6:37

DAY 6: BFF

There are several people in my life with whom I've been friends forever. Once you've known someone for more than half your life, you start feeling less like a friend and more like a sister or some kind of a faithful go-to who is wild enough to help you egg your ex-boyfriend's house. Friendships like that evolve with you and eventually fit into all the right places of your story, becoming the instant classics you never really grow out of.

There's a certain vulnerability that comes with spending time with a person who has known you through nearly every season of your life. There's safety to share secrets and expose the hidden parts you think no one else will understand, because you're confident that person is there for keeps. Although it might be scary to have that kind of transparency in newer relationships, I've always taken comfort in knowing there are people who know me from the inside out and still love me; even though they've seen me at my worst, they're still willing to call me friend.

I don't know where you stand with Jesus, but I want you to know that this is the kind of love He has for you. He knows all your parts—where you're wrong, where you lack, where you've strayed—and He still loves you. He desires relationship with you even when you flake on Him or pass over Him for something else. He's like that friend you've had forever—He'll always make room for you, no matter what you bring to the table.

Where does Jesus fit into your story? Do you know Him as a friend? Just like that longtime BFF, you can bring your baggage to Him. Today, share your heart and your secrets, whisper your dreams and your fears, and He will take care of it all.

 **JOHN 15:12–17**

DAY 7: Preserving Fruit

My father-in-law has a giant fig tree that produces abundantly every summer. Once a year, when the time is right, I fill grocery bags with those juicy rounds of fruit and make jars of strawberry fig preserves, his mother's recipe, to share with family and friends. We spread it on toast, stuff it inside pop-tarts, and savor every last bit of that fruit all year long.

This is a perfect example of God's economy. I love the idea that the fruit from one season of our lives is a lasting thing that can be shared with others too. God has beautiful, creative uses for the blessings in our lives, ways to preserve, repurpose, and spread the goodness of our story into the lives of others. The fruit and evidence of His presence in our lives is an amazing, rewarding gift, and He loves to see us share it with the world around us.

What's God doing in your life right now? If you find yourself in a season of abundance, don't leave that fruit hanging on the tree—share your overflow with the people around you. We are blessed to be a blessing, and His work in our lives is too good to keep all to ourselves. Bottle and share whatever gift He's pouring out in your life with someone else, right now.

 **DEUTERONOMY 28:1–14**

DAY 8: Brown-Butter Peach Berry Crumble

Baked fruit crumbles are a favorite in the South, particularly in the summer when warm temperatures offer fresh berries, ripe peaches, and loads of other fruit perfect for baking into a dessert. This rendition features browned butter, which contributes a warm, almost nutty flavor and delightful texture. We like to serve Brown-Butter Peach Berry Crumble with vanilla ice cream, but whipped cream would also be terrific here; my recipe for homemade whipped cream (see Strawberry Shortcakes, p. 142) would be more than enough.

....

BROWN-BUTTER PEACH BERRY CRUMBLE

Serves 6 to 8

TOPPING

½ cup unsalted butter

⅓ cup packed light brown sugar

¾ cup all-purpose flour

⅓ cup quick-cooking oats

¼ teaspoon ground cinnamon

¼ teaspoon table salt

FILLING

2 cups peeled, pitted, and cut-up peaches
  (from about 2 large ripe peaches)

2 cups hulled and cut-up strawberries

½ cup granulated sugar

2 tablespoons all-purpose flour

Pinch of table salt

1½ tablespoons lemon juice

TO PREPARE THE TOPPING

Preheat the oven to 375 ºF. Lightly grease an 8- or 9-inch baking dish with butter or cooking spray. To brown the butter, cube it into tablespoon-size pieces and place it into a small, heavy-bottomed pan over medium heat. Stir frequently as the butter melts, bubbles, and begins to foam. Then stir continuously and look for small, amber-colored flecks beginning to form on the bottom of the pan. Once the butter is fragrant and golden brown, immediately remove it from the heat and pour it into a large heat-proof bowl. Stir in the sugar. Then add the flour, oats, cinnamon, and salt, stirring just until combined into thick clumps. Place the bowl in the fridge to cool briefly while you assemble the filling.

TO PREPARE THE FILLING

In a medium bowl lightly toss together the peaches and strawberries. In a small bowl, mix the sugar, flour, and salt, and sprinkle it over the fruit. Add the lemon juice, and gently mix until the sugar-flour mixture is evenly distributed.

TO PREPARE THE CRUMBLE

Pour the filling into the prepared baking dish. Sprinkle the topping over the fruit and bake about 25 minutes or until the topping is golden and the fruit beneath is bubbling. Allow it to cool slightly before serving with ice cream or whipped cream.

DAY 9: **Weightless**

I recently traveled by myself to visit a friend and her family, and I was amazed at what a different person I was there. I splashed in the pool with her children and laughed at my own terrible jokes as if I was kid myself—all smiles and silliness and fun. After dinner, instead of rushing to do the dishes or begin the bedtime routines, we lingered at the dinner table to tell one more story and relive our memories, a few shared words at a time. Untethered from my roles as wife and mom, I turned into this lighter version of myself, and, honestly, it felt really good.

I don't want to wait for a night away or an empty house to experience this kind of joy. I want to be able to laugh even when my house is a disaster and I'm behind with work. I'd like to feel at peace even when my kids are running wild, my hair is greasy, and dinner is reheated pizza, again.

I'm not sure it's possible to fully shed the layers of responsibility that come with adulthood, marriage, and motherhood, but I don't think those roles are intended to be perpetually burdensome. We can seek out opportunities to laugh at ourselves and be silly, lingering in the moment as if we've got nowhere better to be. There will always be jobs to do and needs to meet, but even in that responsibility we can embrace the joy and peace that God wants to pour out on us right now. We can rest in His fullness, and let the circumstances and roles of our lives nudge us ever closer to Him.

Bring it all to God today—your heaviness, your responsibilities, and the self-imposed rules and restrictions you've tied yourself to—and exchange them for the weightless freedom found in Him. He has more than enough joy and peace for you, so grab hold of them today.

 **EXODUS 33:14; PSALM 116, ESPECIALLY V. 7**

DAY 10: Knowing Your Portion

There was a time when yes was my go-to answer: to responsibilities, to social invitations, and to the various needs that popped up within my reach. If I was *able* to do it, I did, with little thought to how that stretch of my time, energy, and emotions would affect other areas of my life. Unsurprisingly, I wound up worn thin and burned out on more than one occasion and was forced to learn how to take care of myself by stepping away from some of those things that were bidding for my attention.

Sister, I want to remind you to be gentle with yourself. It's okay to do less in order to be more, and doing less does not make *you* less. We all have a portion that God has given us to operate in, and that portion looks different for each of us in various seasons of life. If we continue to add to our plate, heaping up emotional responsibility, social expectations, and insurmountable self-imposed goals, we may miss out on the opportunity to savor each bite of what God has served us. We simply can't do it all.

Today, give yourself the grace to do less and embrace the freedom of saying no. Be gentle with yourself and others, remembering that it's all right to enjoy what's on your plate before going in for seconds. Instead of stuffing yourself with things that won't satiate you, find satisfaction in what God is working out in your story right now. He's the One who assigns your portion and cup.

 **PSALM 16, 73:23-26**

DAY 11: Grace Upon Grace

When I was in college, there was an ice cream shop in our neighborhood that made the best sundaes. I'd pay for a small cup, and they'd give me one heaped tall with scoop after scoop. Toppings like whipped cream and toffee bits would cling to the sides of the ice cream and caramel would ooze and melt into the crevices, filling every last inch of the bowl. My small portion there was always abundant, entirely delightful, and more than I could ever have expected.

A verse in John talks about our inheritance in Christ: *For from his fullness we have all received, grace upon grace* (1:16). The language here gives a picture of grace flowing over you like an ocean, wave after wave crashing to the shore, one after another. In those waters, you can barely catch your breath before God rolls in with another wave of grace, another wave of grace, another wave of grace.

Our portion in Christ is so full, more than you or I could hope for or imagine. In Him, grace is heaped upon grace, favor scooped upon favor, and all of it is saturated with the rich spiritual blessing that comes from communion with God. This morning, take a moment to reflect on your helping. Thank Jesus for the complete work He did on the cross, for the kindness and compassion He offers so abundantly each day; open your heart to savor the goodness of His grace.

 **JOHN 1:1–16**

DAY 12: The Golden Rule

I grew up hearing about the Golden Rule: "Do unto others as you would have them do unto you." My parents taught me the value of extending kindness toward others in all circumstances, but somewhere along the way to adulthood I found myself changing the rules. Instead of treating people the way I wanted to be treated, I operated according to my own set of requirements and conditions, only offering as much love and respect as I believed their character and behavior had earned them.

Although many of us have left the Golden Rule in the dust, I think God is inviting us to extend radical love to *everyone*, not because it's what they deserve, but because that's who He's called us to be. As believers, we have the opportunity to be a reflection of the love and grace we've found in Him, and that brand of love comes free of charge, without conditions or restrictions.

Although we can't control how other people treat us, we can decide, right now, to extend love, kindness, patience, respect, and dignity in every circumstance. God hasn't called us to demand justice or decide who deserves our goodwill—He's called us to love everyone, no matter what.

Are there people in your life who are harder to love right now? You can share those thoughts with God and ask Him to show you how you can be the hands and feet of Jesus to them this week. It may not be easy, but the rules are that simple. Start practicing the Golden Rule, and carry Christ with you wherever you go.

 **MATTHEW 22:37–40**

DAY 13: Just the Way They Are

There are few things as terrifying as hearing your husband call himself the "meat man." After two go-rounds with an electric smoker and a mint copy of the *Franklin Barbecue* cookbook, Brett had basically taken on the persona of a redneck Bobby Flay. After reading the cookbook for barely a week, his meat-master alter ego had taken over, powered by the fumes of bacon grease and cedar woodchips.

For some reason, this annoyed the heck out of me. We were early on in our marriage, and yet somehow his bolstered confidence and barbecue peacocking just about made me want to pack my bags. Lucky for him, the brisket was fabulous, so instead of leaving I just made it my mission to knock him down to size. I rolled my eyes as he exaggeratedly licked his fingers at the dinner table and refused to take seconds even when those smoky dry-rub wings were basically waving to me.

I'm not sure who told me it was my job to make myself feel more comfortable by bringing him down. Sure, he was being a little cocky, but was it too much for me to just cheer him on while I quietly laughed to myself? Brett's ability on the grill didn't mean that my dinners were any less delicious, and his pride in himself didn't mean he thought he was better than me. Condescending words and snide remarks rarely change a person; in fact, the opposite is true—most people are far more likely to respond positively and grow when they feel loved.

Are there people in your life who are sometimes hard to love? A husband? A coworker? A friend? Ask God for the grace to love them just the way they are. Whether they're right, wrong, or weirdly invested in smoked meats, you owe them the respect and kindness that God has offered each one of us.

 **EPHESIANS 4:29; PHILIPPIANS 2:1–18; HEBREWS 3:13**

DAY 14: Eyes on the Horizon

When Brett and I were dating, I joined him on a deep-sea fishing boat for what I wrongfully assumed would be a short morning of snapper fishing. I was more familiar with cruise-size boats and smaller varieties intended for calm lakes and rivers, so when we jetted out toward the horizon on a turbulent ride, hours away from the shore, I slowly became unglued.

Twenty-seven miles was a long way from home, and by the time we got to our fishing spot, my stomach was rolling. My hands, clammy with sweat, clutched a fishing rod as the boat rocked with the waves under my feet, and the more I willed myself not to throw up, the more certain I became that I'd be tasting my breakfast again soon. Brett, seeing that I was deteriorating, encouraged me to look up from the waves and out onto the horizon, and soon the feeling passed. My sea legs returned, I caught my first red snapper, and the day turned out to be not half bad.

When we fixate on the waves, the swirl of chaos and activity in the world around us, we can be consumed by the churning waters. Instead, Hebrews 12:1-2 tells us to endure challenging times by looking to Jesus as our point on the horizon, a constant source of hope even in the midst of rough seas. He doesn't shake when the ground beneath us rolls, but instead remains the security and confidence that steadies our troubled hearts and minds.

Are you up against some challenging seas today? Take your eyes off the water, the catch, and the other people in your boat, and instead look to the horizon. Jesus is the One who leads and lights your path, and if you'll fix your eyes on Him, He will bring comfort to your heart.

 **MICAH 7:5-7**

DAY 15: Blackened Snapper

Although I still don't love fishing, I love the reward of fresh-caught Gulf fish for supper. Every year, my husband and our friends catch loads of red snapper, which they filet and freeze for the coming months. For some time, I followed Paul Prudhomme's recipe for blackened redfish when preparing snapper, but over the years I've modified that recipe to suit our family's preferences.

This Blackened Seasoning recipe is plenty for two rounds of fish, so save any leftovers for future use. If you plan to make this on an indoor stove, be sure to turn on a fan or at least crack a few windows—it gets smoky! Once prepared, I like to serve Blackened Snapper with rice or Southern Cheese Grits (p. 39).

....

BLACKENED SNAPPER

Serves 4

BLACKENED SEASONING

1½ tablespoons paprika

1 tablespoon table salt (fine salt
   is better than kosher or coarse salt)

1 teaspoon black pepper

1½ teaspoons garlic powder

1 teaspoon onion powder

1 teaspoon dried thyme

½ teaspoon dried oregano

½ teaspoon cayenne pepper

SNAPPER

4 (6-ounce) pieces of red snapper, about
   1 inch thick (skin on or off; redfish, tilapia,
   and grouper work well here too)

½ cup unsalted butter, divided

Blackened Seasoning

Kosher salt and pepper as desired

TO PREPARE THE BLACKENED SEASONING

Thoroughly mix all of the seasoning ingredients together. Place about half of the mixture in a shallow bowl, and then store the other half in a jar for future use.

TO PREPARE THE SNAPPER

Melt ¼ cup butter in a large cast-iron skillet over medium-low heat. Once melted, pour the butter into a shallow bowl and carefully wipe the pan out with a paper towel. Place the pan back on the stove and heat it on high for 5 minutes. Pick out any remaining bones in the flesh of the fish, and dredge both sides of the filets, one at a time, in the melted butter. Generously coat each piece with the blackened seasoning. Once the pan is heated, place the fish into the skillet, skin-side down, if applicable. (If your cast-iron pan is smaller, prepare the fish in two batches so as not to overcrowd the pan.)

Once the fish is in the pan, turn the heat down to medium-high and cook for 2 minutes. Flip the fish and add the remaining ¼ cup butter in tablespoon-size chunks. Carefully swirl the pan to melt the butter and use a spoon to baste the fish with the melted butter in the pan. Cook for an additional 1½ to 2 minutes until the fish is cooked through and flakes when tested with a fork. Remove the fish from the heat to cool briefly before serving.

DAY 16: Even More Undignified Than This

My mom recently uncovered some home movies from when I was twelve. I was 110 pounds of lanky prepubescence, dancing in my bathing suit with friends to a poorly choreographed rendition of the Spice Girls. There was no hesitation, no embarrassment about my uncovered body and ill-timed moves, and as I watched those videos I found myself wanting to be more like that younger person—brave, confident, and unashamed of who I was.

In 2 Samuel, David is described as dancing in the presence of the Lord. In his nightshirt, he leaped and shouted, blew horns and worshiped with all his might. He paid no attention to the people nearby who could see him dancing wildly in his nightclothes, undignified by the world's standards, because his intention was to honor the Lord—David knew who his audience was.

Sometimes we forget who we're dancing for. It's easy to become distracted, constrained even, by the opinions of those around us, but God desires us to experience the joy and freedom of undignified passion for Him. We have an audience of One, a King on high who called David a man after His own heart, and He is honored when we worship and love without restraint. Don't worry about the people around you—just worship God with your whole heart. Honor God with your body and words and actions, because it doesn't matter who's watching, so long as God is there.

2 SAMUEL 6:12–22

DAY 17: Leavening

Sometimes, as a mother of small children, I'm unsure how to best teach them about God. We pray and read their Bible, go to church and talk about heaven, but they're still so young. Some days I'm left wondering, *Is there anything going on in there? Are they getting it? Is any of this seeping through to their little hearts?*

In Matthew, Jesus likens the kingdom of heaven to bread baking: *The kingdom of heaven is like leaven that a woman took and hid in three measures of flour, till it was all leavened.* Although normally a pinch of yeast would only be enough to make a single loaf of bread, here it is far more effective, leavening enough flour to make a hundred loaves. This parable illustrates the exponential impact of God's power. He's always at work, growing and expanding hearts until they're transformed and aligned with His. Even when we don't see Him at work, we can remain confident that, if there's leaven there, God can make it grow.

I'm not sure if we'll ever know the impact of our lives and words on our children and the world around us, but I do believe that God can use every act of love to the glory of His name. He's at work, in the lives of your family, friends, and neighbors, producing abundantly with every bit of leavening we add to the mix. When you're unsure if your words, prayers, actions, or love are making a difference, take heart: the kingdom is at work, and God can multiply whatever you offer in His name.

 **MATTHEW 13:33**

DAY 18: Behind the Velvet Curtain

In my dining room, a velvet curtain hangs in front of a storage nook that serves as a catchall for last-minute cleanups and homeless pieces of clutter. It's not uncommon for me to throw stray toys, sippy cups, and stacks of mail behind the curtain to make the house look tidy, particularly when we're expecting guests. For a minute, I trick myself into believing my home is as spotless and put-together as I'd like it to be, but the area behind the velvet curtain tells a different story.

Like my house-cleaning trick, I've spent years rearranging and cleaning up my life from the outside. I've shuffled around the dirt and the wounds—the sin and secrets and shame—draping it in some sort of a velvet curtain, so that people primarily see what I want them to see. Sometimes it's easier to cover up a mess than it is to expose it to the world.

Behind the velvet, our brokenness looks different, but the bottom line is the same: we each have the opportunity to draw back the curtain and bare our hearts to a really kind Savior. He's not overwhelmed by the chaos, the clutter, and the secret things we've hidden from everyone else. Instead, He wants to help clean it up, to get rid of the things that aren't ours to harbor, and to find a home for the lost and broken parts we've hidden along the way. Jesus is a good catchall. He takes good care of all our bits and pieces, because He doesn't just tidy up our mess—He restores it and uses it for His glory.

Bring your whole heart to the Lord today. You don't need to clean up or shove the yucky parts behind the curtain. Just welcome Him in to partner with you in the restoration.

 **1 CORINTHIANS 1:26–31**

DAY 19: Nurturing by Nature

Building our home in the country has meant that there's a lot of wide-open out-door space to take care of. It's far too much grass for Brett to cut on his own, so we opted to set aside some natural areas that would look beautiful without much maintenance. Over time, the grasses and wildflowers have grown, and those areas have begun to attract wildlife to our home. At any given time, you can look out the window to witness birds and critters enjoying the sustenance, shade, and beauty of what has grown in our backyard.

There's good stuff growing in you too, things that will feed, nurture, and attract the world around you. God has planted all sorts of beautiful qualities and gifts in His people, even His very own Spirit, which provides life-giving sustenance to a world in need. As children of God, we have the opportunity to share that goodness and walk in a manner that points to Him, not out of obligation, but as a love offering of our life to the glory of His name.

Does your life point to Jesus, attracting people who are thirsty for the kindness and hope of the gospel? There's no condemnation for those areas you're working on, but this is a good opportunity to take inventory. Maybe today is the day you plant new seeds of habits and a lifestyle that will cause love to grow and spread, offering beauty and sustenance to the people around you. Ask God to remind you of some simple ways you can be a source of life to others this week, because He's already put it inside of you—you just need to let it grow.

 **TITUS 2:11–14**

DAY 20: Prescription for Brokenness

The prescription for any brokenness that might be in your life can be found in Jeremiah: *Then you will call upon me and come and pray to me, and I will hear you. You will seek me and find me, when you seek me with all your heart. I will be found by you, declares the Lord, and I will restore your fortunes and gather you from all the nations and all the places where I have driven you, declares the Lord, and I will bring you back to the place from which I sent you into exile* (29:12–14).

Let's not miss the depth of this promise. God's Word says we will find Him when we seek Him. He doesn't hide or turn a blind eye to our needs; instead, when we cry out to Him or seek understanding in our lives, He responds by showing up. He is *found*. What's more, in His graciousness, He has promised to tend to the broken areas, providing healing and restoration after our devastation. He doesn't leave us how He finds us, because His plan is to offer us welfare, the fullness of His peace and hope resting within the workings of our lives.

God is so for you and for relationship *with* you. He desires to be found by His people and to lead them into the rest of His loving-kindness. Is there a cry in your heart this morning? Are there places of exile, circumstances marked by brokenness and suffering and the unknown? Seek His ways, His understanding, and His relationship with your whole heart, and when you find Him, remember, He never lost track of you—He's been waiting for you all along.

 JOHN 6:37

DAY 21: What We're Known For

A few years ago, I went to Philadelphia and got the greasiest cheesesteak I could find, because I was determined to get the full experience. I do the same thing everywhere I go: lobster in Maine, deep-dish in Chicago, and hot dogs at every ballpark game. Whether I'm tasting pineapples in Hawaii or croissants in Paris, my goal is the same: I want the taste that place has become known for.

Over the course of our lives, we'll all become known for something. We might build our name upon our career, our successes, or our ideas, or people may recall things like the sound of our laughter or our nuggets of wisdom. Even though our days are made up of millions of little choices and words and actions, in the end it will all be boiled down to a single highlight reel. So the question bears asking: What will we be known for?

In 1 Corinthians, Paul whittles our must-do list down to three things: faith, hope, and love, and then he says the greatest of these is love. We might give away our words and time and money and skills all the days of our lives, but the stuff that counts most of all, the one thing that will remain when it's all said and done, is our love.

I don't know about you, but I want my story to be a legacy of love. Fortunately, Jesus is the perfect coauthor for that kind of narrative, because He *is* love. Today, ask God how you can introduce more of His heart into your everyday life, the choices and words that will be boiled down for your own highlight reel, and I can guarantee you that the end product will be love. With Him, we can be a people known for our love.

 **1 CORINTHIANS 13:1–13**

DAY 22: Award-Winning (??) Guacamole

Fun fact: On that trip to Philadelphia I mentioned yesterday, I randomly won a guacamole-making contest, which entitled me to a year's supply of avocados. Each month, crates of avocados showed up at my door, and guacamole became my new go-to party trick.

Bright and zesty with fresh citrus, jalapeño, and garlic, my go-to guac features roughly cut avocadoes for a thick and toothy texture. I like to enjoy this with cantina-style tortilla chips or cut-up veggies, but it also makes a terrific topping for my Blackened Snapper (p. 210).

....

AWARD-WINNING (??) GUACAMOLE

Serves 4 to 6 as an appetizer

3 large Hass avocados

¼ cup fresh cilantro, finely chopped, plus more as desired

3 tablespoons finely diced red onion

3 tablespoons fresh lime juice

4 teaspoons seeded, minced jalapeño pepper, plus more as desired

1½ teaspoons minced garlic

¾ teaspoon kosher salt, plus more as desired

½ teaspoon black pepper

On a cutting board, use a paring knife to cut around the circumference of the avocadoes down to the pit and twist to separate the halves. Remove the pits and squeeze the flesh out of three halves into a medium-size mixing bowl. Use the back of a fork to mash the flesh until smooth. Add the cilantro, onion, lime juice, jalapeño, garlic, salt, and pepper, and stir to combine. Next, use the paring knife to carefully score the flesh of the remaining avocado halves into cubes and scoop them into the bowl. Stir just until the avocado cubes have been incorporated into the mixture, leaving it thick and chunky. Taste and add more salt, pepper, or cilantro, if desired. Store refrigerated in a covered container up to a day in advance of serving.

DAY 23: Dinner at the Zoo

You would laugh if you witnessed the dinnertime scene at my house. A far cry from the Martha Stewart visions I had for my life, preparing for supper in our home is more akin to feeding time at the zoo—the "animals" are ravenous, barking and clawing for food and attention. Imagine bubbling pots and beeping timers, usually right about the same time the baby fills his diaper. Imagine toddlers quite literally hanging on my legs, as if by being attached to me they might somehow will their dinner to appear faster. There are cries for milk, for nibbles before dinner, and for help getting off the potty, all happening at once while I'm trying to get dishes to the table.

Forget peaceful—dinnertime is straight-up pandemonium, but so are a lot of other parts of everyday life, right? I have battled with myself for years, convinced that maybe if I was more prepared, more present, or more relaxed from the get-go, somehow things would be easier. The truth is, active family life will always be an unreliable source for peace.

Instead, the Bible says true peace is found by forever fixing our eyes on Jesus, our only reliable source of hope and grace (1 Pet. 1:13). When the zoo at home, the chaos at work, and the whirlwind of friends, social media, and daily activities come at us with Mach speed, depleting energy and causing stress, we can remain rooted in the solid ground of Jesus.

Where is there tumult in your world? If there are places where you're prone to losing peace, you can welcome Jesus into that space. His presence won't mean the end of wild dinnertimes or hectic schedules, but it does mean that you can operate in those moments with supernatural love, perseverance, and grace. Invite Jesus into your zoo, and ask Him to transform your mind and heart, right here, right now.

 **ISAIAH 26:3-4**

DAY 24: Letting Your Hair Down

A year or so ago, I went out of town to have dinner with two of my best friends. We were celebrating my birthday at a special restaurant, and with no kids to run home to, I let loose. We ended up dancing in the parking lot and laughing for what felt like hours—it was pure joy and weightless freedom.

I don't do that often enough. I get too busy to fully embrace fun and allow fear to keep me from letting my hair down long enough to start a full-on dance party. I bind myself to my need to perform and take care of everyone else, forgetting that laughter is good medicine. Pure, unabashed joy changes the atmosphere of our hearts, and although my version of joy looks different from yours, both are entirely essential.

Friend, we need to take better care of ourselves. There are fundamental needs and tasks that must get done, yes, but the condition of our heart is just as crucial. God desires for us to experience joy that comes from Him, and let me tell you—that's not nearly as serious as it sounds. It can be as simple as a mindless book, or a game of charades, or dancing in a parking lot with your two best friends. There's an inner strengthening that happens in the release of joy in our lives and for me it feels a whole lot like freedom. Walk in the freedom of joy today. Ask God for childlike joy and more reasons to laugh and He will give them to you.

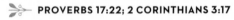 **PROVERBS 17:22; 2 CORINTHIANS 3:17**

DAY 25: Adding Salt

If you've ever eaten unsalted potato chips or pretzels, you know: they're just not that good. I accidentally bought a bag of unsalted pretzels, and it was about as bad as it sounds. Up until then, I didn't realize it was the salt I was craving, those little granules of flavor and crunch that transform ordinary pretzels into something desirable.

Jesus said we are the salt of the earth (Matt. 5:13). Our job here on earth as believers is to impart flavor and season the world with a taste of heaven that transforms our homes and communities with the love of God. What good are we if we stay in our pantries and salt shakers, hidden from a world that is starving for something good? Instead, we're to seek out the people lacking the love and hope of heaven, to impart to them His goodness and transform their lives.

Sister, you have flavor. You bring variety and beauty and goodness to this world, and there are people within your reach who need to taste the goodness of Jesus through your life. Today, consider where there is opportunity to share God's love in a new and fresh way. Ask God to point out people craving His salt and His love, and be brave enough to share it generously. Just be you—people will know the difference when they see Jesus in your life, so offer up His love freely.

 ACTS 13:47

DAY 26: Sweeter Waters

The months after I moved to Selma were a weird and lonely time. There were lots of changes, lots of crying in the shower, and long phone calls to old friends, because my new life felt so foreign. Everyone told me I should be so happy—I was married now! No more long-distance relationship! The future I had longed for was beginning! But when I left my home, my job, and my friends, the lingering flavor in my heart was bitter, as if I had somehow given up more than I received.

Well, you know the story. God eventually changed my heart and opened my eyes to the gift of our new life. He overwhelmed the bitterness of my loss with His goodness, and it completely shifted my experience. It reminds me of a story in Exodus where the Israelites found themselves in need of water in the wilderness. They stumbled upon a new source of water, but the water was bitter and useless for drinking. God commanded Moses to throw a log into the water, and instantly the water became sweet. Because the Israelites trusted His voice, their experience shifted and they were offered water that was more sweet than bitter.

We're all bound to stumble upon bitter waters, but I don't believe that cup is ours to drink forever. God is always faithful, and if we find ourselves in a wilderness with bitter water, He has the power and goodness to replace it with something sweet. He can heal us from our former brokenness and provide in foreign circumstances. If there are places in your life marked by bitterness, ask God to change your heart and fill it with the sweet satisfaction of His love. In His grace, He will offer His provision, changing the sour parts of your story into something that is palatable in Him.

 **EXODUS 15:22–27**

DAY 27: No Disguises

Sometimes my kids dress up in their daddy's clothing. They emerge from his closet wearing oversize button-down shirts and hats and shuffling along in size 11 boots, and I laugh, because I remember doing it too. It's as if kids believe that with different clothing on, they'll somehow trick people into believing they're someone else. Little do they know any mom can spot her children from a mile away.

What kind of disguises have you been wearing lately? A smile? Contentment? Bravery? Maybe you wear extra makeup to cover the parts that feel ugly or feign an air of holiness to hide the places where you've been mad at God? I've been there, and I know: sometimes we shove all the emptiness and disappointment below the surface to conceal our own brokenness, but we're not tricking everyone; God sees our heart from a mile away.

Hebrews 4:13 says: *And no creature is hidden from his sight, but all are naked and exposed to the eyes of him to whom we must give account.* He knows our hearts, our fears, and our thoughts, and you know what? He still loves us. Like the Samaritan woman at the well, Jesus already knows the secrets of your heart, and He's not disgusted; He just wants to relieve you of those burdens.

We don't have to fool God with any disguises. If there's pain, fear, or sin hiding below the surface, we can be real with Him about it. We can be transparent with Him, even in our darkest deficiencies, because He has promised to forgive us for every single bit of it (1 John 1:9). Be transparent before Jesus today, and ask Him to heal any wounded places that have been covered in shame for some time. God loves the person beneath the mask, so be yourself with Him.

 **JOHN 4:1-26**

DAY 28: Trimming the Ends

My childhood summers in western New York smelled like charcoal grills and chlorine. Days were spent listening for the ice cream truck from the comfort of my inner tube, and nights were lit up with fireflies and those last bits of glow from the sun. We'd often visit family out in the country, where the kids would be put to work on the back porch snapping off ends green beans and shucking corn. It felt like a lot of work to me as a kid, but I enjoyed the reward of buttered corn kernels and salty fingers at the supper table later that night.

Since then, there have been many times in my life when I felt a bit like that summer produce. There have been seasons of pruning and trimming, times when I felt like parts of my identity and story were broken off or pulled back like the ends of those beans and those corn husks. You've probably been there too—feeling at a loss or searching for a sense of normalcy, distant and separated from things you've grown used to. We lose a relationship or a job, make a move, or are forced down a road we didn't envision for ourselves, and suddenly our lives can feel bare.

Jesus's illustration of the vine and the branches reminds me, first, who it is who gardens and tends to our lives and, second, that pruning is a good and necessary thing. God will often trim back the parts of our lives that no longer serve us in order to make room for more fruit. He doesn't prune just to make us feel vulnerable or lacking; He wants to see us grow. Looking back on my life, I'm able to see instances where seasons of pruning made room for His goodness in my life, and all that snapping, husking, and trimming of ends gave me something so much more delicious.

Are there places in your life that feel as if they're missing a few pieces? Maybe some comforts that God has been pruning in your life? Ask God to tend to your story like the good gardener He is, abide in Him, and you can trust that fresh abundance is on its way.

 **JOHN 15:1–2**

DAY 29: Balsamic Grilled Chicken

I've come to rely on some simple marinades that, when combined with the heat and flavor of the grill, make for a great everyday go-to dinner. This Balsamic Grilled Chicken makes an easy and flavorful addition to salads, sandwiches, and dinner plates alike.

BALSAMIC GRILLED CHICKEN

Serves 6

¼ cup olive oil

¼ cup balsamic vinegar

3 tablespoons packed brown sugar

2 teaspoons Italian seasoning

1 teaspoon garlic powder

1 teaspoon onion powder

1½ teaspoons kosher salt

1 teaspoon black pepper

6 boneless, skinless chicken breasts
(about 2¼ pounds)

Combine the olive oil, balsamic vinegar, brown sugar, Italian seasoning, garlic powder, onion powder, salt, and pepper in a gallon-size plastic bag. Add the chicken breasts and toss to combine. Seal the bag and allow the chicken to marinate in the fridge for at least 2 hours or overnight.

When ready to cook, preheat the grill or a seasoned indoor grill pan on high; also preheat the oven to 350°F. Place the chicken breasts on the grill, evenly spaced, and lightly season with salt and pepper. Cook the breasts for 4 minutes without flipping. If you're using an indoor grill pan, you may need to cook these in two batches to avoid overcrowding the pan. Use tongs to carefully flip the chicken and cook for an additional 4 minutes, or until grill marks appear and the edges of the chicken have begun to caramelize from the marinade.

Once the outside is browned to perfection, remove the chicken to a rimmed oven-safe pan or baking dish and place in the oven to finish cooking, until a thermometer inserted into the thickest part of the chicken reads 165°F. Remove it from the oven and allow it to rest 5 minutes before cutting or serving.

DAY 30: Good on the Inside

This past summer, I spent an afternoon making homemade ice cream drumsticks with my children. We painted the inside of each cone with a thin layer of chocolate and filled it to the rim with various ice creams, sauces, and toppings: mint cookie for Aimee, vanilla with chocolate sauce and sprinkles for George, and caramel pecan for me. Each cone was finished with an additional scoop of ice cream and then dipped into liquid chocolate to give it a coating that hardens when frozen to keep all the inner goodness protected. We enjoyed the drumsticks over the next few weeks, and each time it was a surprise to bite through the shell and discover the flavors and fillings that were hidden beneath the surface.

In a way, a lot of us are like those cones. Because we live in a society that values outer appearance and achievements more than what's on the inside, most of us have no problem obsessing over cellulite and skin care and fashion trends, but how often do we give a second thought to what's happening on the inside? *What is the status of my heart? How do I feel about myself, about life, about my relationships, and about God?* We can have perfect hair and glowing skin, a myriad of outfits and handbags and shoes, but if we fail to protect our heart, the rich, delightful goodness just beneath the shell, it doesn't mean anything.

Proverbs 31 says that a woman who fears the Lord is to be praised. The stuff on the outside isn't bad, but your heart is where the treasure is. So the question is, are you taking care of *you*? Not your hair or nails or body, but your heart? Spend time this week doing some inner housekeeping. If there are recurring points of pain, sin, or shame in your heart, don't wait for them to bubble up again—offer them in prayer to God. Commit your heart to the Lord, and let Him participate in working out the transformation. He says you are beautiful, and that has absolutely nothing to do with your appearance; all of your treasure is on the inside, so offer that up to the Lord this morning.

 **1 PETER 3:3–4**

DAY 31: Pressing In to the Hard Stuff

How do we continue life in the midst of crisis? When political and social injustices are brought to our attention, how do we respond? What do we say to the people who have lost parts of themselves to poverty or drugs or infertility or cancer? And what about those who feel alone in their communities because of their race or religion or sexuality? Can one person really make a difference?

The honest to God truth is, most days I'm reluctant to take on the role of advocate. Instead, I buy into the lie that my voice won't make a difference or that my action won't meet the needs I see around me. But rather than fixating on my own inability, I'd like to remember how big our God is. He's always good, always there, always ready to extend His hand toward His people. He moves toward the hurting and seeks after the searching, because it's part of His nature. He's a Good Shepherd who longs to care for His sheep, and He often uses *our* hands and feet to take care of His people.

When you feel overwhelmed by the smallness of your humanity, put it at the feet of the Father. Refuse to allow fear or the unknown to keep you from loving and serving with the heart He put in you. Instead of inching away from the hard stuff, press in and meet people where they're at. Let His love meet them there, and He'll do the rest.

 **ISAIAH 61:1-2**

DAY 1: Brown Bananas

I am never without bananas. It seems no matter how many I eat, how many I shove in the kids' lunchboxes, or how fresh they are when I buy them, my countertop is destined to be forever adorned by one or two brown bananas. The one benefit to all that produce is the possibility of delicious breads and muffins and cakes and scones. Bakers never fret over a few brown spots, because in our economy overripe bananas are gold.

I want to start seeing more things in my life from this perspective. So often, I can get discouraged by inadequacies, the blemishes and shortcomings that make me think less of my story. I rarely view those imperfections as the opportunities they are, because I lack vision for what they could be—for what God could make of them all.

Luckily, God's kingdom doesn't work like ours. In His upside-down economy, we live by dying, go first by being last, and get rich by giving away all that we have. He looks beyond the brown spots of our lives and makes something fresh and beautiful with it all. Those parts of us we see as weak and broken down God sees as jumping-off points for strength in Him. Doesn't it encourage you to know there's hope for all our parts in God's kingdom? He has purpose for every single bit of us.

In what areas do you feel weak or broken down today? I want to encourage you to shake off any discouragement or fear that God can't use what you bring to the table. He has creative, beautiful purposes for every single bit of you, and, if you'll let Him, He will make you shine.

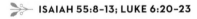 **ISAIAH 55:8-13; LUKE 6:20-23**

DAY 2: Remember What You Have

Getting out the door of our house practically requires an act of Congress. "Where are the keys?" "Why are your pants on backwards?" "Who spilled their sippy cup in my purse?" There's misplaced homework to find, shoelaces to tie, and a baby who, without fail, will make a mess of his diaper right on our way out the door. For years, I've prayed for more patience, sure that these moments would be easier if I could just muster up the wherewithal to keep my cool. But instead I'm usually just one traffic jam, one long grocery line, one miniature household catastrophe away from losing my sanity.

On bad days, left to my own devices, it's a struggle to access my joyful, loving, kind side, and, instead, I'm left without a stitch of self-control or forbearance. The same is true for all of us—on our own, it can seem impossible to muster up enough love and humility, but thankfully in Christ we are one with the One who is adequate for everything we will face. There's no daily allowance or rationed portion of what He shares with us, because He's already freely given His Spirit to reside in us. When we need more patience or joy or self-control, we simply abide in Him, and He is sufficient to meet our needs.

Today, instead of praying for more, rejoice in what you already have. Christ in you will never run out and is always abundantly supplied. Abide in Him today, and rest in the provision He offers freely.

 **JOHN 15:1–11**

DAY 3: Do It Again

Some people collect coffee mugs and others collect T-shirts, but for years I've brought home aprons as souvenirs from my trips abroad. I have frilly embroidered ones from France, hand-stitched ones from Honduras, and about thirty more in between, each one telling a story of a place I visited and the memories I made there. When I use them, I'm reminded of my time spent away, the aprons serving as testimonies to the places I've been.

In Joshua, the Israelites set up stones to memorialize God's faithfulness. After they had wandered for forty years in the desert, God made a way for them to safely cross the Jordan River and enter into the promised land. Twelve stones were erected at that site to serve as a reminder of how God performed the miraculous to care for His people, and those stones, like my aprons, told a story of their own, each one describing the goodness of God and His provision for His people.

You have stories too, examples of God's faithfulness, and although you don't need to collect aprons or stones to memorialize those moments, it's important that you do share them. Your experiences in life, specifically those you've shared with the Lord, tell a story of who you are, where you've been, and how far He has carried you. That testimony is an offering of hope to yourself and others, because if God provided for you in the past, surely He can do it again.

So tell your story. Write it down, say it out loud, or even collect reminders that your children will ask about someday, but don't miss your opportunity to remember. Today, ask God to bring to mind the evidence of His favor in your life, perhaps a story of deliverance or an unplanned event that ended up working to your benefit. Whatever the case, thank Him for His provision, and let those experiences bolster you with hope for the future. If He's done it before, He'll do it again.

 **JOSHUA 4:1-7**

DAY 4: Troubled at Heart

Let not your hearts be troubled. These words, some of Jesus's last to the disciples, are hard for me to swallow. I've heard similar sentiments throughout my life when a bad day or season of despair has found me toting around my own troubled heart like a grocery bag full of bricks. Friends mean well when they tell you, "Cheer up!" or "Just be happy!" but sometimes what you'd really like to say to them is, *Yeah, right.*

Jesus knew we would have days of trouble. He knew we would bump into depression and grief, heartache and fear, and that sometimes those feelings would leave a mark. But look at the next words out of His mouth. Right after He tells the disciples to shake off their troubled hearts, He says, *Believe in God; believe also in me.* There it is: belief. Belief in God is our hope in days of trouble, our lifeline in times of crisis.

Being followers of Christ doesn't mean we're excluded from feeling the depth of human emotions, but it does offer us hope beyond that pain. Belief in God, His goodness, His promises, and the future we have with Him can shift our focus from the momentary troubles of earth to the reality of eternal glory that is ours in Him (2 Cor. 4:17). In Christ, the buck doesn't stop with our trouble, because that is where He meets us. In the midst of suffering, we have hope in the Comforter.

How are you troubled today? If something comes to mind immediately, or even if there's just this looming sense of feeling a little off, you can tell that to God. Jesus has enough hope, joy, and love for you, even in the middle of your pain, and He wants to share that with you. If you believe in Him, bring your heart, full of emotion and humanity, to Him and let Him care for it like the comfort that He is.

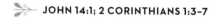 **JOHN 14:1; 2 CORINTHIANS 1:3–7**

DAY 5: Sweet Heat Popcorn

On a girls' night in or a family movie date, popcorn is the simple, social snack that everyone wants a handful of. Look for plain varieties of bagged popcorn or pop your own quickly by microwaving loose kernels of corn in a large paper lunch bag; ¼ cup of kernels makes about 4 cups of popped popcorn. If you're ready to take your party to the next level, you can add in the cayenne pepper for an extra kick of heat; otherwise, leave it out! The end result, sweet and smoky popcorn, is delightful either way!

....

SWEET HEAT POPCORN

Makes 4 cups

1½ tablespoons unsalted butter

1½ teaspoons granulated sugar

½ teaspoon garlic powder

½ teaspoon chili powder

¼ teaspoon table salt

¼ teaspoon cumin

¼ teaspoon paprika

⅛ teaspoon cayenne pepper (optional)

4 cups plain popped popcorn

Melt the butter in a small saucepan over low heat and stir in the sugar, garlic powder, chili powder, salt, cumin, paprika, and cayenne, if using. Place the popcorn in an oversize bowl and drizzle the butter mixture over the popcorn, tossing as you go. Continue tossing until the popcorn is evenly coated in the mixture and enjoy!

DAY 6: Words and Prayers We Don't Have

So many of us have asked the same question: *What is God's will for my life?* We search and hunt with a genuine desire to align our lives with His purposes, but so often we have absolutely no clue how to hear from the Lord. Where do we start? An open door? A sign? A prayer? *Okay, God, not my will, but what exactly is Yours?*

God doesn't expect us to be mind readers. Instead, Jesus told the disciples that the Holy Spirit was to be for the benefit of them and all humankind, because rather than simply observing heaven at work in Jesus's life, we would experience it for ourselves via the power of the Holy Spirit *in* us. Thankfully, this Helper simultaneously knows our heart *and* the heart of the Father, so when our human attempts with words fail us, the Holy Spirit can intercede, petitioning God on our behalf with words we don't even understand and prayers that don't even occur to us to pray.

Don't miss the incredible gift of the Holy Spirit. He knows the Father's will for your story and will give you the words when you're unsure of what to write into it. Through Him, we have guidance in the pursuit of God's purposes, access to the same power Jesus walked in, and understanding that will comfort and encourage us all the days of our lives. Look to Him this week for counsel and wisdom, an everpresent source of help that always leads you to heaven.

 **ROMANS 8:26–27**

DAY 7: Fishing Without a Guide

My mom always dreamed of traveling to Alaska to experience the glaciers and formidable landscape of that little-traveled terrain, and her dream came true with a family vacation a few years back: seven days of whale watching, hiking, and outdoor exploring that was well beyond the scope of our normal weekend trips. On the third day, we chartered a fishing boat that puttered out into the fog, and before long we were pulling massive fish from the depths of the dark blue water around us. One fish after another was piled into the cooler below deck, and just as soon as our guide unhooked our catch, there was another tug on the line, another wild catch.

I'm not a fisherman. None of us were. On our own, we would have been more likely to catch a cold or a maybe even an old sunken shoe, but because of our guide we had the equipment, the location, and the know-how to catch the most beautiful (and delicious!) fish we'd ever seen. There was no need to rely on our own sufficiency when we were captained by an experienced guide—we just had to follow his instructions.

As believers, we don't have to rely on ourselves, because we have partnered with the ultimate Guide. When faced with challenging tasks and unknown terrain, we can remain confident and without fear, because He's already charted the waters before us. We're no longer a people mustering our own strength, reasoning, and ability, because our hope and trust reside in the One leading the excursion.

Are there areas of your life where you've been striving to do it on your own? Why not take a breather and try out life with God as your guide? He is sufficient to lead and provide in every terrain, and He does so as a loving Father. Ask Him to reveal any areas where He's asking you to trust in His sufficiency, and rest in Him knowing He's the best guide there is.

 **ISAIAH 41:13; LUKE 5:1–7**

DAY 8: For Such a Time as This

Esther might be the coolest woman in the Bible. Not only was she a queen, but she was a smart one too. Passionate, brave, and quick as a whip, this girl, whose heart was full of love for God and compassion for her people, had all the makings of a modern-day heroine. Anyone else want to be just like her?

Her story reminds me how God positions unsuspecting people to serve His purposes. He doesn't need us to carry out His plans; after all, He is God. Instead, He welcomes us into His purposes, so we can witness the beauty and wonder of His hand at work. That participation increases our faith and bends our heart toward Him, opening our eyes to His goodness in action in the world around us. He did it in Esther's story, and I believe He wants to do it in ours too.

God doesn't have to use you to accomplish His will, but He wants to. Just as He positioned Esther "for such a time as this," He's put forth plans and purposes in your life that are intended for His glory. He's allotted each one of us a portion and position from which to pursue His plans and glory while we're here on earth.

If you find yourself feeling uncertain about how God could ever use you, that's good news—He always chooses the unsuspecting people. Today, submit your heart to the Lord and ask Him to show you how you can partner with Him in furthering His kingdom. He has big, Esther-size plans for your life, and when you make yourself available to Him, He will most certainly welcome you into them.

 **ESTHER 4:14**

DAY 9: The Fire

I've watched every season of *The Office* an embarrassing number of times. For years, one of my favorite scenes was the one where Dwight sets a fire in the office to simulate a drill for emergency preparedness. I could barely catch my breath from laughter as Angela threw her cat through the ceiling tile and Stanley passed out on the floor next to his desk. The ridiculousness of it all was comedy gold.

That is, until last summer when I received a call that my grandparents' house was burning to the ground. This was the home where Brett and I were married, a place that had come to feel like home to me. Fortunately, everyone got out safely, but the house was a total loss. The trauma shook our family to the core, and it was weeks before the knot in my stomach disappeared.

Months later, I watched that same episode of *The Office* again, and the whole scene felt different in light of my recent experience. Having witnessed the devastation and confusion playing out in my grandparents' lives changed the way I viewed that episode, and I could no longer separate the silliness of the scene from the reality I knew.

The point is this: the world looks different in light of your personal experiences. Just because you've experienced the world one way doesn't mean your neighbor knows that same reality. Be gentle with one another, and open your heart to the idea that their truth, the characters and laughter and scenes of their world, might be entirely different from yours. Today, love, listen, and seek to grow in understanding and compassion for the hearts of the people around you.

 **JAMES 1:19-27**

DAY 10: Warm with Delight

Some days I get so caught up in how I feel about myself that I forget to experience the Father's love. Has this happened to you? Maybe you've beaten yourself up over a mistake, felt discouragement about areas of your life where you're a work in progress, or been unable to fully appreciate the beautiful contributions you make to the world? Until we fully grasp how big and long and wide God's affection is for us, we'll never be able to truly love and care for ourselves and one another. So, today, if that's you, here's a snapshot of the Father's heart for you:

The Lord your God is in your midst, a mighty One who will save; He will rejoice over you with gladness; He will quiet you by His love; He will exult over you with loud singing (Zeph. 3:17).

Even when you struggle to delight in yourself, on days when you feel dark, unlovely, or full of despair, God is singing a song of adoration over your life. No longer is your name "Forsaken," for the King of heaven has called you delightful. Read the verses below, and soak in the loving-kindness of Jesus; His affection is so real, so tangible—it is enough to transform your heart today and forever. Ask for a fresh revelation of His care for you and let your spirit be warmed by the glow of His love. Remember, no matter how you feel about yourself, God's love remains unchanged; He's called you delightful.

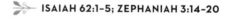 **ISAIAH 62:1-5; ZEPHANIAH 3:14-20**

DAY 11: The Right Time

I met my husband in a hospital cafeteria. He likes to say it was "love over fish sticks," but I can assure you, there were no fish sticks involved. Although we were both finishing school, the timing was never right, so for the next year we wove in and out of each other's stories in a series of near misses, until our lives finally intersected for good.

It was one of the first times in my life I didn't try to force the timing of it all, and that in and of itself is all the proof I need to know that God's hand was in it. When we finally made it to that first date, I knew we were onto something good, and I was so grateful that I hadn't muddied the waters by trying to make it work during those earlier months. I wouldn't have been ready, and our lives might look much different today.

Only now am I beginning to value the framework of God's timing. In the past, I haven't been patient enough to see it all work out, but I've since had enough big life experiences to know that His timing is always best. It doesn't matter if I think my schedule and plans are great, because it's finally settling in my heart that God's ways are always best-case scenario.

Are there things in life you've been waiting for? Maybe a job opportunity, a breakthrough, a child, or a move? I'd encourage you to bring your desires to the Lord this morning. Just plop your heart at His feet, and thank Him for the rest He has offered in the waiting. Make His desires—the fulfillment of His timing, His plans, and His methods—your greatest desire, and trust that He's actively at work on your behalf.

 **LAMENTATIONS 3:22-26**

DAY 12: Texas Hot Sauce

My favorite part of a ball game is the food, and my very favorite is ballpark hot dogs. I grew up enjoying hot dogs with my family's favorite Texas Hot Sauce, a chili topping that's very flavorful but not nearly as spicy as its name would suggest. This sauce, plus relish and a squirt of mustard, is what my summer dreams are made of—truly. If you want a chili topping that is actually quite spicy, opt for the addition of Tabasco sauce—it definitely brings the heat.

....

TEXAS HOT SAUCE
Serves 6 to 8

1 pound ground sirloin (or ground turkey)

1 yellow onion, finely chopped

2 (10¾-ounce) cans condensed
   tomato soup, undiluted

1 tablespoon granulated sugar

1 teaspoon ground mustard

1 teaspoon chili powder

½ teaspoon cayenne pepper

¼ teaspoon paprika

¼ teaspoon ground cloves

4 bay leaves

Tabasco sauce (optional)

Salt to taste

In a large skillet over medium heat, cook the beef and onion, stirring occasionally, until the meat has browned and the onion is tender. Add the soup, sugar, mustard, chili powder, cayenne pepper, paprika, cloves, and bay leaves and bring just to a boil. Immediately reduce the heat to low and allow it to simmer for 15 minutes, or until thickened slightly. Carefully taste, and add salt if desired (I usually add about 1 teaspoon). Add Tabasco sauce, 2 dashes at a time, until the desired heat level is reached. Serve immediately or reheat to serve over hot dogs or hamburgers as a chili topping.

DAY 13: Our Champion

People say mean things on the internet. I've been lucky enough to remain mostly unscathed, but a few times ugly things have been said about me, my photos, or my recipes. I've got to admit—it hurts. Of course, we're all familiar with painful words and the effects of bullying to greater or lesser degrees. But when people and life come at us in a way that burns, it's empowering to remember who is fighting for us. It's Jesus.

Jesus is our champion, the One who goes before and behind us, defeating our enemies on our behalf and for His glory. All things in heaven and on earth come under the feet of Jesus, the One to whom all power and authority are due, and as believers we're on His team. He's not just fighting for us; He's already won.

Jesus has the final say about who you are. When the enemy tries to intimidate you with lies and threats, remind him that Jesus is your champion. He fights on your behalf and has already established power over sin and death. As His child, you no longer fight for victory, but fight from a place of victory alongside a God who knows no defeat. He's already won, and He says He's yours, so today rest in the victory that is yours in Christ.

 **JEREMIAH 20:10–13**

DAY 14: Thirsty

The habitual nature of my personality means that sometimes I just do too much. I indulge in too much coffee, too much wine, too much dessert. I dive head-first into hobbies, binge-watch television when one or two episodes would suffice, and often find myself in a proverbial sprint, searching for one more thing to get my hands on.

Overconsumption plagues a lot of us, even right down to our spiritual life. We read books, listen to sermons, and subscribe to podcasts, as if overconsumption will somehow get us closer to God. In the rush of it all, I often find myself still feeling distant, because in the race to consume knowledge, I've passed over re-lationship. I may *know* more about God's love, but I haven't truly *experienced* it.

I heard someone say recently that knowledge does not equal understand-ing. It's important that on our journey to know more about God we actually *get to know Him*. It's not enough to memorize scripture and acquire knowledge; we need to be encountering His love regularly, because that is where relationship and transformation happen.

Are you thirsty for more of Him? Today, instead of being satisfied by mere knowledge of His goodness—experience it. In your quiet time this week, ask God to point out any areas where you may be striving for relationship, and ask Him to replace those efforts with worshipful time that nourishes your desire for Him. God desires deep connection with you, and if you seek that out, you'll be sure to find it.

 **MATTHEW 5:6**

DAY 15: Order Envy

We sat down to dinner at a new restaurant the other night, and I was out-ordered. We were there with a couple of friends, and although my dish sounded great on paper, it paled in comparison to the food that arrived on my friends' plates. I wanted to be excited about my dinner, but I couldn't help but look around, wishing I was nibbling on the meals in front of everyone else.

A case of order envy isn't so bad, but we should be aware of those times when our lack of contentment is seeping into other areas of our lives. Just as our wandering eyes long for the food on other people's plates, our hearts wander too, taking in the gifts, prosperity, beauty, and attributes of others, wishing they were our own. Sometimes we even take it a step farther, wondering why there seems to be so much blessing and favor in someone else's story. *Does God love them more than me? Why does their portion seem to be so much more abundant than mine?* The truth is, everyone's allotment is different, but when it comes from God, it is always secure. He only gives good gifts, and He's delighted when we seek to fully enjoy the ones He's given to us.

Let's keep our eyes on our own plate. It's okay to admire the portion others have been given, but don't let their helping distract you from yours. God loves you and desires to see you operate in the fullness of whatever He's allotted for you, so if you find yourself feeling discontent, you can bring that to Him with honesty. Ask Him to shift your heart and open your eyes to the beauty in your story. He has delightful things to serve you, so open wide and get ready to savor the goodness of your portion.

 **PSALM 16:5–6**

DAY 16: Coming to Terms

I have an early memory that I can see in my mind, clear as day: five-year-old me, dressed in a leotard, crying in my seat in a time-out. Earlier that day, I had broken into our family's medicine cabinet for a swig of orange-flavored cough syrup (something I apparently found delicious), and when my mom found the half-empty bottle (with the lid off, no doubt), I lied about it. I went to a time-out, tap shoes and all, while my mom phoned the doctor or poison control to find out what to do. I was fine, but I knew I had done wrong, and the crushing weight of that realization made a lasting impression.

Coming to terms with our own sin can be painful. When we are faced with our shortcomings, the enemy will often whisper words delivering shame or fear or regret, words that tell us all the ways we've failed or hurt the ones we love. We're not alone here; Romans 3:23 says *all* have fallen short and sinned against God. The cure for that sin was provided for by the blood of Jesus, with the body of the One who knew no sin and was sufficient to cover our faults. Because of Him, we have the opportunity to know grace, a concept so big and inconceivable that many of us have a hard time dealing with it. *How can He forgive me when I can hardly forgive myself?*

When faced with your sin, don't hide from Jesus; run to Him. He meets us as an advocate, as the sufficiency for our sins, and His blood serves as our bridge from sin into the kingdom of heaven. Shame and fear have no hold over you because He's already paid for your freedom. Grace is His gift, and it's ours to receive by faith.

Have you opened your heart to the forgiveness that has been purchased for you by Christ? If God has forgiven you, you can forgive yourself as well. When the Holy Spirit opens your eyes to the sin in your life, don't wallow in shame or regret—hand it over to Jesus in exchange for His gift of grace. He's already forgiven you, so you can forgive yourself too.

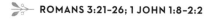 **ROMANS 3:21–26; 1 JOHN 1:8–2:2**

DAY 17: Admitting

One Saturday not too long ago my husband and I got into a silly spat in which we were each convinced we were right and the other was wrong. Armed with arguments and evidence to support my claims, I testified on my own behalf and held my ground, until we eventually parted in silence. Within the hour, conviction crept in, and I knew I had to apologize. I was wrong. But something about it was gut-wrenching, so instead, I spent the afternoon with my tail between my legs, avoiding any confession of guilt.

For me, it's not the *being* wrong that's so hard—it's the *admitting* wrong that feels impossible. It's coming face-to-face with my own humanity, looking it in the eye, and acknowledging the sin out loud that hurts so badly. Lately I've been learning that one of the hardest parts of marriage is not just living with another imperfect human—it's living with an imperfect *me*.

I'm grateful for a husband who sees beyond so many of those humbling moments, and his offerings of grace remind me of the much bigger dose of grace God is administering on my behalf daily. With Jesus, I still temporarily feel the weight of that humility, but I'm finding that at my lowest points He offers me a chance to stand more upright. He meets our humility with compassion and kindness, always lifting us up out of any shame or disgrace. If anything, marriage has moved me to become more vulnerable in my faith, and the revelation of my own need has pushed me nearer to the arms of Jesus—it's a terrifying and beautiful thing.

Pride leads to conflict, but humility will send you closer to Jesus. God has offered you healing and forgiveness if you are willing to humble yourself, so don't hesitate. It might be momentarily painful, but it's a surefire route to wholeness.

 **1 PETER 5:5-11**

DAY 18: Saving for Later

Biscuits are the ultimate comfort food in our home. My kids all have their favorite toppings—butter for George and Charlie and jam for Aimee. They perch on their stools at the counter and peel the biscuits layer by layer, nibbling on pieces one at a time. I keep a stockpile of homemade biscuits in the freezer to pop in the toaster oven at a moment's notice, and I secretly hope it will end up being one of those things my kids remember about life in the home they grew up in—Mama and her freezer full of biscuits.

I like this idea of saving good things, morsels of butter and flour and sugar, for a rainy day. It's comforting to know I have a reserve to fall back on that will nourish and delight my family when the need arises. Truth be told, I'm good at preparing for those needs, and my freezer and pantry will attest as much, but in my heart I know their cravings extend beyond physical nourishment. I want to be stockpiling treasures that will meet the needs of their hearts too.

The Bible repeatedly references the value of storing up kingdom treasures in our hearts. The Psalmist says that the person who meditates on God's word is *like a tree planted by streams of water that yields its fruit in its season, and its leaf does not wither. In all that he does he prospers* (Ps. 1:3). There's life and abundance and hope in those places where we've feasted on riches from heaven, and we can have confidence that, when our lives have a foundation in Christ, we will be prepared no matter what comes our way. We're like a freezer stockpiled for a rainy day.

Are you filled up on Christ today? Is your foundation, the very framework of your life, rooted in things from heaven or things from earth? Take time this week, even now, to stockpile His word and promises and principles in your heart, and be comforted knowing that a life filled with Jesus is secure.

 **JEREMIAH 17:5–8**

DAY 19: # Buttermilk Biscuits

I have loads of favorite biscuit recipes, and it was hard to settle on just one to share in this book. At the end of the day, though, I felt that what everyone needs is a perfect everyday option to serve at home.

....

BUTTERMILK BISCUITS

Makes 14

2¾ cups all-purpose flour plus
    2 tablespoons, divided

1 tablespoon granulated sugar

2 teaspoons kosher salt

2½ teaspoons baking powder

½ teaspoon baking soda

1 cup chilled unsalted butter, diced

1 cup chilled buttermilk

3 tablespoons butter, melted,
    for brushing

Preheat the oven to 425°F. Line a baking sheet with parchment paper. In a large bowl, combine the 2¾ cups flour, sugar, salt, baking powder, and baking soda. Use a pastry cutter or the backs of two forks to cut in the butter until it is evenly dispersed, with pea-size clumps throughout. Gently stir in the buttermilk until a scrappy dough forms.

Sprinkle the 2 tablespoons flour over a clean work surface and dump the crumbly dough. Gently and quickly work the dough together and pat it out to a 1-inch-thick rectangle. Cut the dough into three equal-size rectangles and stack them on top of one another. Gently press or roll it out again to a 1-inch-thick rectangle. Repeat the cutting and stacking process two more times (this process laminates the dough, making those delicious flaky layers), and then roll it out to ¾-inch thick. Use a 2¼-inch round biscuit cutter to portion out rounds of dough. Flour the cutter well and press down straight, being careful not to twist the cutter at all. Reflour and continue cutting out until all the dough has been used.

Place the biscuits about ¼ inch apart on the baking sheet. Brush with a bit of the melted butter and bake for about 20 minutes, or until the biscuits have risen and the tops are golden. Allow them to cool slightly before serving.

DAY 20: Marching to the Beat of Your Own Drum

I attended a middle school with a dress code that mandated uniformed culottes and collared shirts. The look certainly didn't win me any fashion contests, but, thankfully, we were allowed to choose shoes and accessories of our own. For the first few weeks of sixth grade, we all wore our favorite hair clips, sneakers, and necklaces, until one day two girls showed up wearing the exact same sandals. In true prepubescent fashion, it took less than a month for most of us to have purchased those same black platforms followed by matching purses, hair ties, and more. Although we each had the freedom to pick our own things, what we wanted most of all was to look just like each other.

With the rise of social media, I'm finding it much more difficult to "be myself." It's hard to march to the beat of your own drum when everyone else's music is so loud and wonderful, isn't it? Although it's very tempting to do or be what everyone else is doing or being, it's important to remember that God has called us to *His* purposes, crafted uniquely and individually for each one of us and set apart from the work He is doing elsewhere. Instead of looking more and more like one another, the goal of our heart should be to look more like Him from the inside out.

It's okay to admire and even take inspiration from the beauty in someone else's life, but remember that God has plans that are custom-built just for you. He's less concerned with outer appearances and more interested in doing work on the inside, softening and shaping your heart until it aligns with His.

So what does God say about who you are? What are the purposes and dreams and ideas He's given specifically to you? Today, instead of worrying about looking more like everyone else, let God make you more like Him. He's the only One who will truly satisfy.

 **1 SAMUEL 16:7**

DAY 21: Winning Fights

I've been in exactly one fist fight in my entire life. It happened when I was in second grade while riding the bus to school. A boy in my class (one I had a crush on, no less) called me a name, so I punched him in the stomach. He cried, we both went to the principal's office, and that was the first and last time I decked anyone.

Jesus said that when people hurt us we, should turn the other cheek (Matt. 5:38–39), but most of us would rather get even. When a friend wrongs us, when a coworker behaves pettily toward us, or when a spouse offers up their own fighting words, it's tempting to step into the ring, armed with words intended to cut that person down to size. I do it so often that I can tell you from experience: it never makes you feel better in the long run. The temporary glow of a won argument or quick-witted comeback leaves you feeling smaller, more in need of the love and kindness and respect you desired in the first place.

God said that vengeance was His, not so we would gloat over our enemy's forthcoming demise, but so we would know it's not our fight. Becoming more like Jesus means we move toward our spouses, children, and friends with the same gentle humility that He walked in. It means seeking understanding, believing the best about a person, and knowing when to stand down. Bowing out from a fight doesn't make you weak; it shows your strength of character, the transforming work of God at work in your life.

Instead of getting even, get real. Be vulnerable when the wound of a fighting word has cut you deep, and bring that pain to the Lord. Stand down, walk away, or bow out, because the fight is never yours to manage; God always fights and wins on behalf of His children.

 **ROMANS 12:16–21**

DAY 22: Pipeline of Love

A few weeks ago, I made a cake for a friend's birthday, and it was a reminder of why I'm so head-over-heels in love with baking. He called to thank me for the cake, and instead of just saying, "It was good!" or "Thanks a bunch!" he told me that the gesture made him feel special. He felt set apart, and that evidence of our friendship made him grateful.

This is why we share our gifts with people. It's not to show off or fill a slot on a birthday menu. We don't do it out of obligation or so that everyone can know what a great person we are. We share our gifts—the cookies, our brain power, our hugs, *whatever*—to love people! It's a token of our affection that lets them know they are worth our time and resources. We share our skills and the things we're good at to remind people they matter to us.

Let me encourage you to take the initiative. Share whatever it is you're doing with the people around you, and just wait till you see the difference it makes. When we extend ourselves on behalf of others, it lets them know we value them, and that love becomes a revolving door of kindness within that relationship, extending to all others within proximity.

In a world where it's all too common to look out for ourselves, I want to be the person who shares my gifts in a way that lets people know they matter, and if that happens to involve macarons and pies and tall stacks of cake, well, I'm all for it. How do you express your love for the people in your life? What are your gifts? Who are the people in your circle whom God wants you to love in big way? Start small and share generously, even today, knowing that the gift rarely stops there— love given freely keeps going and going.

 **1 CORINTHIANS 13:1–3**

DAY 23: Scheduling Rest

I know Disney World is supposed to be the most magical place on earth, but all of my fairy tales are set in the rolling hills of the Smoky Mountains. There, nestled in the foggy haze of peaks and valleys, is Blackberry Farm, a charming resort that, to this day, is my favorite place on earth. We've traveled there for years, and I have yet to find a place that brings me so much rest, so much comfort, and so, so much delicious food.

We weren't made to be the Energizer bunnies that some of us force ourselves to be. Rest is the simplest form of self-care, yet we've made it an impossible task by filling every minute with more stuff, more tasks, and more outlets that suck us completely dry. Although God built rest into His original framework for our schedule, we've somehow decided to be a people who can do and have it all. I'm learning that making time for rest doesn't make you weak or old or incapable—it offers a space for you to breathe, to refocus, and to nourish yourself with the things that make you whole.

Find a place you feel at rest, and actually schedule time for it in your week. Bring your grind to a standstill and completely unplug from the stuff that wears you thin. Invite God into your rest, and take time to feed on things that make you whole. Every day can't be a vacation, but you can trade in your hustle for something that's better than a retreat in the mountains—you can rest in Jesus.

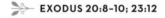 **EXODUS 20:8–10; 23:12**

Stewarding Success

Every once in a while, I forget that I'm not entirely responsible for my own suc-cess. When my bank account is brimming, my family is thriving, or I find myself advancing up career and social ladders, I think, *My work is paying off. I did it!* I start to believe that the goodness in my life—the joy, the prosperity, the blossom-ing relationships, or any other set of chips that seems to be falling in my favor—is nothing more than the well-deserved result of my choices and actions.

As children of God, we have been lavished with rich, abundant blessings. We get to partner with God to achieve His purposes and steward the millions of gifts He has offered us, but in the excitement of it all, we must remember who the source of those blessings is. We play a role, yes, but God is the author of every good gift.

Take time this morning to realign the posture of your heart into one that is bowed in gratitude. Maybe even take out a pencil and paper and jot down the list of wonderful things in your life right now. Can you see where God's hand was at work in those blessings? Where is the evidence of His favor? Offer up a prayer of gratitude and ask Him to forgive you for any places where you've overlooked His goodness. The good news is, we're never solely responsible for the happenings of our lives—only stewards. Ask God to show you how to steward His goodness with grace and thanksgiving, and carry that disposition with you throughout your week.

 **ROMANS 11:36**

DAY 25: Effort over Perfection

It was a friend of a friend who first taught me how to frost cakes. I stood next to her in the kitchen, amazed at how she finessed frosting onto the layers, smoothing out wrinkles and smears until the cake was seamless on all sides. Her work appeared effortless, perhaps just the magic of the tools she worked with, but when my turn came around, it quickly became apparent that she just knew what she was doing. My first attempt had tilted layers and lumpy buttercream, but over time, each of the cakes I made began to look a little better than the last, and I learned that a little practice can go a long way.

That first try is always hard, isn't it? Sometimes fear keeps us from fresh attempts, making us think we're safer on the sidelines than risking our efforts on something new, but I'm thankful to know that Jesus isn't at all concerned with our perfection. Instead, He's pleased when we work with integrity, doing all things to the best of our ability, particularly when it comes to things He's called us to. As with most things, Jesus values our heart, our desire to honor Him with our efforts, and there are boatloads of grace for the parts we get wrong. If you find yourself being called outside the boundaries of your qualifications, that's great news—Jesus is about to show off.

You don't have to do it perfectly to do it well. God knows your heart, and it blesses Him to no end when He sees His children pursuing His will to the best of their abilities. Is there a task, a job, or a calling you've avoided because you're scared to fail? God values your intent more than your perfection, so you can trust Him when it comes to trying something new. Look to Him for the bravery to step into a new thing, and dedicate your efforts to the glory of His name. When your efforts honor Jesus, there's always reward on the other side of trying.

 **1 CORINTHIANS 3:10–15**

Fudgy Chocolate Sheet Cake

Fudgy Chocolate Sheet Cake is a potluck all-star. With a tender, moist crumb and a fudgy, pour-on icing, this cake comes together quickly, serves a crowd, and tastes delicious for days. Bonus: no fancy decorating tools required here. For a darker, more intensely flavored cake, try substituting dark cocoa powder for the regular unsweetened variety. Just don't skip the sprinkle of sea salt at the end—it really makes this cake shine!

....

FUDGY CHOCOLATE SHEET CAKE

Makes 1 (9 × 13-inch) cake

CAKE

1 cup unsalted butter

1 cup brewed coffee

3/4 cup unsweetened cocoa powder

13/4 cups all-purpose flour

13/4 cups granulated sugar

1 teaspoon baking soda

3/4 teaspoon table salt

2 large eggs, at room temperature

1/2 cup sour cream, at room temperature

2 teaspoons vanilla extract

ICING

1/2 cup unsalted butter

6 tablespoons water

1/4 cup unsweetened cocoa powder

1 teaspoon vanilla extract

31/2 cups confectioners' sugar

Maldon sea salt (optional)

TO PREPARE THE CAKE

Preheat the oven to 350ºF. Lightly grease a 9 × 13-inch pan with baking spray.

In a saucepan over medium heat, combine the butter, coffee, and cocoa powder, stirring frequently until melted. Bring the mixture to a boil and cook for 30 seconds. Remove it from the heat and set it aside while you assemble the dry ingredients.

In a large bowl, combine the flour, sugar, baking soda, and salt. Add the butter mixture and stir just until combined. In a separate small bowl, whisk together the eggs, sour cream, and vanilla, and fold this mixture into the batter. Pour the batter into the prepared pan and bake until a toothpick inserted into the center comes out clean, about 20 to 25 minutes.

TO PREPARE THE ICING

When the cake is about halfway through baking, combine the butter, water, cocoa powder, and vanilla in a saucepan over medium heat. Whisk frequently and be careful not to boil the mixture. Once the butter is melted, remove the pan from the heat and carefully whisk in the confectioners' sugar until smooth. Pour the icing over the warm, finished cake and enjoy once the icing has set! Serve with a sprinkle of flaky salt if desired.

DAY 27: Putting on Your Own Mask First

I've been flying with my children since Aimee was six weeks old. Because my kids earned their little plastic pilot wings at an early age, friends often ask how to make traveling with kids easier, but really the secret is simple: snacks.

I'm not talking raisins and applesauce squeeze packs. I'm talking potato chips, caramel corn, candy, and juice boxes. Lollipops? Sure. Gummy snacks? Heck yes. The one food that you normally don't allow your kids to eat is the single best insurance that they'll be happy on the airplane.

On my last flight with my children, I was loaded down with treats and games for the kids, but completely forgot to bring anything for myself. No water, no Clif bar, no frivolous reading for the ride. I was reminded of why flight attendants are quick to remind you to put on your own oxygen mask before you attempt to help others—they know that sometimes, when caring for the needs of others, we forget to take care of ourselves.

Some of us are at risk of losing track of our own selves while on the mission to serve and love the people around us. In an effort to prioritize the wants and success of those around us, we shirk our own physical needs, our mental health, and even the desires of our heart, not realizing that our overgenerosity is sucking us dry. Serving others is certainly within the bounds of what Christ has called us to do (Gal. 5:13-14), but we cannot overextend ourselves, attempting to give from a nonexistent reservoir, a heart that is parched for lack of nourishment. We have to put on our own oxygen mask if we want to be able to help others with theirs.

Sister, you are God's creation, a home that fosters His very Spirit inside of you, and as much as He wants you to honor Him with your love and service toward others, He desires for you to care for His temple as well. Are there places where you've overextended yourself or allowed the care of your own body, mind, and spirit to take a backseat? Ask God to show you where to slow down, draw back, and take much-needed time to receive a fresh filling of His love. Fill up on His affection, love, and grace, and you'll be ready to serve the world.

1 CORINTHIANS 6:19-20

DAY 28: Believing the Best

The other day, I was frustrated by a friend who wouldn't return my call. My mind immediately jumped on a hamster wheel of assumptions, sure that her silence indicated something more. *Is she mad at me? Did I do something wrong? I can't believe she could be so rude.* I later found out she was home sick, a possibility that never even crossed my mind. After all, it's difficult to believe the best about somebody when I'm all too busy assuming the worst.

I'm not alone here. Many of us have become experts in drumming up what-ifs and worst-case scenarios, certain that people and circumstances aren't working with our best interests at heart. Have you ever been cut off on the highway and immediately assumed that person was out to get you? Or have you ever found your husband's cereal bowl on the coffee table, certain that he left it as some kind of passive-aggressive attack on your sanity? Very few get called to the principal's office believing they are there to receive a reward or a gold star for their good behavior, because our brains are wired to jump to the worst conclusion.

Most of the assumptions we make about others are based on our own fears and insecurities. What felt like an attack may have truly been just a misunderstanding, and God is glorified in our lives when we choose to believe the best. He always has our best interest at heart, so even when other people hurt or disappoint us, we can rely on Him to be a steadfast source of kindness and hope.

Spend some time in prayer today and ask Him to soften your heart in relationships or circumstances that seem to be strained by mistrust and offense. And remember, you can always assume the best about God.

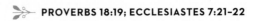 **PROVERBS 18:19; ECCLESIASTES 7:21–22**

DAY 29: Lowering the Bar

There's a lot they don't tell you when you get pregnant. You hear about the lack of sleep, the stretch marks, and the infinite loss of personal space. You're prepared for birthing classes and diaper changing, the terrible twos, and endless renditions of "Rock-a-bye Baby." But there are other things that people don't tell you about, and that's the kind of stuff that keeps me up at night.

People don't mention night sweats and cracked nipples and that weird upper-lip discoloration that looks like a mustache. They don't tell you that everything, even your little pinkies and nose, will swell, or that postpartum hair loss might leave you looking a little like Danny DeVito. Women are told they should be "glowing" and at peace as they await the arrival of their bundle of joy, but let me demystify something for you: that is not everyone's story. Life changes, even the ones we have ten months to prepare for, can throw us for a loop, and in the midst of it all we may lose track of who we are.

Whether its motherhood or another big life event, remember to be patient with yourself in the midst of changes. Lower the bar a little, and know that you don't have to figure this all out today. As roles change and life begins to look different than you thought it would, remember that one thing is certain: you are a child of God. Your identity is not rooted in a baby or your abilities or your mental-health status. Your identity is Christ in you. He has the final say on who you are, and what He says is weightier than any of the judgment we pile on ourselves.

Enter change knowing that your identity is daughter of the King of heaven. You aren't the sum of your relationships or postbaby weight loss or diaper-changing skills—you're worth the price He paid on the cross. Let that be enough today.

 **COLOSSIANS 3:1-3**

DAY 30: Midnight Worship

It's two o'clock in the morning. I'm standing over the remains of yesterday's box of donuts eating forgotten pieces of apple fritters and crullers. A midnight cry from one of my children woke me, and sleeplessness has convinced my brain that I'm starving, despite the fact that I ate a massive dinner and a late-night dessert just hours ago. Clearly the only reasonable thing to eat at such a time is stale, sugary breakfast foods. Please, someone persuade me otherwise.

There's something about the midnight hour that makes only cold pizza, butter crackers, and leftover pastries the suitable cures for hunger. Just as I crave coffee in the morning or a glass of red wine on a cool evening, my mind has become accustomed to the comfort of a pantry raid when I find myself restless in the dark of night. I'm not saying this is healthy, but it's one of the weird parts of sleepless motherhood I've come to know.

My other cure for sleeplessness is worship. Three rounds of postpartum insomnia made me well acquainted with the Psalms and the comforting hum of songs that soothe me from the inside out. Now, if awakened anytime between twelve and four, I retreat to a secluded corner of the house and read. I flip through familiar pages and meditate on the comforting words they contain. Sleep eventually does come, and it's nice to find it somewhere between "The Lord is my Shepherd" and the tune of a familiar song. For me, worship is the midnight craving that can actually be satisfied; it is like a visit to the Father who gently rocks me back to sleep.

Are there areas of your life that need the encouragement and comfort of worship? Ask God to remind you of some spaces where your heart may benefit from time spent with Him, and rest knowing He'll take care of you there. He's better than a run to the pantry—love from Jesus really satisfies.

 **PSALM 4:6-8**

DAY 31: Changing Seasons

The beginning of fall always marks a change of pace in my kitchen. Grills are stowed away and large Dutch ovens emerge for stews and chilis. In lieu of ice cream cones, pumpkin and caramel reign supreme, and where there were rosés and beachy cocktails, bourbon and jammy reds appear. It's as if that first glimpse of fall serves as an opportunity for an inner reset, the permission to shift gears and do a new thing.

Just as food, clothing, and activities change from one season to the next, it's okay if you do too. If the busyness of summer has left you feeling tired or overwhelmed, ask God to show you how to slow down in the coming season. If you find your heart starved for connection after a lonely past few months, ask Him where to begin building relationship in the ones that are coming. You don't have to be or do the same things you've done before, and it's important that we use this new stretch of time to assess where we are, how we are feeling, and what God wants to do in the coming days.

God is constant, never changing from age to age (Heb. 13:8), and we, as believers, have been promised the consistency of His presence, regardless of where we find ourselves. Today, take time to check in with Him. Do you sense God is drawing your heart into something new this season? What are you looking forward to in the coming months? Whatever it is, talk to Him about it, and don't be afraid of a reset if it's required; God will be with you no matter what is at hand.

 **ISAIAH 43:18–19**

DAY 1: Supporting Characters

Several Septembers ago, Aimee and I flew to Michigan for a girls' weekend with my mom, nana, and great-grandma. The weather was perfect, the leaves on the trees were turning, and we spent an afternoon at an apple orchard, filling our baskets to the brim with Braeburns and Jonagolds. I love looking back on photos from that day—Mom and Nana pushing baby Aimee in a stroller, sweet Grandma sipping fresh cider from a paper cup. The setting of the story was picture-perfect, but the characters . . . well, they stole the show.

The people we welcome into our lives will always be what makes our days memorable. Sure, circumstances and plotlines can work in our favor in remarkable and beautiful ways, but it's the people who will make those moments worthwhile and life-giving. Today I want to remind you that, regardless of where you find yourself—whether in picture-perfect, undesirable, or unexpected life circumstances—the relationships you participate in with love are what will leave a lasting mark.

Who has God written into your story? Who are the supporting characters who breathe life, creativity, passion, truth, and joy into your world? How is God using those relationships in your life? On the other hand, are there people in your story to whom you might need to give a different role? God is responsible for all the beautiful details of your life, and He always gives you enough grace to play your part well. Work on building a cast of characters who will surround you well and make your life shine.

 PSALM 133

DAY 2: Dutch Apple Pie

Dutch Apple Pie is, without a doubt, the best apple pie I've ever made. Ever. That includes the ones I've made with cider, and the ones made with salted caramel, extra brown sugar, or even cheddar cheese. Here, a simple flaky pie crust is filled with spiced fruit and topped with a buttery crumble that adds texture, salt, and loads of deliciousness to an already great pie. I love to serve this à la mode, but a little whipped cream works well too. Rest assured, this will be the best use for any apples you gather this fall.

....

DUTCH APPLE PIE

Serves 8

CRUST

Homemade dough for 1 single-crust pie (see Sun-Dried Tomato Quiche, p. 134) or 1 refrigerated deep-dish pie crust

FILLING

8 cups apples, peeled and sliced ¼-inch thick (I use Golden Delicious apples)

2 tablespoons fresh-squeezed lemon juice (from about 1 lemon)

¼ cup packed light brown sugar

¼ cup granulated sugar

¼ cup all-purpose flour

2 teaspoons apple pie spice

TOPPING

1 cup all-purpose flour

2/3 cup packed light brown sugar

1 teaspoon cinnamon

¼ teaspoon table salt

½ cup unsalted butter, melted and slightly cooled

TO PREPARE THE CRUST

Move one rack to the bottom third of the oven and preheat the oven to 400°F. If possible, preheat a baking steel or heavy-bottomed sheet pan on that lower rack.

Use a lightly floured rolling pin to roll the dough out on a well-floured surface into a 1/8- to 1/4-inch-thick circle about an inch larger than your deep-dish pie plate on all sides. Roll the dough loosely back onto the rolling pin and lift it into the pie dish. Gently fit the dough into the pie plate and trim off any excess dough, leaving a 1-inch border around the edge of the dish. Fold the lip of the dough under so that it extends just over the edge of the pie plate and crimp the edges as you prefer. Place the dish in the freezer while you mix up the filling.

TO PREPARE THE FILLING

In a large bowl, toss to combine the apple slices, lemon juice, brown sugar, granulated sugar, flour, and apple pie spice. Pour the mixture evenly into the prepared pie crust and place it in the fridge while you prepare the crumble.

TO PREPARE THE TOPPING

In the same bowl that you used for the filling, combine the flour, brown sugar, cinnamon, and salt. Stir in the melted butter until it becomes a sandy mixture with pea-size clumps. Sprinkle the topping onto the apple filling.

TO PREPARE THE PIE

Bake the pie on the preheated baking steel or sheet pan until the crust is brown and the filling in the center of the pie is bubbling, about 60 to 70 minutes. If you notice that the crust is getting too brown before the filling is bubbling, you can use a pie crust shield or a ring of aluminum foil to carefully cover the outer edge to prevent burning. Allow the pie to cool completely, at least 4 hours, before cutting and serving with ice cream, if desired.

DAY 3: **Balloon Rides to Heaven**

After my daughter's sixth birthday party, I was cleaning up paper plates and left-over cupcakes when she brought over a handful of inflated helium balloons and asked, "Mama, how many balloons would it take to carry me up to heaven?" I laughed, because it's just the kind of thing I would have wondered in the days before my mind was tethered to the ground by grown-up logic and facts and practicality. Children have a way of bringing out the wonder, the whimsy, and the imagination that I believe God desires for us all to have.

All of creation whispers of the wonders of heaven: in sunsets and sea crea-tures and lofty mountains extending high above the clouds. The evidence of God's majesty and beauty can serve as a pointing arrow, stirring up our holy imag-inations to dream and question in pursuit of the depths of His glory. Like a child with a handful of balloons, we can let that beauty inspire wonder and awe of the One who is responsible for creating it in the first place.

This morning, search your heart for the questions and desires you have for Him. You can bring your curiosity to Him, because He relishes the innocence of childlike wonder. All of creation beckons you to the Lord, so delight in it, in Him, and thank Him for a heart and mind that longs for heaven.

 **ACTS 17:24–28**

DAY 4: Take a Load Off

Last year, Brett and I flew to California for vacation. The goal was simple: connection. We wanted a few days without the responsibility of children and jobs, days where our purpose was simply to relax and enjoy each other's company. Not all vacations go according to plan, but thankfully this one did. We laughed over glasses of wine and lingered at the breakfast table to talk, just because. No agenda, no ulterior motives, just a deep longing to rest with one another.

Every life comes attached with its own strings of responsibility, but we don't need to let them encircle our spirits and choke out all the joy God has put inside of us. He longs to see His people thriving and living in freedom, relishing the blessings He's offered to the fullest measure.

Are there areas you need to let go and unwind in order to grab onto the goodness God has called you to live in? Are there places in your everyday life where you can say yes to life-giving laughter and fun? Ask God to show you parts of yourself you haven't explored in a while, and be brave enough to step into those attributes. There is freedom and joy when we rest in the Lord, so take a load off yourself and spend time in Him today.

 **ECCLESIASTES 9:7–9**

DAY 5: Hot-Air Balloon Perspective

The first time I went to Napa was during harvest season, when the wineries were bustling with workers gathering grapes while they were ripe for picking. One morning, we rose with the sun for a hot-air balloon ride above the valley, and from up in the sky, separated from the rush of farmers and equipment and large vats of fruit down below, our balloon pilot showed us where the work was being done. From our point of view, we could see it all: the fields that were in process, the ones that weren't quite ready for picking, and the ones that had already been turned over.

As humans, we don't usually get the hot-air balloon perspective. With two feet on the ground, we can only see the field that is right in front of us, and that limited perspective can make the work ahead feel overwhelming. In those moments, we have the opportunity to trust in the Lord and seek His understanding for our lives, knowing that He has the vantage point and wisdom to direct our steps. He sees it all: not just where we're going, but also the places where we're in process and the ones where we've already seen victory. In Him is all the direction, encouragement, and peace we could want for this life, because when our eyes can't see, we believe that His do. That's the essence of faith.

Are there areas of your present days or future that feel big or overwhelming? Maybe there's work to be done in a relationship, something you're struggling with, or a goal you've set? You can trust God with the big picture; He knows which parts of your life are in season, and He'll lead you toward a harvest of His blessing when the time is right. Today, submit your plans and trust to Him, and ask for a much-needed change of perspective: one that looks to Him.

 **PSALM 37:5; HEBREWS 11:1**

DAY 6: Free from Smoke

We arrived in Sonoma shortly after wildfires had ravaged much of the land and crops in the area. The ash hadn't even settled before most of the experts had agreed that the 2020 crop could possibly be a wash. Weeks' worth of smoky air had likely penetrated into the skins and flesh of the grapes, and what started as a promising crop was now tainted by the air it had been exposed to.

Like those grapes, our surroundings, for better or for worse, will influence the harvest in our lives. As believers, it's important that we're being exposed to the good stuff: hope, joy, peace, love, respect, and kindness. The world can be pretty noisy with things that don't line up with God's word, but we can guard our heart by saturating our mind and spirit with things that look, taste, and sound like Jesus.

Be real with yourself: Does your life point to Jesus? Remember that Jesus Christ in you is a beautiful flavor that will season the world around you. Instead of soaking up the metaphorical wildfires around you, be an aroma of heaven in every circumstance and relationship you find yourself in. Ask God to intensify His presence in your life, and love people from the overflow of what you've received from Him. A life that points to Jesus always has bountiful harvest in good time, and it's not affected by a little smoke.

 **PROVERBS 13:20**

DAY 7: Wanting More of Jesus

Whether in fitting rooms, on test scores, at potluck dinners, or with our own children, we've all played the game of comparison. I've compared my appearance to a friend's, compared my Christmas gifts to my siblings', and even compared the tidiness of my home to the ones I see in magazines. The comparison game is maddening, but my hunch is that I'm not alone here. We all look around at what other people have and wish we had those things.

Early on the in the Bible, God gave Moses a commandment about wanting things other people had, saying: *You shall not covet your neighbor's house; you shall not covet your neighbor's wife, or his male servant, or his female servant, or his ox, or his donkey, or anything that is your neighbor's* (Exod. 20:17). Did you catch that? We're not to covet *anything*. Not our neighbor's brand-new car, or her husband who seems to do all the chores, or his talents, or her spiritual gifts, or anything else. It's as if God knew our eyes would be prone to wander and wonder whether we had it as good as everyone else, whether our lives were as rich and full as the ones we saw around us.

I like what author Bob Goff says in *Live in Grace, Walk in Love*: "We'll never be like Jesus if it's more important for us to be like each other." Isn't that the truth? Friend, don't be distracted by the blessings you see around you. Keep your eyes on your own plate and feast on the goodness God has set before you. Today, consider the blessings that you can give thanks for. Honor Him with your gratitude, and let the desires of your heart reflect His: for you to look more and more like Him.

 **2 CORINTHIANS 10:7–12**

DAY 8: Starved for Connection

Sometimes my girlfriends will come over after the kids have gone to bed, and we sit together in our pajamas to talk, drink wine, and eat crispy rice treats straight from the pan. It's nothing fancy, but I find those brief moments of face-to-face conversation and intimacy with dear friends to be deeply nourishing, feeding an inner craving to share life, to be known, and to occupy common ground.

As we get older, it can become harder to carve out the time to take care of ourselves. Our calendars are so full of claims already made on our time—our job, our family, social organizations—that we forget to pencil in time for our hearts too. Sometimes, I don't even realize how starved I am for connection until I have a night when I get a big gulp of it with a few good friends. Afterwards, I lie in bed, rehashing the stories and witty banter, thinking how good it felt to be in relationship, to be heard, to be known.

We weren't designed to take on life by ourselves. God designed us for connection, and there's so much comfort to be experienced by being known. Are there people in your life who feed this need in you? Or is there anyone in your corner who needs the love of a close friend today? Take time to participate in the exchange of friendship this week, and thank God for the opportunity to know and be known.

 **ACTS 2:42-47**

DAY 9: Sweet and Salty Crispy Rice Treats

I'm not sure if there's such thing as a crispy-rice-treat expert, but if there is, my friend Rayne definitely qualifies. She rarely comes over for dinner without bringing a plate of crispies for us to share with the kids, and those sweet and salty treats have become synonymous with her in my mind. These Sweet and Salty Crispy Rice Treats are our favorite: a brown butter and marshmallow base with rice cereal and honey grahams throughout. They're heavenly, and if you've ever thought crispy rice treats were just for kids, you're dead wrong.

....

SWEET AND SALTY CRISPY RICE TREATS

Makes 20 squares

½ cup unsalted butter, diced

½ teaspoon table salt

1 teaspoon vanilla extract

1 (16-ounce) bag mini marshmallows

2½ cups honey graham cereal, crushed into large bits

4½ cups crispy rice cereal

Lightly grease a 9 × 13-inch pan and set it aside. In a large pot over low heat, stir the butter until melted. Continue stirring frequently. It will begin to sizzle and foam slightly before little golden bits start forming on the bottom of the pan. Continue stirring until the butter has browned. You'll know it's done when there are golden flecks throughout the butter and you notice a sweet, nutty fragrance. Immediately remove it from the heat and add the salt and vanilla, stirring carefully. Add all but 1 cup of the marshmallows and stir over low heat until they're melted completely. Add the remaining marshmallows with the two cereals and stir just until combined.

Turn the mixture out into the prepared pan and use the butter wrapper or a clean, lightly greased hand to pat the crispies flat in the pan. Allow them to cool completely before cutting and enjoying!

DAY 10: Setting the Table for Connection

In a few weeks, we're hosting a wedding and reception at our home. It'll be a small affair with just a few family members, an iPod playlist, and a homemade cake, courtesy of yours truly. I normally like the challenge of piecing an event together, of working out details and planning things down to the minute, but something about this is slightly intimidating. The perfectionist in me wants it all to be pressed and dressed and free from blemish like a bride on her big day.

What I've had to remind myself is that, as easy as it is to get wrapped up in designing menus and tablescapes, creating an atmosphere of love is more valuable. When you invite people over, they may not remember if the linens matched or if they ate off of plastic plates or fine china, but they'll remember if they were welcomed generously. The warmth of genuine kindness and good conversation will make up for cold sandwiches and mismatched chairs, because what people long for is connection.

The next time you have people over, don't get so caught up in the details that you miss the opportunity for community. Jesus is honored when we set aside our own convenience to make room for love and connection around the table, and I believe you'll find that any love you serve in your own home will end up nourishing you too. Ask God to show you some simple ways you can free up your home and hands for hospitality, and remember that love will cover most of the mistakes you make along the way.

 **1 PETER 4:8–10**

DAY 11: Hand-Me-Downs

At the upcoming wedding, the bride and groom plan to say their vows under the same wooden arbor Brett and I used for our wedding ceremony. My grandfather built it years ago for our big day, and since then it's made a home in our backyard. Other things from our wedding have been repurposed and used at other events too—my dress and veil, the flower vases, and even the white bistro lights that hung at our reception. I like the idea of sharing our treasures with other people, and it makes me pause to consider what other kinds of things we can pass on to the people around us.

The Bible talks a lot about generational blessings, and since having children, I've become increasingly interested in sowing good seeds for future generations to harvest. There are countless places in scripture where God's goodness and favor in one person's life trickles down and into the family line that follows. It's because of His faithfulness, the endurance of His love, and promises to His people that He honors the discipline and love of former generations by extending that same generosity and affection to future ones. Not only do we get to reap some of the treasure that was earned by the people who came before us, but we also get to pass on our own blessings to the ones who come after! Hallelujah!

Today, take pleasure in knowing that the growth and spiritual maturity you're pursuing in your life will outlive you. It has nothing to do with your own merit or good works, but rests solely in the steadfast love and kindness of the Lord. Ask God to reveal what you can pass along to someone else and any new seeds He wants you to sow for yourself and the generations to come. Get excited about the work He is doing in your life and be delighted knowing that the harvest doesn't stop with you—there's always more to come.

 **EXODUS 20:5–6; DEUTERONOMY 7:9; PSALM 89:1–4**

DAY 12: Holding Our Hands

The weeks following the birth of each of my babies are now a blur, a hazy memory of sleeplessness and nursing and new baby smells. During those days, my husband and I experienced an outpouring of help from neighbors, church friends, and even people we barely knew who wanted to bring a meal, a gift, and or a handwritten note. Family and the friends who feel like family served in big ways too by picking up groceries, taking the other children for play dates, or even staying awake to comfort our new baby while we got some rest. As hard as those days were, they offered us the opportunity to feel the full weight of love and support from the people who were in our corner.

In the Bible there's a story about the Israelites entering into battle against the Amalekites. Moses carried his staff to the top of a hill, and as long as his arms were raised to the sky, Israel prevailed. When Moses grew weary, Aaron and Hur propped his body up with stones and held his hands to the sky. The Israelites won the battle that day because of the Lord's provision, but God allowed Aaron and Hur to play a part by literally providing support to Moses at the critical time.

God will always provide, even in the seasons of life that feel like a battle, and often He does so by sending us a lifeline in human form. The friends and family who hold up our arms when we can't anymore, when we've all but lost the war we're in, are a physical manifestation of God's grace right here on earth. Just as Moses grew weak, we'll get tired too, and when that happens, we can trust that God will prove Himself to be strong and surround us with the support we need.

Who are the people in your corner? Has God surrounded you with one or more friends you can trust during whatever challenge you're facing? Spend time in prayer and thank God for the hands and feet of others that He's provided for you here on earth. Ask Him to show you how you can express your gratitude to the people in your corner and remain humble in the moments when you can't do it on your own. He desires that you rely on Him, and when you do, He will never fail to be faithful.

EXODUS 17:8-16

DAY 13: Warming to Friendship

Our dear friends live in a beautiful home outfitted with a cozy study featuring dark walls, plush furniture, and a wood-burning fireplace. It feels like the kind of room that takes you back in time, where people should be smoking pipes or browsing rows of leather-bound books, but we just show up in our pj's with take-out pizza and a bottle of red wine. Within minutes, our bones and hearts begin to thaw, and I'm never sure if it's the fire, the wine, or the warmth of the conversation, but it's comforting to experience something so real and rich, right there, in my slippers.

Early on in life, I made friendships a numerical thing, always most concerned with having a sizable number of friends to my name, but as I get older, I want fewer people on my speed dial but more who feel like family. I want the ones who accept me in my pajamas and will feed me cold pizza, because we're beyond putting on a show. I want friends who ask the hard questions, laugh about mistakes, and speak truth when I've bought into a lie. I want friends who expect me to curl up on their sofa and don't hesitate to make themselves at home on mine either.

Take a moment to inventory your friendships. Are there people you can go deeper with in the coming months? Who are the friends God is calling you to grow alongside this week, this month, and this year? Today, ask God to nurture those friendships that honor Him, and make time in the next few days to experience the joy of life-giving relationship.

 **PROVERBS 27:9; EPHESIANS 4:25**

DAY 14: A Lot like Camping

I have a friend who says that following Jesus is a lot like camping. In theory, it sounds great: adventure, soaring views, babbling brooks, s'mores, and moonlit renditions of "Kumbaya." But let's be clear—camping is not a stay at the Ritz-Carlton. There are bugs and temperature changes and that whole business of doing your business outdoors. There's tending to a fire, carrying your pack, and, sweet mercy, how does everything always end up wet?

Like camping, following Jesus can get messy and uncomfortable. He's honored when we say, "Yes, I'll follow you there," but let's not fancy-up what that actually means. Like camping, sometimes you'll find yourself in foreign, uncomfortable terrain.

Luckily, Jesus has all the qualifications any leader worth following should have. He has ointment for the sunburn and rashes you'll get along the way, and He's the voice that will whisper to you from the next sleeping bag when you're scared and alone at night. Christ in you is equipped to manage any terrain you find yourself in, and (bonus!) He is the only one with a good trail map.

If you're sure you're ready for this, let Jesus fill your pack with all the stuff He'll help you use along the way. He hasn't promised it will be easy, but He's a really good guide. He'll equip you wherever you go, and your only job is to follow His lead.

 **LUKE 9:57–62**

DAY 15: Midnight Pizzas

When I was a kid, my favorite Fridays included sleepovers. My best friend would spend the night, and we'd stay up for hours telling secrets and debating life's most important questions like, "Who is the cutest Backstreet Boy?" and "Which is better: Dr. Pepper or Mountain Dew?" Sometime after midnight, we'd tiptoe to the kitchen for cold pizza and Girl Scout cookies and giggle as we ate, because we had nowhere to be in the morning.

Late bedtimes and sleepovers are no longer a part of my regular lifestyle, but do I miss the simplicity of those early friendships. Looking back, I recognize those silly conversations and contemplative whispers as things that forged understanding, a widening of common ground that is hard to come by as an adult. Friendships nowadays require intentionality that many of us forget to make time for. I get it: life is busy, and some things just end up on the back burner, like making the phone call, asking the hard questions, and digging in beyond surface-level interactions.

We weren't intended to do life alone. God designed each of us with an innate desire for relationship, and I'm here to remind you that those bonds are *good*. They can be sources of the encouragement, hope, accountability, and fun that most of us could use more of these days.

Today, spend some time in prayer and ask God to show you who your community is. Who are the women He's placed alongside of you to share an authentic, life-giving relationship? Who can you reach out to in an effort to build relationship? Life is busy, but friendship is worth the effort. Thank God for the ones He has in store for you, and make time for deepening those relationships in the coming weeks.

 **1 JOHN 4:7-12**

DAY 16: Sheet-Pan Pizza

My kids absolutely love making homemade pizza, pepperoni smiley faces and all. The dough recipe for this Sheet-Pan Pizza is the simplest one we use in our house, and it yields a chewy, soft crust. If you prefer a slightly crisper crust, you can pre-bake the dough for about 3 to 4 minutes before adding the sauce and toppings. Keep in mind that some toppings (for example, fresh vegetables and uncooked meats) can make your pie soggy, so it is best to precook those.

SHEET-PAN PIZZA

Makes 1 (9 × 13-inch) pizza

DOUGH

2½ cups all-purpose flour

1½ teaspoons instant yeast

1 teaspoon table salt

1 cup lukewarm water

3 tablespoons olive oil, divided

PIZZA

3 tablespoons grated Parmesan

¾ teaspoon garlic salt

⅓ cup pizza sauce

2 teaspoons Italian herbs

2 cups shredded mozzarella cheese

Toppings: pepperoni, cooked sausage,
ham, veggies—your choice

TO PREPARE THE DOUGH

In a medium bowl or the bowl of a stand mixer, stir to combine the flour, yeast, and salt. Add the water and 1 tablespoon of olive oil. Stir to combine into a shaggy dough and then, using the dough-hook attachment on your mixer (or your hands on a floured surface), knead the dough until it becomes smooth, elastic, and slightly tacky, about 5 minutes. Use a ½ tablespoon of olive oil to lightly grease a large bowl and place the dough inside. Cover the bowl with plastic wrap or a tea towel to rise in a warm spot in your kitchen until doubled in size, about 1½ hours.

Once risen, you can punch down the dough and store in the fridge for up to 6 hours, or you can go ahead and prep the pizza!

Use 1 tablespoon of olive oil to grease the sides and bottom of a rimmed quarter-sheet pan (9 × 13 inches) or casserole dish. If you refrigerated the dough, allow it to come to room temperature before rolling out. Use your fingertips to press the dough into the pan, extending it all the way to the edges. It may shrink back a little—just keep pressing—or set it aside for 10 minutes to let it relax and then press again. Cover the pan with a tea towel and let it rest for about 30 minutes. Move an oven rack to the lowest position in the oven, and preheat the oven to 500ºF.

TO PREPARE THE PIZZA

Drizzle the remaining $\frac{1}{2}$ tablespoon of olive oil on top of the crust and use your fingers or a pastry brush to smooth it out. Sprinkle the grated Parmesan on top, making sure to thoroughly cover the edge crust area. Repeat this process with the garlic salt. Use a pastry brush or spoon to spread out the pizza sauce and sprinkle the saucy area thoroughly with the Italian herbs. Cover the sauce with shredded cheese and then lay out your toppings. Bake on the lowest rack in the oven for 16 to 18 minutes, or until the crust is turning golden and the cheese is bubbling and browning. Allow it to cool slightly before slicing.

DAY 17: Less Is More

Aimee recently helped to make some of her own birthday cupcakes. She picked out all her favorite colors, minty green and pale pink, dusty purple and a blue that reminded me of cornflower, and together we piped swirls on each cupcake, finishing them off with white sugar pearls and rainbow sprinkles. When we got to the final cupcake, she eagerly mixed together all the remaining frosting colors to make what she thought would be the most special color, saving the very best cupcake for last. Much to her dismay, what she found in her bowl was a color I would best describe as brownish-green, not what she had hoped for, and the cupcake that was supposed to be her favorite ended up a hot mess.

She learned a lesson that afternoon that I am still learning even now as an adult: sometimes less is more. Many of us are prone to taking on too much, saying yes to every good invitation and well-meaning request, because if doing a little is good, then surely doing more must be better. We add more and more good colors to our bowl, stirring it all together in hopes that we'll mix up something really special: fulfillment, joy, purpose, or the recognition we've been hoping for. The truth is, sometimes when we do too much, we lose sight of the goodness we had to begin with. We muddy the waters with our own frustration and exhaustion, until we eventually figure out that, however many good deeds or fruitful activities we do, they will not bring us the peace and joy we've been looking for all along.

Let's be content with the colors God has given us. If you find yourself on the hunt for purpose, for things to fill voids or areas of discontentment in your life, remember, you won't find them by doing or acquiring more stuff. Instead, look to Jesus for the beauty and peace and love your heart is desiring. As Psalm 63:1 says, He is the water in a dry and parched land; the answer to that thirst you're feeling is Him. Fill up on Jesus, look to Him before you fill your plate with things that won't satisfy, and know that His portion is where you'll find fulfillment.

 **MATTHEW 6:24**

DAY 18: Pots on the Stove

In the weeks after I had each of my three children, friends and family came out in droves to support us with love and gifts and meals. The doer in me doesn't like to rely on anyone to pick up the slack, but during a time when I was tired and overrun with emotion I was grateful to surrender my own expectations of myself and to be accepted exactly as I was: with bleary eyes, greasy hair, hormones, and the whole nine yards.

I'm comfortable with lots of pots on the proverbial stove, but I've learned that proficiency can become an idol. God didn't intend for us to take on life on our own, and when we trick ourselves into believing we can and should be able to do it all, have it all, and to be it all, there's bound to be a fall from grace.

Friend, the sufficiency of Christ would mean so little if you had it on your own already. Your need for help, from Him and from others, does not make you weak or incapable; it makes you human. If you're currently operating under weighty expectations of yourself or others, take some time to rest in the sufficiency of Christ. Ask Him who you are and how little or much you can manage at this particular phase of your life. Your capacity may vary from season to season in life, but His power and abilities are constant. You can rest in that today.

 **2 CORINTHIANS 3:4–6**

DAY 19: Foundation Work

When we began building our house, I had a big vision for the end product. There'd be white marble counters, shiny brass fixtures, and wheat-colored wood floors flecked with green and gray undertones. I spent months picking out the finishes and, quite often, became frustrated with how long the more tedious parts of the building process took. For weeks there was plumbing, electrical wiring, and inspections, those lackluster essentials that seemed to be getting us nowhere, but that were setting up an important foundation.

Quite often in life I want all the end results—a beautiful home, a healthy marriage, well-behaved kids, blossoming friendships, satisfying work, and brimming health—without the work it takes to get there. I skip over the delicate tasks of hard conversations, inner healing, and persistent everyday choices, opting instead for quick-fix outcomes that never seem to last.

The task in front of us as believers is to establish a foundation that lasts. There will always be temporary satisfactions that distract us from addressing the structural necessities of our lives, but we will absolutely crumble without doing the work. The shiny finishes and beautiful aesthetics will come, but first we need to let God do the groundwork. Invite Jesus to do work in your life. On days when it doesn't seem as if there's much progress, you can trust that He's in there, digging and wiring, adding screws and nails to make your foundation firm. Your hope for a future worth living is only secure when it's built with Jesus, a solid rock on which to build an eternal home.

 **MATTHEW 7:24–27**

DAY 20: Never Move-In Ready

Just as I had big plans for our home-building process, I also had some pretty grandiose expectations for how I'd fill the home too. There'd be overstuffed armchairs and crisp bedding, tailored window treatments and organized shelves. I filled Pinterest boards with stylish photos and made plans to outfit each room with unique pieces that represented the classic English style I had come to admire. Sure, the process might take a *little* time, but, convinced of my own drive and promptness, I was certain this project would be over in a jiff.

If you've ever furnished your own home, you know this is laughable at best. Even after a couple of years under this roof, it's still a work in progress, and although our home is beyond lovely, it's nowhere near done. Early on, our guests slept on my old college furniture and hand-me-down sheets, and the curated dinner parties I had imagined involved take-out boxes and mismatched dining chairs. As much as I wanted to stick a fork in the project and call it done, there was no amount of hustle that could get us past the pace of slow progress.

Thankfully, God's okay with slow progress. He doesn't need you to be move-in ready for Him to claim you as His own. The Bible says we are *being transformed into His image with ever-increasing glory* (2 Cor. 3:18, NIV), which lets me know we're still a work in progress. He's the One transforming, and He's the One who has promised to complete the work.

Get comfortable with the places in your life that are unfinished. You can let Him be the One to do the refining work in your heart. In the meantime, have grace for yourself, and remember that if He started the work in you, He will finish it too (Phil. 1:6).

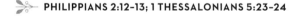 **PHILIPPIANS 2:12–13; 1 THESSALONIANS 5:23–24**

DAY 21: Making Your Home a Haven

After years of unsuccessfully dropping hints to my husband, I've finally just started buying myself flowers. Ladies, I have zero regrets. Flowers are an instant mood lifter for this woman, and it takes little more than a bunch of wildflowers or a couple of hydrangeas to make me feel as though my home is sparkling. Those fresh signs of life, whether on my table or in my yard, bring beauty into my home, one tiny bloom at a time.

There's something to be said for creating a home that feels good. Look through the Bible—God was crazy specific on how His temple was to be adorned, and that lets me know that it's okay to treasure beauty. Fresh flowers are a favorite of mine, but you may prefer pretty music, bright colors, or plush, cozy blankets. Either way, don't hesitate to make your home just that—yours. Whether it's a temporary or forever place, a single room or a million acres, make your space a haven that prompts you to rest and joy.

Today, allow Jesus to show you where in your physical spaces you can make room for rest, for peace, and for enjoyment. Look for ways to feel at home wherever it is you find yourself, and thank Him for the secure haven you have in Him.

 **ISAIAH 32:18**

DAY 22: Balance Is Everything

Most people are surprised to find out that I'm a dietitian by trade. It must have something to do with my butter- and sugar-laden blog, the cookies and cakes and biscuits I splash all over social media. Sure, there's nothing healthy about the food on my website, but nutrition was my first love, and I'm slowly coming to terms with this professional paradox of mine.

Here's the thing: I understand that balance is everything. Jesus said, "Man cannot live by bread alone," which is true, but man also cannot live solely on caramel sauce and browned butter—we all need something of substance in order to survive.

As I explore balancing food as a source of nutrition with food as a source of enjoyment, I'm trying to find that same equilibrium in other areas of life too. What does it look like to be a supportive friend without being a doormat? How can I learn to work to the best of my abilities without becoming a workaholic? What does it look like to diligently seek the Lord without striving as a means of relationship? Life is made up of all sorts of balancing acts, and the truth is that sometimes we mess up; we can lose our balance and, in the process, lose track of ourselves.

Are there areas in your life that feel out of balance? Remember that God has grace for the parts you're still figuring out. You give it all to Him—your responsibilities, your time, your efforts, and your heart—knowing that He is big enough to work it all out. When life gets out of balance, reset your heart on Him, and He will steady your steps.

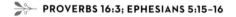 **PROVERBS 16:3; EPHESIANS 5:15-16**

DAY 23: Roasted Vegetable Orzo Salad

On nights that I serve roasted veggies to my family, I add a few extra to the pan to toss into Roasted Vegetable Orzo Salad the next day. Flavored with Parmesan and a tangy dressing, this pasta salad is a seriously delicious and adaptable recipe to serve all year long. In the summer, try adding fresh basil or briny olives; in colder months, add wilted greens or winter squash. The best thing about this dish is that you really can make it your own, so follow your taste buds and enjoy.

ROASTED VEGETABLE ORZO SALAD

Serves 6 as a side

4 to 5 cups cut-up mixed vegetables for roasting (I like the combination of bell pepper, red onion, carrots, tomatoes, and zucchini, but mix and match as you choose)

5 tablespoons olive oil, divided

2 teaspoons minced garlic

Salt and pepper to taste

1½ cups vegetable or chicken broth

1 cup orzo pasta

1 tablespoon apple cider vinegar

2 teaspoons stone-ground Dijon mustard

½ teaspoon dried parsley

½ teaspoon dried oregano

½ cup grated Parmesan cheese

Preheat the oven to 400°F. Toss the vegetables on a large rimmed sheet pan with 2 tablespoons olive oil, the minced garlic, 1 teaspoon salt, and ½ teaspoon pepper. Remove half of the vegetables to a second sheet pan and evenly distribute the vegetables on both pans. Roast for 30 minutes, tossing the vegetables and rotating the pans halfway through. Once the vegetables are browned, remove the pans from the oven and set aside.

In the meantime, pour the broth into a small saucepan and bring it to a boil over medium-high heat. Once boiling, add the orzo, stirring to combine, and then cover the pan and reduce the heat to low. Cook the pasta until al dente, about 10 minutes. (The orzo will absorb most of the broth, and any leftover broth adds nice moisture to the salad.) Remove the pan from the heat and set it aside, stirring occasionally.

While the vegetables and pasta are cooking, prepare the dressing. In a large bowl, stir together 3 tablespoons olive oil, the apple cider vinegar, mustard, parsley, oregano, and Parmesan cheese. Toss in the prepared vegetables and pasta, gently mix, and adjust the salt and pepper to taste. I usually add an additional 1 teaspoon salt and ½ teaspoon pepper. Enjoy as a warm or room-temperature side!

DAY 24: Unveiling

I take comfort in this verse from 2 Corinthians: *And we all, with unveiled face, beholding the glory of the Lord, are being transformed into the same image from one degree of glory to another. For this comes from the Lord who is the Spirit* (3:18). Did you catch that? We are actively being transformed; there's change happening, a work is in progress, and it's God who is making it all happen.

Almost daily, we'll come face-to-face with our humanity. It can be tempting to feel discouraged when our sin and insufficiencies are uncovered and we realize there's a long way to go in this mission to fully abide in Christ, but this verse is full of all the encouragement we need. It's God who does the work and has the power to transform us, and if we're resting in Him, He is constantly sharpening the image of His Son in us until that's the picture most in focus.

Our job as believers is to depend on Him. We can trust God to do the work if we're willing to be obedient to His Spirit in us. When the Holy Spirit offers conviction as an opportunity for course correction, let His voice be the gentle nudge that moves you into the arms of your refining Savior. Expose your heart to His forgiveness, and allow His grace to be transformative in your life today.

 **ROMANS 12:1-2**

DAY 25: Reflected Desires

When I started working on the proposal for this book, a part of me felt hesitant. *Was I pursuing this for myself? Was it a selfish desire, a narcissistic hope that would only serve my own agenda?* I had a hard time separating my fleshly wants from the ones God put in my heart, and for a long time I wondered if my prayers for open doors and big opportunities were just another self-serving act. Ultimately, I came to rest in the sense that the desire wasn't my own—it was one God had given to me.

Some of us have bought into the lie that God is tired of hearing prayers about our lives, but that couldn't be farther from the truth. He longs for His children to come to Him, to experience the love and revelation found in Him, and His Word says that when we return that love to Him, our hearts will begin to desire the right things. Psalm 37:4 says, *Delight yourself in the Lord, and He will give you the desires of your heart*, meaning, love God and He will put His own desires in your heart. Sure, our humanity will pop in from time to time, but when we pursue Him in prayer, our wants will slowly begin to reflect His.

Remain in close relationship to the Lord, in prayer and affection. He's not in the business of returning prayers unanswered, and if you have a heart that reflects His love, you can rest knowing that He is working to carry out your prayers in beautiful and purposeful ways. Bring your heart to Him in prayer, and ask for a deposit of His desires; He'll make your desires His own.

 **1 JOHN 5:14–15**

DAY 26: Breaking Out the Good China

I recently went to a friend's house for a birthday dinner. The table was set with the host's wedding china—dishes, glasses, and stemware that she'd displayed in a glass cabinet for the better part of a decade without ever using. We sat around the table, everyone's faces all pink-cheeked and glowy from champagne and candlelight, and celebrated the birthday girl.

Later, we vowed to be fancy together again. Instead of waiting for birthdays or holidays to gather and celebrate the good things in one another's lives, we determined to make occasions out of ordinary moments. There's something special about pulling out the fancy dishes, a good dress, or that special bottle of wine as an offering of your best for the people you love most.

Today, take time to make a list of things you can celebrate *right now*. Ask God to show you opportunities for gratitude and joy both in your life and in the lives of the people you love. It won't always require a white tablecloth or candlelight, but it's encouraging to be reminded of the good things in our lives by treasuring those blessings as the gifts that they are. Instead of overlooking the everyday and not-so-everyday occasions in your life, make time in the coming weeks for celebration (fancy wedding china is totally optional), and remember to give God thanks for the treasure of community.

 **1 CORINTHIANS 10:31**

Making Room

My favorite family days are the ones where we make room for absolutely anything. We play dress-up and whisper secrets, tell stories and snuggle. We might stir bowls of cookie dough or make biscuits, draw pictures of dinosaurs or just sit still. Although it's easy to fall into the habit of doing the same thing every day, I'm finding that it's the out-of-the-ordinary days, the ones on which schedule and time take a backseat, where rich conversation and connection happen.

Our family has been blessed with so much, but with that comes the responsibility of managing it all. It requires daily discipline, an intentional slowing of my brain and body, to stop and embrace the opportunity for true relationship. Without that practice, I blow through weeks' worth of moments without truly settling into a pace that is compatible with connection.

Be honest with yourself. Where is your struggle? Do you rush through life? Are you guarded in a way that makes genuine connection impossible? True relationship, the kind that is memorable and life-giving, requires presence and authenticity, and the first step is to make room for it. Today, set aside purposeful time for connection with God and with others, and know that your efforts are delightful to Him.

 **PROVERBS 21:5**

DAY 28: Being Bold with Our Gifts

For women in today's world, it's easy to feel pressure. When staring into the face of Goliaths like Pinterest, the DIY Network, and the ever-present Instagram Supermom, it's easy to feel a little uncertain about what we bring to the table. We're often left disappointed, or even feeling shameful, about what we have to offer.

The phrase "Comparison is the thief of joy" comes to mind. We step up on the scales of comparison time and time again to measure ourselves against the success in others' lives, failing to remember that we are all equipped with different gifts. When our identity is tied to our achievements, our "likes," or our abilities rather than to God, we can lose track of who we are. Ultimately, we undervalue the beauty He created and the price He paid for our lives.

Friend, lift your head and honor the work God is doing in and through your life. Celebrate the people around you for the grace that is present in their lives and stand proud of the refining that is happening in yours. Let's be bold with our gifts and content in the places where we're still learning. God is honored when we share what He's put inside of us and He's proud when we make room for the greatness in others too.

Whose story can you celebrate today? Is it a sister, a friend, a neighbor? Maybe your own? Your gifts don't pale in comparison to others, and God is illuminated most when we let our gifts shine to His glory. Shine brightly today, and encourage others to do the same.

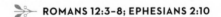 **ROMANS 12:3–8; EPHESIANS 2:10**

DAY 29: Who's in Your Corner?

For years, I dreamed of writing a cookbook. It felt big and far-fetched, but over time I eventually got to the place where I could voice that dream out loud. Even as I said it to friends and family, I feared rejection and judgment, as if their reactions would expose the fact that I wasn't good enough or my dream didn't stand a chance. Of course, I was wrong; the community I'm surrounded with is supportive, and I walked away from those conversations feeling emboldened to press in.

One friend took it upon herself to check in regularly, encourage me, and pray for me and my work. We weren't even particularly close at the time, but she sent occasional texts cheering me on and celebrating the small victories along the way. I don't know if she would say the same, but for me that time felt like a deepening of our relationship. I knew that she was unequivocally for me, and my heart was so moved with gratitude at the amount of care and support she offered.

Who are the people in your corner? Who has laced their gloves to fight with you for your dreams? It's so important to find the friends and neighbors who will encourage you, remind you of who you are, and agree with what God has said about you. Those are the people who challenge us to move forward and won't let us settle for less than what God has promised.

Sometimes we give more weight to the voices that try to tell us all of the reasons our dreams aren't worthwhile. Today, listen for the voices who will cheer for you in truth and in love. Let their encouragement embolden you to press forward toward the dreams God has put in your heart.

 **EPHESIANS 4:29; HEBREWS 10:24-25**

DAY 30: Whole-Wheat Pumpkin Muffins

Some people nurture with words or hugs, but my friend Blair encourages with food. It's not uncommon for her to show up with a bag of muffins and a handwritten note just because—it's just the kind of friend she is. For years, her pumpkin muffins have been a staple favorite of mine, and I was lucky enough to snag the recipe.

If you're new to the kitchen, these Whole-Wheat Pumpkin Muffins are a great place to start. They're simple and incredibly rewarding for the little work they require. You can omit the butterscotch chips or use peanut-butter or caramel chips as an alternative, but the butterscotch adds a warm sweetness that coordinates well with the pumpkin.

....

WHOLE-WHEAT PUMPKIN MUFFINS

Makes 48 mini muffins

1 cup all-purpose flour

3/4 cup whole-wheat flour

1 teaspoon baking soda

1/2 teaspoon baking powder

1 1/2 teaspoons apple pie spice

1 1/2 teaspoons ground cinnamon

1/4 teaspoon ground nutmeg

1 teaspoon table salt

3/4 cup packed light brown sugar

1/2 cup granulated sugar

1/2 cup canola oil

2 large eggs

1 cup canned pumpkin puree

3 tablespoons water

1 cup butterscotch chips

Preheat the oven to 350°F. Lightly grease two mini muffin pans (48 muffins total) with baking spray.

In a medium bowl, combine the all-purpose flour, whole-wheat flour, baking soda, baking powder, apple pie spice, cinnamon, nutmeg, and salt. Set aside.

In a large bowl or the bowl of a stand mixer, combine the light brown sugar, granulated sugar, oil, eggs, pumpkin puree, and water, stirring on medium just until combined. Add the dry ingredients and stir until smooth. Scrape the sides of the bowl to stir in any unincorporated bits and then gently stir in the butterscotch chips.

Use a small cookie scoop or a spoon to fill the muffin cups three-quarters full. Bake for about 12 minutes, rotating the pans halfway through as needed to ensure that they bake evenly. Once a toothpick inserted into the center of a random sample of muffins comes out clean, remove them from oven and allow them to cool slightly for a couple of minutes before removing them from the tins.

NOTE: If you prefer, this recipe can be adapted to make standard muffins. Prepare the batter as directed and fill lightly greased muffin cups two thirds of the way full. Bake for about 17 to 18 minutes, until a toothpick inserted into the center just barely comes out clean. Allow the muffins to cool briefly before removing them from the pans.

DAY 1: Plugged into His Word

There was a time when my sweet George was afraid of the dark, uncertain of what might be hiding in the shadowy corners of his room. The solution was simple: I bought a little plug-in nightlight for his wall, and within no time he was back to sleeping like a rock.

The Bible says God's word is a lamp to our feet and a light to our path. It illuminates the darkness, eliminating the shadowy questions and fears and murmurings of our heart. It reveals the truth about His heart for us and offers wisdom for our circumstances. In Him, there is no darkness, no fear, no worry to be found—only love.

So often, the uncertainties of life create a fear in my heart that can feel overwhelming, but I'm comforted when I remember that God has already decimated darkness with the illuminating power of His truth and love. If you've found the darkness of uncertainty, shame, or unbelief in the hidden corners of your heart, bring those questions, confusions, and doubts to Him today in prayer. Hold up the inner workings of your mind against the illuminating truth of His Word. There's power and direction for your life, even now, so plug in that nightlight and let Him reveal His truth.

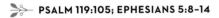 **PSALM 119:105; EPHESIANS 5:8–14**

DAY 2: Finding "The One"

I grew up dreaming of fairy tales, believing that one day I would find "the one." My Prince Charming would sweep me off my feet, and in an instant my whole life would change. We'd ride off into the sunset and begin our happily-ever-after.

As I grew older, my beliefs started to shift, and I learned that it's not really about finding the person you just can't live *without*—it's finding the person you can live *with*. It's identifying the person you're willing to bend for, to honor and care for day in and day out, offering your heart in all its mess and vulnerability in exchange for theirs.

When I met Brett, there was no shortage of romance and starry eyes, but I realized there was more below the surface too. I had finally met someone I desired to be united with for forever, and, miracle of miracles, he felt the same way. There weren't any games or wondering where he stood, and for the first time I knew I had met someone who desired my heart as much as I desired his.

There may not be a romantic soul mate or "the one" waiting out there for each of us, but I've seen how God satisfies our soul's craving for deep relationship. One of the beautiful things about relationship with Jesus is that any ounce of affection you pour out to Him is always matched with an abundant return of His own. He never leaves you wanting or wondering if His love will run out or grow cold. Instead, He meets our hearts with kindness every time, and we can count on His love to meet the deepest and most vulnerable places of our being.

Have you found a love relationship in Jesus Christ? Do you know what it feels like to be tended and cared for by the loving affection of your Heavenly Father? Know that, here on earth, there may not be "the one," but there certainly is in heaven. As believers, we each have the opportunity to be at one with the One who has loved us since the beginning of time and will continue to do so forever. His love never changes, never fades, and will always be sufficient to meet you. Lean in to that today.

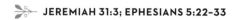 **JEREMIAH 31:3; EPHESIANS 5:22–33**

DAY 3: On Disappointment

Our marriage counselor once told Brett and me that we needed to become comfortable with disappointment. After years of seeking out resolutions for the exact same fight, we sat side by side in his office feeling tired and defeated. Why couldn't we come into agreement? Why were we continuing to run into the same challenges? We each had our own list of unmet expectations and were coming to the realization that our relationship would never be perfect—we had to learn how to work through our disappointment.

Pain, whether intentionally inflicted or not, is an inevitable part of relationships, and instead of avoiding those feelings or looking the other way, it's important that we submit them to the Lord. The disappointment we experience on earth will keep us relying on God, pressing in to Him for the transformational grace our relationships so desperately need. We don't always need more mediators or solutions or quick fixes in our marriage—we need the God who is all about restoration.

Only communion with Christ can provide the heart change necessary in marriage and other close relationships. Let the disappointments you experience in life nudge you closer to a God who never fails, and allow Him to shape your marriage into something that looks more like Him.

 **JEREMIAH 17:5-8**

DAY 4: His Grace Is Sufficient

My kids are screaming.

His grace is sufficient.

I'm behind with work.

His grace is sufficient.

I feel lonelier than I ever have in my life.

His grace is sufficient.

My husband seems distant.

His grace is sufficient.

I don't think I can do this anymore.

His grace is sufficient.

There just isn't enough time.

His grace is sufficient.

This diagnosis is scary.

His grace is sufficient.

We'll never run out of reasons to keep relying on God. The reality of a broken world is evident in our day-to-day, but the truth remains that His grace is sufficient. He is able to do more with our tiny mustard seed of faith than we could ever do with our strongest efforts, and regardless of how perilous, impossible, or painful our circumstances appear from a human perspective, His grace is sufficient and worthy of our trust. He is big enough, wise enough, and loving enough to care for all of our needs, so I'll say it again for the ones in the back:

His grace is sufficient.

 **2 CORINTHIANS 12:1–10**

DAY 5: Take It In

Alabama autumns are unpredictable but lovely. For a few short weeks, when the weather is right, the kids and I spend hours outside on a quilt on the grass, taking in the change of scenery. All summer long we avoid the muggy, relentless heat, but those first few days of fall are enough to lure us outside to take it all in: jewel-toned foliage, an occasional cool breeze, and all of nature moving, coming alive again.

How often do we take the natural beauty of the world around us for granted? My eyes always seem to catch those big, majestic displays like waterfalls, snowy mountainsides, and ocean sunrises, but I forget to take in the beauty right in my backyard. I see the bugs and the sweat and a yard scattered with plastic toys, forgetting to pick out the hints of God's glory that are right in front of me.

The Bible says that all of creation was formed in His image—you, me, the plants and animals and rivers and clouds and oceans—and I'm beginning to think that those moments of astounding beauty, like the first perfect days of fall, are really just a revelation of His splendor. Those orange leaves, gentle breezes, and bab-bling coos from the baby in your lap are intended to point to a holy, magnificent Creator.

Find a moment this week to take it all in. Don't just admire the beauty and move on—really take it in, and thank God for a creation that hints at His power and beauty. It is truly awe-inspiring, so don't miss it.

 **PSALM 19:1-6; COLOSSIANS 1:16-17; REVELATION 4:11**

DAY 6: Working Overtime

My kids are trying to grow up too fast. Gone are the days when they asked for stuffed animals and baby dolls. Now all they want is to ride in the front seat, stay up past bedtime, and have their own smartphones. Why hold hands and walk across the street when you could run?

While they're trying to flex their independent muscles, all I can see is the danger looming around every corner. Moms can sniff out risk from a mile away, and we foresee potential harm because we've rehearsed most of these scenarios in our nightmares. Part of our job as parents is to shield our kids from pain until they're old enough to work through it themselves, but I don't think we're alone in this business—God does the same for us too.

Although many things that happen in this life don't make sense at the time, I wholeheartedly believe God is there, working overtime to protect us from the pain and sin in the world. Aren't you thankful some things didn't work out the way you wanted them to years ago? Have you had those moments when you sensed God protected you from physical, relational, or even self-inflicted harm? All throughout His Word, God has promised to care for His people and meet their needs. Like a mother warning a child before crossing a street, the Holy Spirit is there, urging us toward the best path to follow.

Are there things in your life you need entrust to God today? Maybe an area of life that feels treacherous or uncertain? God is working overtime for your benefit, and if you rely on Him you will forever be led by a good shepherd. Your Heavenly Father is capable and willing and has promised to never forsake you, so even when it doesn't make sense, you can follow Him.

 **PSALM 9:10; 28:7**

DAY 7: Fluffernutter Pretzel Pie

When I was a kid, my favorite dessert menus were ones that included peanut butter pie. Our whole family loved it, and I was always able to convince one of my parents to order it as an after-dinner treat. Fluffernutter Pretzel Pie is a spin on the classic Southern icebox pie made with cream cheese, whipped cream, and loads of peanut butter, but the pretzel crust is the star of the show. Regular whipped cream is fantastic here, but I love adding Marshmallow Fluff for a little extra sweetness to balance out the salt. This is bound to be a favorite for all the peanut-butter lovers out there!

....

FLUFFERNUTTER PRETZEL PIE

Serves 9

CRUST

5 ounces mini salted pretzels

¼ cup packed brown sugar

½ teaspoon table salt

½ cup unsalted butter, melted

TOPPING

1 cup heavy whipping cream

5 ounces (about 1 cup) Marshmallow Fluff

FILLING

1 cup heavy whipping cream

3 tablespoons granulated sugar

3 ounces cream cheese, at room temperature

¾ cup creamy peanut butter

¾ cup confectioners' sugar

TO PREPARE THE CRUST

Preheat the oven to 350°F. In a food processor, pulse the pretzels, brown sugar, and salt together until the pretzels are crumbs (if you don't have a food processor, seal the pretzels in a large heavy-duty plastic bag and crush them with a rolling pin). Add the melted butter and pulse to combine. Pat the crumbs into the bottom and up the sides of a standard (not deep-dish) 9-inch pie plate. Bake for 8 to 10 minutes until set. Allow it to cool completely before using.

TO PREPARE THE FILLING

Whip the cream and sugar together in a medium-size bowl until stiff peaks form. Set aside. In a separate large bowl, beat the cream cheese, peanut butter, and confectioners' sugar together until smooth, about 3 seconds. Fold in the whipped cream until smooth. Spread the filling into the prepared pie crust and set aside while you make the marshmallow topping.

TO PREPARE THE TOPPING

In a large bowl or stand mixer fitted with the whisk attachment, whip the cream on medium speed until thickened and soft peaks form. Add the Marshmallow Fluff and continue whipping until thickened to a cloudlike consistency. Dollop the topping on the pie and decorate with additional pretzel crumbs if desired. Chill in the fridge for 2 to 4 hours before serving.

DAY 8: Glory to Show for It

There's a story in the Bible in which Jesus heals a man who was blind from birth. The disciples ask, "Whose sin made him blind? This guy's or his parents'?" Jesus responds that no one was to blame; his blindness simply made room for the glory of God to be present in His life. After a little mud and a quick rinse, the man was on his way, changed because he had experienced the miraculous provision of his Heavenly Father through Jesus's touch.

We've all lived through a diagnosis, a disaster, or a horror committed against someone we love and wonder, *How could God have let this happen? Where is God when bad things happen to good people?* I'll be honest—I struggle with this question more often than I feel comfortable with it, but just as Jesus met the blind man on the road, I know He'll meet me in my pain too. He has healing and provision for my story, and if I welcome Him into it, there will be glory to show for it too.

God doesn't abandon us in our pain, and He certainly isn't the author of it either. If you find yourself living with the weight of sickness, heartache, or devastation, you can bring it to Jesus. You may not understand why or find the solution you hope for this side of heaven, but He will meet you, even in the suffering. He will uncover His glory in the midst of trouble, provide salve for your wounded parts, and always prove to be sufficient to meet all of your needs (Phil. 4:19).

 **JOHN 9:1-34**

DAY 9: Our Lineage

Last year, I received a book of recipes written by my Pops's great-grandmother. The pages were browned with age, but her stunning script could be seen as clearly as if it were written yesterday. The book was filled with her recipes, most of them for baked goods, and I was so overwhelmed by the treasure I was holding. It was just an old book, but also so meaningful—a piece of my history, a window into a part of my family that I'd otherwise never know.

The Bible says that we as Christians have been adopted into the family of God. Next time you're in the New Testament, pay close attention to the life of Jesus. Meditate on His character—His peace, love, joy, wisdom, gentleness, and self-control. Read about the intimacy He had with God and observe how He walked in power, in miracles, and in faith. Find the evidence of His glory shining off the pages, and then consider this truth—this is *your* inheritance too.

Every good gift that the Father gave to Jesus is one He desires to be a part of your life too. If Jesus had patience, He has that for you too. If Jesus healed the sick and walked in freedom, then that's in your story as well. The mystery of Christ in us is that we get to share in the glory and gifts and personality of Jesus, having been grafted into His lineage forever.

We all have different family histories. Maybe you have heirlooms, treasured books, and keepsakes, or maybe not. Maybe there are a lot of question marks or painful stories in your family tree. Regardless of who you are or who you've come from, you can stand confident that, in Christ, your inheritance is secure. If you're in God's family, you now share *His* lineage. Let the enormity of this truth fill you up with love today: You are a child of God.

 **ROMANS 8:1–17**

DAY 10: Return on Investment

During grad school, I worked two jobs and lived on a minuscule budget so I could pay off student debt. I had been lucky enough to live my entire life in the financial security provided by my parents, but now it was up to me to make ends meet, and I had the crappy apartment and empty wallet to prove it. In that season, when my resources were slim, I found it difficult to trust God with my finances, and it took some time for me to be willing to offer what I had to Him.

When our own resources are slim, it's tempting to believe that God's resources will run out too. We clutch our pocketbooks for fear that any generous contribution, however big or small, will leave us with less security. What I'm beginning to learn is that God honors our offerings, small as they may be, because He's less concerned with a dollar amount and more concerned with where our heart is. God doesn't need our money, our time, or our resources to have meaningful impact on this earth, but He does desire to partner with His children in pursuit of His purposes. Like the widow who donated two mites, we honor Him most when we hold our worldly possessions with loose hands, offering all we have to the glory of His name.

Has God been calling you to give generously of your money, time, or resources? God's not going to leave you high and dry. Instead, you can trust that He will provide and make abundant use of whatever offering you bring to the table. If there are any areas where you've held back bits of yourself or your resources, ask God how you can partner with Him to use what He's given you to the glory of His name. There's always a return on investments made to the kingdom, so hold fast to King Jesus and don't worry about the rest.

 **1 KINGS 17:8–16**

DAY 11: Bloom

One of my favorite sayings is "Bloom where you're planted." It means we should learn how to grow and thrive wherever we find ourselves, and it's a reminder to me that we always have the choice to make the most of our circumstances.

There have been periods of my life when I failed to bloom because I was waiting for a different season of life; times too, when my stubbornness, fear, or haughtiness prevented me from authentically engaging with the world around me. What I've learned is that we bloom when we're willing to do the hard work of digging in deep and stretching out our roots to absorb the goodness that is all around us. We don't grow by uprooting every time life gets hard, and we certainly can't make it someone else's job to water or nurture us; instead, we grow when we settle into the soil God has us in, trusting that He's better at tending to our lives than we are.

I think the harvest of a well-planted life is contentment. You may not be in that same soil forever, but don't you want to grow where you are anyway? Today, be okay with wherever God has you. You may not be where you thought you'd be or where you'd like to end up, but God has purpose for you right where you are; begin blooming into it.

 **JEREMIAH 29:11**

DAY 12: Staying for the Tailgate

Fall in the South means one thing: football. I began my tenure as a Southerner with little to no interest in football, but after I had my first taste of tailgating, I was all in. On game days, we load our cars with coolers and pompoms and folding lawn chairs, drive to the stadium, and set up our gear next to friends under big white tents where we share all sorts of delicious food together. Among tailgaters, there's an understanding that, although the game is the main event, the most delicious treats are always found at the tailgate.

Although Jesus is the main event of our faith, I wonder how often we miss out on His fullness because we never tap into a deeper experience of life in Him. We might miss out on spiritual gifts, words of encouragement, and manifestations of His presence here on earth, or we may dabble in His rest, peace, grace, and mercy without ever truly abiding in it. We'll never get to the end of Jesus, so if you find yourself in a relationship with Him that feels underwhelming or routine, ask Him to show you where He wants to draw you into more.

Do you sense that God may be leading you into a deeper relationship with Him? Like the spread at a good tailgate, God has wonderful, delightful things for you to taste and experience in Him, so dive in for the real thing.

 **EPHESIANS 3:14-19**

DAY 13: Hail Mary

My husband grew up cheering on his favorite football team, the Auburn Tigers. The first year we were married, Auburn had a terrific season, but one game will forever stand out in my mind. Auburn was playing the Georgia Bulldogs, and with a fourth down and thirty-six seconds remaining, our quarterback threw a massive Hail Mary pass that was accidentally deflected into the hands of his teammate. In an unbelievable, hold-your-breath kind of moment, the receiver carried the ball into the end zone, and Auburn took the lead to win the game. The stadium erupted with elation and disbelief, as everyone knew we had just witnessed something incredible.

We all throw our own versions of Hail Mary passes from time to time. Desperate times call for desperate measures, so when faced with difficult or treacherous circumstances, we do the unthinkable, whatever it takes, to get the ball into the right pair of hands. A story in the Bible describes a few good friends who bring a paralytic man to see Jesus. Jesus was speaking in a home so crowded with listeners that the group could not get near him. But the friends didn't let a traffic jam stop them. In an act of desperation, they carried their friend to the top of the house, cut a hole through the thatched roof, and lowered their friend into the room where Jesus was standing. It's a crazy story, an attempt to secure healing and provision, but the friends' big faith made room for big outcomes, and the paralytic was healed that day.

Desperate times call for Jesus, but everyday happenings do too. He's always a good pick for your team, because He's already gone up against everything we will face in our days on earth. We don't have to wait for a critical or hopeless situation to become desperate for Jesus; instead, ask God to make you hungry for Him, desperate now for an encounter with the King of creation. He has beautiful things in store for your big acts of faith, so welcome Him to work wonders in your life today.

 **MARK 2:1–12**

DAY 14: Bacon–Pepper Jelly Pinwheels

I'm always looking for tasty finger foods to share with friends at various events, and Bacon–Pepper Jelly Pinwheels fit the bill for just about every one of them. Here, a simple, almost sconelike dough is filled with the Southern staples of bacon, pepper jelly, and cheddar cheese. For tailgates? Sure. For weekend brunch? You betcha. As an appetizer for a Friday-night cookout? You got it! Roll up your sleeves, find a few friends to share them with, and get baking!

....

BACON–PEPPER JELLY PINWHEELS

Makes 20

DOUGH

2½ cups all-purpose flour

1 tablespoon baking powder

1 tablespoon granulated sugar

¾ teaspoon table salt

½ teaspoon black pepper

½ cup chilled unsalted butter, cut into chunks

¾ cup plus 2 tablespoons chilled heavy whipping cream

1 chilled large egg

FILLING

6 tablespoons pepper jelly, divided

¾ cup shredded cheddar cheese

½ pound bacon, browned and finely chopped

TO PREPARE THE DOUGH

Preheat the oven to 375°F. Line a sheet pan with parchment paper.

In a large bowl, combine the flour, baking powder, sugar, salt, and pepper. Use a pastry cutter or the back of two forks to cut the butter into the dry ingredients until pea-size clumps are present throughout and the butter is well integrated. In a separate bowl, whisk the whipping cream and egg together. Pour the liquid ingredients into the dry ingredients and stir together until a shaggy dough forms. Dump the mixture onto a floured counter and work it together until a dry dough forms, being careful not to overwork it. Cover the dough with a tea towel while you prep the other ingredients, but don't let it sit out more than 15 minutes.

TO PREPARE THE PINWHEELS

When ready to bake, roll the dough out on a lightly floured surface into an 8 × 20-inch rectangle, about 1/8-inch thick. Use an offset spatula to spread 4 tablespoons of the pepper jelly evenly over the dough. Sprinkle evenly with the cheese and finely chopped bacon. Starting with the longest end closest to you, begin to roll the dough somewhat tightly away from you until the roll is complete. Pinch to seal the seam along the length and turn the log so the seam is on the bottom. Slice the log into 1/2-inch rounds and arrange them on the sheet pan. Bake until the crust is golden brown, usually about 20 minutes, depending on the size of your rolls.

In the meantime, combine the remaining 2 tablespoons of pepper jelly with 1 1/2 tablespoons of water in a small saucepan on the stove on low heat, until water and pepper jelly are gently warmed so the mixture can be brushed on. When the pinwheels are done, use a silicone basting brush to lightly brush the pepper jelly mixture onto the top of each pastry. Allow them to cool slightly before consuming them. The rolls are best eaten the day they're prepared, but can be reheated the following day.

DAY 15: Unseen Things

Fall in Alabama is beautiful, but the weather can be unpredictable. Last year, my daughter insisted on carving faces into a few oversize pumpkins, so we spent an hour in the sun, cutting toothy smiles and scooping out the sticky, seedy insides from each one. We were pleased with our efforts, but less than two days later our pumpkins were soft and sagging, having rotted in the heat of the sun. We were so disappointed.

Our pumpkins were a silly reminder that few things last forever. The Bible reminds us that the things of this earth will pass away, and when it's all said and done, only God's truth will remain (Matt. 24:35). Most of us spend our time engrossed in the here and now, but God has called us to fix our eyes on Him (2 Cor. 4:18) and to take part in conversations and acts and gifts that offer eternal value.

I'd like to grow into a person who invests the majority of her heart and time on things that will outlive this world. If that's you too, take some time today to consider how you spend your time and where you might be able to realign parts of your life to serve God's purposes. If you find yourself in a place where your priorities primarily have a temporary impact, ask God to expand your desires to meet His. You have access to beautiful, holy things on this side of heaven, and God desires for you to get a taste of them, even now.

 **MATTHEW 6:19-20**

DAY 16: Going for It

I recently traveled out west for a ski trip with friends. To say I was a train wreck is an understatement, and I have really embarrassing video footage to back it up. It took about four lessons for me to be comfortable on the same slopes my five-year-old was skiing, but as pathetic as that sounds, I was really proud to have tried. Sure, it wasn't pretty, but I silenced my fear long enough to do something I didn't think I could and, honestly, sometimes that's enough.

Although it's okay to stay in your wheelhouse and plug away at whatever your gifts are, it's also incredibly fulfilling to step out of your comfort zone and into something new. It offers the chance to learn from someone else and to persevere under the weight of a challenge. In those moments when you succeed, even if it's as small as skiing the beginner hill, something changes—you're bolstered with a confidence to do more, press in, or risk it with something new, and that accomplishment readies you for the future mountains you might face.

Is there something you've been curious about trying? A skill or activity you've longed to attempt but never had the chance? Remember that there is often breakthrough and reward on the other side of fear. God loves to see us persevere and stretch to experience His world in new and fresh ways, so don't hesitate—go for it.

 **JOSHUA 1:7–9**

DAY 17: # Daughter

For the majority of my Christian life, I viewed God from the vantage point of a servant. Sure, there was love, gratitude, and a healthy dose of fear mixed in, but mostly I felt indebted to Him. There was recognition, but no relationship. I honored Him, but there was little joy.

Then, about seven years ago, my eyes were opened to who I was in Christ. For the first time, I experienced God as a Father who loves His daughter, and it changed my identity. I was beloved. Chosen and adored. For years, I had groveled on my knees like a servant, and when I finally crawled onto His lap and experienced His love in a face-to-face, so-real-it's-almost-tangible kind of way, it changed my heart forever.

I still fear the Lord and desire to honor Him with my life, but most of all I want to be His friend. I want to experience His love in deep and intimate ways and receive His fatherly blessings. So what about you? Have you met Jesus as daughter? Does your relationship with Him reflect the intimacy that His heart so desires? Today, let the truth of God's love sink deep into your heart, and know His deepest desire is for you to love Him back.

 **JOHN 15:15; ROMANS 8:12-17**

DAY 18: Proud of Progress

You know how, at fancy hotels and restaurants, they always ask you if you're there to celebrate? Don't tell anyone, but I usually make up an occasion, even if there's no actual one, because I really like the special treatment. Please, just give me *all* the candlelit desserts and champagne toasts.

As fun as it is to celebrate the big occasions, I'm finding there are plenty of opportunities to honor the moments in between too. Stopping to acknowledge where we are right now allows us to be proud of ourselves and offer gratitude for how far we've come. Even in more difficult seasons of life, I find it encouraging to celebrate the fact that I'm still in the fight, in pursuit, and in motion. A friend of mine recently shared a quote that I think is fitting: "What a good day to be proud of all the progress I've made." Isn't that the truth? We're always progressing, always in process, and our perseverance is certainly worth celebrating.

Don't wait for the end zone, the finish line, or the big milestone event to celebrate; instead, put your chin up and honor your efforts right where you are. Take pride in how far you've come and the work God is doing in and through your life, remembering that any road you follow Jesus down is bound to lead to victory. You can trust Him with your process today and every step along the way.

 **PHILIPPIANS 2:12–13**

DAY 19: Celebrating Everything

A few years ago, I started making a conscious effort to celebrate more frequently. I had grown tired of waiting for another birthday or wedding and decided there was no time like the present. I'd pull out the tinsel and balloons every chance I got to revel with my family and friends.

God is the source of every good gift in our lives, and I really believe He is honored when we take time to celebrate them. Maybe it's a new child, a career change, or your last day of school; maybe you're celebrating recovery, a fresh start, or a new friendship. God's goodness doesn't always come with fanfare, but it's always there, and I believe He's honored when we make a point of seeking out opportunities to recognize the rich, beautiful blessings He has written into our story.

The opportunity to share love and appreciation for life's treasures and triumphs is a gift that is available for all of us. Your version of a celebration may look different from mine, but honoring those moments with gratitude and fun is a decision you won't regret. Where is God working overtime in your story? Take some time to thank Him for the amazing gifts in your life, and make a point of celebrating those things this week.

 **PSALM 105:1–3**

DAY 20: He Exceeds My Expectations

Early on in motherhood, I had grandiose expectations for dinnertime. I envisioned the supper table as a place of connection and love and togetherness, and because I worked hard to make meals that I was proud of, I assumed they would be welcomed by my kids with appreciation and enjoyment.

Wrong. Instead of a peaceful wonderland, dinnertime with my kids turns into a full-blown assassination of this mother's morale, as not one but three pairs of eyes stare at their dinner with despair. There's no cafeteria mystery meat on the table either, just a simple meal of what I wrongfully assumed were dinnertime basics—broccoli, chicken, and quinoa. During the torturous minutes that follow, Aimee goes to time-out twice and has to be hand-fed broccoli florets in order for her to consume her second and third bites. The floor around George's and Charlie's chairs is covered with food, a million little quinoa granules that someone (read: me) will have to clean up after suffering through this godforsaken meal.

Friend, we can't count on every meal being a peaceful one. We won't always have the cooperation of toddlers, spouses, or despondent teenagers, but we *can* always rely on a good God. He is our peace, our hope, our joy, and our sustenance at all times. Things and people of this world, sometimes *especially* the ones we love the most, will let us down, but He is always true to His word. He's the God of exceeding expectations, always doing abundantly more with whatever it is we bring to the table, so today when you're grasping for a bit of peace, you can start with Him.

 **EPHESIANS 3:20-21**

DAY 21: Cheddar Cornmeal Chicken Pot Pie

My friend Lauren and I have a saying about our country-boy husbands: they're easy to please, but impossible to impress. So when our husbands went for seconds on this Cheddar Cornmeal Chicken Pot Pie I knew I'd hit gold. Since then, this dish has become legendary in both of our homes.

....

CHEDDAR CORNMEAL CHICKEN POT PIE

Serves 4 to 5

CRUST

1 cup all-purpose flour

1/2 cup cornmeal

1 teaspoon granulated sugar

3/4 teaspoon table salt

1/2 teaspoon black pepper

1/4 teaspoon dried rosemary

1/4 teaspoon dried thyme

1/4 teaspoon garlic powder

1/4 teaspoon onion powder

6 tablespoons chilled unsalted butter, cubed

1/3 cup chilled shortening, cubed

1 cup shredded cheddar cheese

4 tablespoons ice water,
   plus more if needed

FILLING

6 tablespoons unsalted butter

1 1/2 cups chopped yellow onion
   (from 1 large onion)

6 tablespoons all-purpose flour

2 1/2 cups chicken stock

1 chicken bouillon cube

3 1/2 cups diced or shredded cooked
   chicken (I prefer breast meat)

1 cup (1/2-inch) diced carrots

1 cup frozen peas

1/3 cup fresh parsley leaves, minced

Salt and pepper

1 large egg

TO PREPARE THE CRUST

In the bowl of a food processor, pulse together the flour, cornmeal, sugar, salt, pepper, rosemary, thyme, garlic powder, and onion powder for about 30 seconds. Add the butter and shortening and pulse until marble-size clumps form. Add the cheese and pulse a few more times until well combined, with pea-size clumps throughout. Add 2 tablespoons of the ice water and pulse until the dough begins to come together in chunks, adding 1 to 2 additional tablespoons of water as needed and being careful not to overprocess. Dump the dough crumbles out onto the counter and form them into a round, flat disk. Cover it in plastic wrap and chill it in the fridge for at least 1 hour or up to three days.

TO PREPARE THE FILLING

Preheat the oven to 375°F. In a large Dutch oven or pot, melt the butter and add the onions. Cook over medium heat, stirring frequently, until the onions are translucent, about 8 minutes. Add the flour and cook for 2 minutes, stirring all the while. Add the chicken stock and bouillon cube and continue to cook and stir for an additional minute. Once the sauce has thickened, add the chicken, carrots, peas, parsley, 1 teaspoon salt, and $\frac{1}{2}$ teaspoon pepper. Mix well.

TO PREPARE THE POT PIE

Pour the pot-pie filling into a deep-dish pie pan or large cast-iron skillet that the pot pie can nearly fill to capacity. If desired, whisk the egg with a tablespoon of water and brush the mixture on the lip of the pan; this will help the pot-pie crust to stick to the pan.

On a floured surface, roll the crust out until it is 2 inches wider on all sides than the size of the pan. The dough may be challenging to work with; be sure to keep your surface and rolling pin well floured to prevent the dough from sticking. Roll the dough loosely back onto the rolling pin and then gently unroll it back out on top of the pan. Trim the edges and crimp them as desired. Brush the top of the pie with the egg wash and cut a few vent slits on the top.

Place the dish on a sheet pan and bake for about 1 hour, or until the top is golden brown and the filling is bubbling underneath. If the crust or edges are browning too fast, before the filling is bubbling, cover loosely with a piece of foil. Allow the dish to rest for about 20 to 30 minutes before serving.

DAY 22: Serving Love

My friend Catherine is the picture of hospitality. She's the kind of person who works tirelessly behind the scenes to make sure there's a seat and a plate for everyone she welcomes into her home, and her kitchen is like a revolving door of shared meals and care and love.

When I try to pinpoint what exactly it is about her that feels so special, I think less about the casseroles and charcuterie boards and more about the love. With Catherine, I'm rarely just receiving the physical nourishment of a warm meal—I'm being filled from the inside out, because she serves in a way that lets people know she cares. Cooking and entertaining are certainly her gifts, but it's the kindness with which she welcomes people into her home that really fills the hearts of her guests.

You don't have to have a fancy kitchen or serious cooking skills to host a feast. You just need some real-deal love and the intentionality to serve it abundantly. Ask God to highlight some ways you can offer care and kindness to the people in your life. You can worry less about the menu and more about making people feel seen, heard, and welcome. Jesus has equipped you to love, and that's basically all you need to be a terrific host.

 **ROMANS 12:9-13**

DAY 23: Aging Well

Thirty is such a milestone birthday. In the days leading up to my big three-oh, people insinuated that the passing of my twenties meant I was on some kind of a downhill slope leading to a monotonous future of dentures and knee replacements. I gotta say, I totally disagree. Turning thirty meant the end of a decade, sure, but it was certainly not the end of life as I know it.

For me, every birthday beyond thirty has nudged me to dust off the bits of myself that I was too busy or insecure to embrace in my twenties. Now older, more settled, and confident in my own skin, I've been able to flourish in a way that the twenty-year-old me simply could not. I'm learning other things as I grow older too, like how to be patient in uncertainty and to expect the unexpected from life, how to relish in the highs and steady myself through the lows. Rather than looking at aging as life's inevitable decline, I see getting older as something more like accumulating another year's worth of wisdom and experience to treasure for years to come.

In Isaiah, God promises to lead His children until their hair is white with age (46:4). Although I'm far from being fully white-haired today, I know I can rest wherever I find myself along life's road, because God is the One leading me. Take time to thank God for the days He wrote into your story. Ask Him to drum up excitement for the years to come, and know that each one is an opportunity for time spent in Jesus's presence.

 **2 CORINTHIANS 4:16–18**

DAY 24: Cake for Breakfast

Growing up, I used to love the birthday tradition my mom started of letting us enjoy leftover cake for breakfast on the morning after our birthday. You can imagine the look of shock on my friends' faces when we saddled up for a slumber-party breakfast of cinnamon rolls and Funfetti cake. For a group of thirteen-year-old girls, this might as well have been Christmas morning! At the time, I thought she was the coolest mom for allowing it, but now I'm pretty sure she just wanted cake for breakfast too.

Mom was never one to throw lots of birthday gatherings or dinner parties, but she's always been terrific at making people feel special. She loves big and is quick to honor others with encouragement and affirmation. Her small but intentional acts of love and fun, like those slices of breakfast birthday cake, forged tradition, relationship, and joy, and looking back on those years at home, I'm so grateful.

We don't always need invitations and party hats and balloons—we just need intentionality and a generous heart. Jesus had a way of sharing his love through ordinary measures too, by opening His arms to the unloved and joining the broken where they felt comfortable. If there is someone in your world who needs extra love, don't wait for a birthday or a special occasion to make them feel valued—today is just as good as any. Ask God to show you who might need to experience His love through you, and go after it—celebrate them big.

 **1 JOHN 4:7–8**

DAY 25: Secret Ingredient

On cooler days, there's a soup I love to make with creamy wild rice, kale, and bits of sweet potato. It's comforting and filling in all the right ways, a recipe that's become a staple I revisit again and again. One evening, on a whim, I added curry powder to the recipe, and the contents of the pot were transformed. Those once subtle flavors exploded to life with spice, heat, and color, and an entirely new dish to enjoy in that season was born.

Life with Jesus is kind of similar. He's like the secret ingredient that transforms ordinary people into rich vessels brimming with uniqueness and nuance and possibility. Even the smallest bit of His presence can bring ordinary people, gifts, and stories to life in new and vibrant ways. When the Psalmist wrote, *Oh, taste and see that the Lord is good* (34:8), I really think he meant it—when we smell and sip and fully consume the presence of God in our lives, we experience how powerful and rich His love really is. One taste of His presence and we're changed—there's no going back to a bland existence.

A life flavored with Christ is exciting, always full of hope and joy. If there are areas of your life that lack the rich, live-giving flavor of heaven, ask God to show you how to invite Him in and ask Him to season your relationships, work, mind, and home in new and creative ways. Then can carry those tastes and aromas with you, sharing the delight and comfort of His love with the world.

 JOHN 8:12

DAY 26: Telling Your Story

There's a running joke about food bloggers and the storytelling that frequents their posts. You might be looking for a simple pie recipe and end up finding yourself twenty-five hundred words deep in a flashback from the blogger's childhood, all written in unnecessarily poetic prose. I'll admit—I'm totally guilty of this. I've shared far too much on the internet, not because I'm just dying to spill my guts, but because for me, and for many of us, the food and stories of our lives are so interconnected that there's no distinguishing the flavors and textures of those bites from the very moments themselves.

We all tell our stories in our own way. For me, making certain recipes feels like an ode to the memorable moments of my life; you may tell your story in a different way. Whether through food, art, words, or songs, I want to encourage you to share your story. Tell people who you are and where you've been. Use your passions to bring salt and light to a seriously hungry world.

Today, consider what stories you have to tell. How can you honor a loved one, a treasured memory, or a cause with your gifts? What life experiences would serve as encouragement to a world in need? Your story is unique and is entirely yours to tell, so ask God how you can let His Son shine bright by sharing it with the world today.

 **2 CORINTHIANS 9:6–15**

DAY 27: On Following Recipes

My mother-in-law makes a mean lasagna, one that is so good she's become known for it in our family. She also makes terrific pot roasts, sausage pinwheels, and basically anything that's loaded with meat and butter. I've asked her for recipes a number of times, and her response is always the same: "I don't really have a set recipe." Like many women in the South, Pam learned the old-school way by watching and listening to the older women in the kitchen beside her. There's no referencing recipes or precise measuring, just a little of this and a little of that.

I want to encourage you to embrace this same kind of freedom in other areas of life. Some of us have gotten comfortable allowing societal norms and widely accepted recipes for living to dictate even the minute details of our story: *Where should I go to school? How should I dress? When should I start a family? How should I spend my time, my efforts, or my money?*

The truth is, there's no standardized recipe for success, and if we're always looking to the opinions and choices of our peers as some sort of benchmark for living, we risk overlooking what God is doing in our lives individually. Instead of looking to others, we can simply look to God: *"Father, what do you have for me in this season of life? What are the hopes and plans you have for me? How can I use my gifts and love to serve you?"*

Sure, there's no magic formula or recipe for living a good life, but we can get pretty close to it by following Jesus. Today, if there areas of your life where you need to let go of the world's standards and listen more closely to what Jesus says about you, ask Him to show you how to release that to Him. Take time to listen to what God has to say about who you are and the life you're living, and let Him decide what comes next. When Jesus is the One at work in your life, you can rest knowing that you're well on your way to something wonderful.

 **GENESIS 28:15, ECCLESIASTES 3:10–14**

DAY 28: Weeknight Spaghetti Sauce

This is a rendition of the weeknight spaghetti sauce my mother-in-law, Pam, uses in her famous lasagna. Her original recipe is terrific as is, but would I really be a normal woman if I didn't try to rebel against my mother-in-law and tweak the recipe, even just a little? Nope.

Pam says this was a go-to recipe when her kids were growing up. If more friends or neighbors showed up during dinnertime, she just added a little more water to the sauce and pulled up an extra chair. I think this is how Jesus intended community to look—everyone is welcome and there's more than enough to go around.

....

WEEKNIGHT SPAGHETTI SAUCE

Makes 2 quarts

1 tablespoon olive oil

1 pound ground sirloin

1 pound ground mild Italian sausage

2 (14.5-ounce) cans Italian diced
    tomatoes, undrained

2 (6-ounce) cans tomato paste

1 cup water

¼ cup unsalted butter

2 bay leaves

2 tablespoons Italian seasoning

2 tablespoons Worcestershire

1 tablespoon granulated sugar

1½ teaspoons kosher salt

2 teaspoons black pepper

In a large Dutch oven or heavy-bottomed saucepan, heat the olive oil on medium. Add the beef and sausage and brown them, stirring and breaking up the meat often. Once browned, carefully drain the fat. Add the tomatoes, tomato paste, water, butter, bay leaves, Italian seasoning, Worcestershire, sugar, salt, and pepper, and stir. Bring the mixture to a low boil, then reduce the heat to low, and simmer for an additional 30 minutes. Add salt and pepper to taste, or a bit of water to thin it out as desired.

DAY 29: Free from Fear

When I was a kid, I was terrified of the dark, but that's long been a thing of the past. But now, as an adult, I find myself faced with other fears that creep in with the night—lies about my identity, my purpose, and the health and future of my family. The enemy whispers that I'm not a good mother, that I'm too much for my husband, or that my work has no value. It's a different kind of darkness, but the fear I experience in those moments can be just as paralyzing.

At his core, the enemy is a ruthless liar who will capitalize on our weaknesses and fears to distract us from the truth. Thankfully, 2 Thessalonians 3:3 says, *The Lord is faithful, and He will strengthen you and protect you from the evil one* (NIV). We aren't left to fend off the enemy on our own, because we stand united with the One who already has victory over the scariest places in our lives. We abide in His ability and trust in Him, knowing that He is advancing on our behalf.

If there are places where fear and darkness have become overwhelming, you can rest assured that God is with you. When you find yourself believing lies from the evil one, run to the Lord, who always leads in truth. Jesus is bigger than fear and death themselves, so rest in the promises of Psalm 91:4–5: *He will cover you with his pinions, and under his wings you will find refuge; his faithfulness is a shield and buckler. You will not fear the terror of the night, nor the arrow that flies by day.*

 **PSALM 115:11; LAMENTATIONS 3:57**

DAY 30: Your Failures Don't Make *You* a Failure

People ask me all the time if I ever have any kitchen failures. Let's just LOL at that one. I could tell hours of stories about soupy pies, dry cakes, and loaves of sandwich bread as flat as pancakes. There's no shortage of spilled ingredients, burned sugar on the bottom of the oven, or greasy, spread-out cookies. As with any craft, mishaps are a real thing. Absolutely no one is excluded from mess-ups.

We should expect the same in life. Failure is a natural part of our world, yet most of us tend to see every failure as a closed door, a setback, or a sign that maybe this isn't God's plan for us. Why are we so hard on ourselves when our plans and efforts flop? Wouldn't a little grace go a long way here?

Sometimes failure isn't as big and terrible as we make it. Just as a failure in one of my recipes teaches me how to try again next time, failure in life can nudge us toward a better plan, and the act of dusting ourselves off develops perseverance. The enemy wants us to feel embarrassed and ashamed about our failures, but God just wants to use them to sharpen us. He wants us to learn and grow and do things even bigger and better than we initially may have dreamed.

Today I want to remind you not to be so hard on yourself. Your failures don't make you a failure. When the efforts of your hands, heart, and mind don't go as you planned, lift your head, make another plan, and try again. Ask God to use your flops for His glory, and He will. He'll have you diving into something better in no time.

PSALM 3:3; 37:23-24

DAY 31: Coffee Chats

When my mom comes to town and stays with us, I wake up extra early, excited to share that first cup of coffee with a friend. I tiptoe out to the kitchen and quietly start preparing coffee, willing my eyes and mind to awaken as the ground beans brew. Without fail, Mom usually emerges about the same time, and we plop ourselves in a pair of overstuffed chairs, warm mugs in hand, for a few moments of conversation before the day begins.

I always look forward to those mornings, knowing that during that conversation time I'll be met with love. As I've gotten older, my mom has slowly become a dear friend, a trusted confidante, and source of wisdom, and in those minutes before sunrise when it's just her and me, there's an unspoken exchange of support and love and vulnerability.

I imagine this is the kind of relationship God has in mind for us too. I envision Him sitting in His chair, waiting to meet us, waiting for us to awaken to His offering of love and connection. He delights in exchanging stories, speaking wisdom to our hearts, and offering us the fullness of His affection, right there in our everyday life. In the pursuit of more knowledge, more spiritual growth, and more church activities, sometimes I forget that, at the heart of it, He's just looking for relationship. He just wants us to come to Him.

When is the best time of day for you to connect with God? Set aside those minutes for Him and come expectant, ready to meet Him face-to-face as if He's joining you for morning coffee. You don't need to clean up or prepare for that time with Him; just come as you are and participate in that relationship.

 **MATTHEW 6:6; JAMES 4:8**

DAY 1: Counting Votes

I can remember the first time I walked into a voting booth. It was 2008, the first year I was old enough to vote in the presidential election, and I was thrilled to have a seat at the table. I could vote! Take a stand! Fight for the causes in my heart! For the first time, I believed in the beauty of democracy, a framework in which every voice is counted and we all have an equal opportunity to cast ballots according to our beliefs, ideas, and opinions.

I still appreciate democracy when it comes to our nation, but I'm increasingly glad that it's not how things work in the kingdom of heaven. Instead of a democracy, we exist as the Body of Christ, a family made up of individual members who are submitted to the authority and love of a Heavenly Father (Eph. 2:19). God *always* has the final say about His creation. The people of this world don't get to cast their ballots about us, telling us who we are and who we can be, mapping out the boundaries of our hopes and dreams, because the only word that counts is His.

So who does He say you are? He calls you forgiven (1 John 2:12), valuable (John 3:16), and full of power and love (2 Tim. 1:7). God calls you daughter (Eph. 1:5), and says your future is full of hope (Jer. 29:11), joy (John 15:11), and peace (John 14:27). The Father's heart for you has been written all throughout scripture, and we have been welcomed to shake off any untruth that doesn't line up with His Word.

Have you been letting the world tell you who you are or what you'll amount to in this life? Instead, look to the Father, the One who has authority over everything in heaven and on earth (Matt. 28:18), to tell you who you are. His vote is the only one that counts, and you can rest in His love today.

 **PHILIPPIANS 3:20**

DAY 2: Flours for You

When I experienced Southern hospitality for the first time, it truly rocked my world. I couldn't understand why people would extend themselves with such intentionality and kindness, looking for absolutely nothing in return. Although I learned that hospitality comes in many shapes and forms, my favorite version, hands down, is anything involving food. It goes like this: "You had a baby? Here's a casserole!" "It's your birthday? I made you cookies!" "Have the sniffles? Let me bring you soup!" In the South, we basically pass around each other's Pyrex and Tupperware, refilling it to celebrate and serve each other whenever possible. If you've been on the receiving end of this, you know that it's a beautiful thing.

I'm realizing that hospitality is rarely just a means of service—it's an act of love too. A batch of muffins or a homemade loaf of bread doesn't just serve as physical nourishment—it fills the friend's heart too. Going out of your way to honor, care for, and serve people, even if it's just with a warm casserole or a glass of tea, lets them know they're valued and worthy of your time.

Now when I want to honor the people in my life, instead of giving flowers, I give out *flours*—cinnamon rolls, biscuits, or whatever else happens to be in my oven. I'd encourage you to consider what hospitality might look like in your own life. A meal? A phone call? An afternoon walk or playdate with your kids? Honor God by sharing your love and warmth with the people in your lives, and let those offerings speak for themselves.

 **HEBREWS 13:1-2**

DAY 3: Not Settling for Artificial

My husband is notorious for his love of pudding packs. I'm talking the processed, store-bought ones that your mom probably put in your lunchbox a million years ago. He licks the plastic wrappers on every top and scrapes the sides so he can consume each and every last bite. This is how I know God has a sense of humor—a food blogger being married to the Snack Pack guy is some kind of a joke.

Knowing how much he loves it, I once made him homemade chocolate pudding, but was shocked to find that he still preferred the store-bought kind. All those years of consuming imitation pudding had engendered a preference for those familiar, artificial flavors, and my homemade variety couldn't hold a candle.

Sometimes we settle for artificial pleasures because it's what we know. God has really good gifts for us, things like grace, love, joy, peace, and truth, but we often become distracted by imitations of those gifts, settling for worldly versions that won't last or satisfy. An encounter with God's brand of love looks, tastes, and feels different from what the world offers, and, unlike the imitation satisfaction we find in money, possessions, social media, and unhealthy relationships, His love is nourishing, whole, and everlasting.

Eat your pudding pack, if you'd like. No one here is knocking a boxed cake mix or instant gravy or imitation butter. But don't settle when it comes to Jesus. If there are places in your life where you've settled for treasures of this world, ask God for a genuine encounter with His love and grace and mercy instead. Once you've experienced love from Him, you'll never be satisfied with any less.

 **2 CORINTHIANS 4:18**

DAY 4: Bourbon Old Fashioneds

My husband doesn't spend much time in the kitchen, but what he does, he does well. A clear winner in our home is the Bourbon Old Fashioned cocktail, always made with Kentucky bourbon and served with a large cube of ice. We order Old Fashioneds everywhere we go, but I prefer the ones at home—slightly sweeter and a bit more drinkable for a casual night in our pj's.

....

BOURBON OLD FASHIONEDS

Serves 2

SIMPLE SYRUP

(Makes 6 Ounces)

½ cup sugar

½ cup water

COCKTAILS

2 orange peel twists

4 dashes orange bitters

4 ounces Kentucky bourbon

1 ounce simple syrup

2 Luxardo or bourbon-soaked cherries

2 giant ice balls/cubes

Splash of club soda (optional)

TO PREPARE THE SIMPLE SYRUP

Combine the sugar and water in a small saucepan over medium heat. Stir with a whisk until the sugar is dissolved and then place the mixture in a small jar or heat-proof container to cool in the fridge. This can be made ahead and kept in the fridge for up to two weeks.

TO PREPARE THE COCKTAILS

Place a single orange peel in each of two lowball glasses and add 2 dashes of bitters to each. Gently muddle the peel and bitters together to allow the orange peel to release its oil. Add 2 ounces of bourbon, ½ ounce of simple syrup, and 1 cherry to each glass, stirring to combine. Carefully drop an ice ball into each glass and top with a splash of club soda, if desired.

DAY 5: Living for the Weekend

Before I became an adult, I lived for the weekend. Now, with a home and family and job to manage, I'm finding that the weekend is less of a reprieve from the work week and more like an extension of it. In adulthood, it doesn't matter what you accomplished Monday through Friday, because there are still groceries to buy, lawns to mow, and cars to clean. Instead of using them for rest, adulthood takes hostage those few hours of weekend solace and ransoms them for nine bags of raked leaves, a sink full of dishes, and few hours' worth of ironing.

Weekends with kids are even wilder, with zero free time and even less personal space. Kids aren't concerned about your rest because they want cereal. Kids want to go to the park. Kids want to unroll an entire roll of toilet paper and then poop their pants while you're in the middle of cleaning up the mess.

The point is, there's a good chance that at some point this coming weekend, you, as an adult, just might lose it. Unless you've found yourself on an all-inclusive vacay to the Bahamas, you're likely to end up with an annoying weekend task or a kid whose face has been colored on by a sibling. So here's a message of solidarity: you are not alone. I'm right there with you, many of your friends are probably right there with you, and guess what! God's in the midst of it all too, just as big and great and good in the mess as He is in the peace. Give Him your weekdays, your weekends, and whatever circumstances you find yourself in, knowing He is big and good enough to help you manage every bit of it.

 **1 THESSALONIANS 5:12–24**

DAY 6: Saying It Out Loud

My daughter went through a coloring phase, filling stacks of blank pages with rainbow drawings of birthday cakes and stick figures. I was proud of her artwork and told her so often, and after a few days of encouragement, she was calling herself an artist. Aimee made drawings for her brothers and teachers and babysitters, because she believed who I said she was and wanted to share her gift with other people.

As a mother, I spend a lot of time calling out the good characteristics in my children because I want them to feel empowered to let those parts shine. I want my daughter to eagerly befriend a new kid at school, because she's confident in the kindness she has to offer. I want my sons to be joyful, sprinkling the world with their silliness and laughter, because they know how clever and fun they are. In a world that screams ugliness and shame and doubt to anyone who will listen, I want my children to be saturated in the assurance of who they are and the beautiful things they have to contribute to this world. I call out the good, because I'm convinced that our words have so much power.

The Bible says our words have power and carry even more weight when they are rooted in God's truth. Today, spend time considering who needs your words, and ask God who He's put within your reach to encourage. Start by calling out their talents, their goodness, and the truth of their identity in Christ. Your words may be the push someone needs to rise up and into their calling, so don't hold back—say it out loud.

 **PROVERBS 12:18; 15:4**

DAY 7: Higher Ground

In college, my friends and I often took a late-night drive up a winding mountain road to stop at a lookout point at the top. From there, we could see our campus, the highway, and a million little streetlights that lit up the darkness below. We would build a fire and roast marshmallows, sometimes staying long enough to watch the sun come up. For a few hours, our lives and friendships felt distanced from the world that waited below, as if the elevation of our vantage point somehow broadened our perspective in a way we couldn't experience down there.

Sometimes we just need a change of perspective. I often forget how little I'm able to see and understand from my place here on earth, and all it takes is a late-night drive or a walk in someone else's shoes for me to remember that my take on life is not the full picture. God doesn't expect us, as humans, to understand it all on this side of heaven, but He has asked that we trust Him with patience and faith as He carries out His vision here on earth. When we're tempted to question, demand answers, or become fearful of the circumstances of our everyday life, we have to remember that God sees it all and has it under control.

As believers, we have the mind of Christ. We no longer are limited by the parameters of our old vantage point, because we are one with the One who is seated on high in heavenly places with the King of heaven. Friend, you can trust God in the places of your life that feel chaotic, uncertain, or just out of your own reach, because He is the only One with the total picture. Are there areas of your life you've been trying to grasp and control and discern with your own strength? Instead, remember who lives inside of you, and rely on His peace, His wisdom, and His strength to carry you to higher ground.

 **PROVERBS 2:1–15**

DAY 8: Essential Ingredients

I once served a cake with no sugar. It was a disaster of epic proportions, and it wasn't until after the cake had been baked, frosted, and sliced that I realized my mistake. The dark chocolate slices were bitter and dry, and although the cake looked beautiful, there was no redeeming the lingering taste of those off-flavors.

In baking, there's rarely a nonessential ingredient. Every teaspoon of sugar, flour, leavening, and salt plays a distinct role in the final outcome of the baked good. Sure, sometimes you can fudge the ingredients, adding a little more here, a little less there, but rarely can you simply omit whole ingredients, because each one serves its purpose.

Similarly, we all play a role in the Body of Christ. Each one of us has different gifts, functions, thoughts, and responsibilities, and we operate best when we each are doing our part, contributing in the way God has equipped us to serve our purpose.

Sister, I want you to know that you are an essential ingredient. You don't need a theology degree, a paid position, or a name tag to have value. God has uniquely equipped you to serve and love your church, family, and community in a way that will have meaningful impact, and if you'll open your heart and hands to do the job you are qualified for, He will most certainly make it count.

Today, ask Him where you fit into the equation, and consider some ways you can contribute your efforts to the glory of His name. Is it your time? Your talents? Your resources? Don't be left out of the final outcome—be a part of what He's doing in your world right now.

 **EPHESIANS 4:15–16**

DAY 9: Dwelling on the Positive

Sometimes it feels easier to dwell on the negative rather than believe the best about our circumstances. Missed opportunities, broken relationships, insecurities, and public mistakes are realities of this world, but God doesn't want our story to stop there. What if, in every failure and hopeless scenario, we were set on finding the good? What if we squinted and searched through the dark to find a glimmer of light that may have, even if only briefly, cast its warm glow on our story? Wouldn't it feel good to be reminded of the bright spots in our days?

The enemy will often try to stir up negative thoughts in order to take our eyes off God, but we can silence those feelings by speaking over them with gratitude. We can fix our hearts on seeing the goodness of God even when the temptation is to become discouraged by our circumstances.

Consider your own life. What would it look like to be thankful in all things? How can you position yourself to be thankful even in the hard, nitty-gritty of everyday life? How can you flood the negative spaces of your heart and mind with reminders of God's goodness and faithfulness?

Share some gratitude today. Thank God for the good days, and the hard ones, and everything in between. The God who gives the best gifts is the same One who promised to never leave or forsake you, so today open your eyes to His beauty in your life and make gratitude your offering to Him.

 PSALM 34

DAY 10: Food Tells a Story

A few years ago, I spent an afternoon making a pot of butternut squash soup with some friends, and now, whenever I pull out my Dutch oven to make it again, I'm instantly transported back to that first meal: chilled glasses, steaming bowls, and the savory scent of spice and crisped bacon. The soup was good, but it was the company that nourished my soul, and over the course of that hour spent at the table, butternut squash soup evolved from a dish that fed me physically into one that is now attached to the faces I shared it with.

Food has a way of melting and mixing into our stories, and when we bring those dishes to the table, we often bring our memories and experiences too. We all share in the universal language of food, but our individual stories are uniquely ours to tell, a dialect that speaks to the past, our relationships, and where we've been. By sharing those dishes and the words that come attached to them, we allow others to become fluent too, participating in the feelings and laughter and lessons they have to share.

When you invite people into your kitchen, don't miss the opportunity to welcome them more deeply into your life as well. You can use the food and minutes spent around the table as a segue into conversation and connection. Today, think back on some food memories that were special in your past—what comes to mind? Invite God to use those stories to create intimacy and love in your kitchen. Connect yourself to the people at your table, and remember, no one can tell your stories better than you; it's your opportunity to share them.

 **ECCLESIASTES 5:18-20**

Butternut Squash Soup

This Butternut Squash Soup tastes like all kinds of home to me. Creamy and fragrant, with herbs and cooked bacon, it's rich and comforting without being too heavy. We like to enjoy it alongside a fresh salad or warm buttered bread, both if you're feeling extra festive. In a pinch, you can substitute onion for the shallot and additional stock for the wine, but don't underestimate the flavor that both contribute. This soup sings with warm, savory notes, and you're going to want to relish each and every one of them.

....

BUTTERNUT SQUASH SOUP

Serves 4 as an entrée, 8 as a side

2 whole butternut squash, about 5 pounds total

2 tablespoons olive oil

Salt and pepper

6 slices of applewood smoked bacon, browned and chopped, fat reserved

1 cup chopped shallots (about 2 large shallots)

2 tablespoons unsalted butter

1 teaspoon dried thyme

½ teaspoon dried rosemary

4 cups low-sodium chicken stock

1 cup dry white wine, such as Pinot Grigio or Sauvignon Blanc

1 cup of whipping cream

Preheat the oven to 400°F. Line a rimmed baking sheet with foil and lightly grease it with cooking spray.

Carefully cut each squash lengthwise into two equal halves. Remove the seeds and lightly drizzle each half with olive oil. Sprinkle the flesh with salt and pepper and place each piece facedown on the baking sheet. Roast for about 45 minutes, or until the squash is tender. Allow it to cool enough to handle. When cool, use a spoon to scoop out the flesh, and set it aside.

Heat a large pot on medium-low. Cook the bacon until crisp, flipping as needed. Remove the bacon to a paper towel-lined plate and set aside it to cool. Add the chopped shallots and butter to the pot with the bacon fat and sprinkle with $1/2$ teaspoon salt and $1/4$ teaspoon pepper. Cook for about 3 minutes, or until the shallots are soft and fragrant. Add the garlic, thyme, and rosemary, and cook an additional minute. Add the squash, chicken stock, white wine, 2 teaspoons of salt, and $1/2$ teaspoon pepper. Stir to combine. Mash any large clumps of squash until broken up. Reduce the heat to medium and bring to a simmer, stirring occasionally.

Once simmering, remove the pot from the heat and stir in the cream. Carefully, puree the soup using an immersion blender or in batches using a standard blender. Once smooth, add salt and pepper to taste. Garnish the soup with chopped bacon bits and serve.

DAY 12: The Weight of Worth

Long before my drawers were filled with measuring cups and spoons, rulers and scales, I was an expert in comparing and measuring myself against other people. *Am I thin enough? Am I smart enough to get the job? Am I a good enough mother?* I carried my invisible scales to measure my appearance, personality, and worth against the people around me, who, more often than not, were completely unaware that this mental appraisal was happening. But, rest assured, there were measuring sticks for them too, and I'd tally up my disappointments and unmet expectations, the ways they failed to meet my impossible standards.

I'll be honest—I still struggle here. I often feel as though I'm somewhere on the short end of the measuring stick, where my allotment, my place, and my skills have always appeared small under the critical magnifying glass I view myself through. It's only been recently that I've realized how hurtful those assaults have been, both personally and relationally.

Sister, I want you to know how valuable you are. The weight of your worth was poured out in the precious blood of Jesus, and there just aren't scales fit for that kind of measure. He saw the sum of your days and said His life was worth that price, so who are we to compare?

Today, set aside the assessments you make about yourself and the judgments you've declared on others to ask God how He feels about you. Spend some time with Him, and ask Him to soften your heart toward any wounded areas that need healing. Thank Him for the price He paid and the value He put on your life. Instead of nitpicking about yourself or others, look at the world through *His* magnifying glass of love.

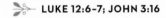 **LUKE 12:6-7; JOHN 3:16**

DAY 13: Remembering

I was in my husband's grandparents' home when I stumbled across an old box of recipes. The cards were yellowed and worn, smudged and stained from a lifetime of spills, and you could identify the ones that were well loved by their crumpled edges and faded writing. We brought the recipes home, where I made copies for a cookbook that we later shared with family members. I love to thumb through that book on occasion, even now, and it's powerful to think about the family who enjoyed meals from those recipes long ago.

It's good to remember. Old recipes, black-and-white photos, keepsakes, and handed-down treasures transport us back in time to recall the relationships, experiences, and words that shaped us. In the life of believers, remembering produces thankfulness, as we recall the promises of His word, knowing that what was true yesterday remains true today, tomorrow, and for all of eternity. Remembering produces hope, because we can rest in His promises, particularly when we recall past examples of how far He's carried us.

Don't forget the goodness of God in your life and the riches that are yours in Christ. Instead, remember who He's called you to be and the promises that are yours in Him. Fix your heart on His goodness and mercy, and let gratitude, hope, and humility prostrate you at His feet to continually experience His love forever and ever.

Today, spend some time remembering, and write down any signs of His love. Consider the big and small ways He has carried you and ask Him to bubble up reminders of His promises from years past. How has God proven to be true to His word in your life? Let the evidence of His love give you hope, thankfulness, and encouragement for the future.

 **1 CHRONICLES 16:8–18**

DAY 14: Making a List

During a time of the year when we're all supposed to be feeling extra thankful, can we just admit that some days it's easier said than done? Sure, gratitude comes easily in seasons of abundance, in weeks where joy and goodness overflow from the corners of your life and the glow of favor warms your heart and tends to your soul. But what about on harder days? What about in seasons of loss, when relationships are fractured, or when feelings of sadness overwhelm your mind? What about when any semblance of gratitude in your life exists only by means of necessity, as a last-ditch effort to remain afloat when you've been flooded with despair?

In 1 Thessalonians, Paul writes, *Rejoice always, pray without ceasing, and give thanks in all circumstances* (5:16–18), and I believe it's because, deep down, he recognized our human hearts required those constant reminders of God's grace in our lives. Without a metronome of gratitude ticking throughout our days, it's easy to lose track of our reasons for purpose and hope. Instead, a thankful heart positions us to recognize blessing in our lives, because our eyes and ears and hearts are open, looking for the evidence of goodness in our story. Gratitude shifts our perspective from the circumstances of the world to the loving-kindness of a God who causes everything to work for the good of those who love Him (Rom. 8:28).

In this season of giving thanks, make a list of your own, with one or ten or a hundred things that are worth appreciating. Know that it's okay if that list is a little shorter on some days than others, and you can submit your wanting heart to a God who desires to encourage and love you in difficult seasons. You have many reasons to be thankful, so seek them out this morning.

 **PSALM 95:1–3**

DAY 15: Bringing Nothing to the Table

On any given Friday night, when presented with an invitation to hang out with friends, the question from me is always the same: "What can I bring?" After all, rule number 236 in the unwritten handbook of Southern hospitality is that one never shows up empty-handed . . . ever. Even when I'm told to bring nothing, my brain is still searching, trying to decide upon a gesture, maybe a bottle of wine or a plate of appetizers, to share in exchange for my friends' generosity.

An offering of grace, whether from a friend, a family member, or even God, can be difficult to accept, and our human tendency will often be to try to reciprocate as a means of earning the kindness we've received. Do you ever feel this? Have you ever wondered how God could offer such kindness—the life and death of His Son, forgiveness of sins, an inheritance well outside of anything we could earn—for absolutely nothing in return? How could it be that grace requires *nothing* of us?

The Bible describes this grace as a gift (Rom. 3:23-24.) It's not something we've earned or are working for, not a gesture we've been offered based on our own merit or good behavior; it's a gift. It's ours to take and use, or not, but it will never require more than our faith. We just show up, empty-handed and undeserving, without a thing to bring to the table, and He welcomes us in because of grace. He loves us not because of what we can bring him, but simply because of who we are in Him.

Spend some time in prayer today, and let your mind wander to the millions of ways His grace has impacted your life. His grace requires nothing of us, but we can honor His gift with a sincere return of thankfulness. Return His goodness with gratitude, and let that thankfulness, the awareness of His love, bless you this week.

 **EPHESIANS 2:8-9**

DAY 16: Joy in the Presence

A few years ago, I went to Chicago with my nana, mom, and sister for seventy-two hours of shopping, sightseeing, and sampling delicious food. On our last evening, we dined at an amazing Italian restaurant and spent hours talking like best friends, laughing through stories to the point of tears. The evening was immediately immortalized in my mind as one of the best nights of my life, and I knew right then that no amount of tiramisu or Chicago skylines would ever be able to re-create the perfect intimacy we experienced in those minutes.

It's common to attach our memories to a place, possession, or phase of life and begin to believe that those things were the reason we were so happy. We think, *If I could just go back to Chicago*, or *If I could just be young again*, or *If only I had that same freedom*, as if our joy is fixed on the locations and circumstances of our lives. The truth is, the treasure in our memories is rarely the stuff or the setting; it is the people we shared it with and the joy we experienced in their presence.

Spending time with the Lord is no different, and the Bible says God's presence brings fullness of joy (Ps. 16:11). It's not where we are right now or the circumstances we find ourselves in that bring fulfillment, because, as believers, we have the opportunity to stay connected to that joy in every setting and season of our lives by abiding in Him. The temporary things of this world may point us to a good and generous Father, but the treasures worth holding on to are always found in Him.

Are there places in your heart that need to rest more fully in the joy of the Lord? Have you found yourself longing for things that, deep down, you know won't truly satisfy? Set your eyes on the eternal, seeking first the kingdom of God, and all the rest will fall into place.

 **LUKE 12:32-34**

DAY 17: # When Love Is on the Menu

Anytime we invite a large crew over for dinner, everyone ends up in the kitchen. It doesn't matter if a game is on the television, the kids are outside, or if an entire tray of appetizers is waiting in the living room—people want to be where the action is. The kitchen is the hub, the place where smells and heat and flavors collide with laughter and the steady hum of conversation, the place where relationships and bodies are nourished by bites and sips and love.

For a long time, I felt the pressure to put on a show every time someone came over, as if a parade of colorful cocktails and warm appetizers was the selling point for spending time in our home, but I'm learning that people care less about the food and more about being loved. Some of my most prized evenings happened over packaged cheese straws and an okay bottle of wine, because our hearts aren't impacted by a set stage—they're transformed by true connection.

During this season when many of us are enjoying parties, meals, and shared tables, remember that love is the most valuable thing you can serve. The food and décor and background music are fun, but best when there's love there too. Is there a way you can better sow love into your relationships this season? Ask God to show you ways to create space for meaningful connection, in your home and in the homes of others, and take the pressure off everything else.

 **PHILIPPIANS 2:1–4**

DAY 18: Shrimp Cocktail

A shrimp cocktail was my parents' appetizer of choice when I was a kid, but this rendition is my favorite. The shrimp are cooked in water that is spiced with black peppercorns and bay leaves. Once done, they are chilled in a saltwater bath until ice-cold.

....

SHRIMP COCKTAIL

Serves 8 as an appetizer

COCKTAIL SAUCE

½ cup ketchup

¾ teaspoon Worcestershire sauce

1½ tablespoons fresh lemon juice

¼ teaspoon Old Bay Seasoning

2½ tablespoons prepared horseradish sauce

Pinch of table salt and pepper

SHRIMP

4 quarts cold water, divided

Ice

Peel and juice of 1 lemon

¼ cup plus 3 tablespoons
   coarse kosher salt, divided

2 pounds jumbo shrimp, peeled
   and deveined, tails left on

1 tablespoon black peppercorns

3 bay leaves

½ teaspoon celery seeds

½ teaspoon dried thyme

TO PREPARE THE COCKTAIL SAUCE

Combine the ketchup, Worcestershire, lemon juice, Old Bay seasoning, horseradish, salt, and pepper in a medium-size bowl. Taste, and add extra horseradish a ½ teaspoon at a time for more heat, or extra lemon juice, as preferred. Tightly wrap the sauce and keep it in the fridge until ready to serve, up to three days in advance.

TO PREPARE THE SHRIMP

Start by preparing the ice bath. Fill a large bowl with 3 quarts cold water and ice. Add the lemon juice and peel and ¼ cup salt. Mix, and set aside.

Combine 4 cups cold water, the shrimp, 3 tablespoons salt, the peppercorns, bay leaves, celery seeds, and thyme in a medium-size pot. Set the pot over medium heat and stir frequently until the shrimp are done, about 6 to 7 minutes total. You'll notice the shrimp go from gray to opaque white with pink spots and pink tails. The shrimp will barely curl. Once there are no more translucent or gray spots, the shrimp are about done—do not overcook!

Quickly dump the shrimp into a strainer, drain, and put them into the prepared ice bath. Stir frequently to cool them completely, about 10 minutes, and then remove them to a plate lined with a paper towels. Tightly cover and place the plate in the fridge to cool for at least 2 or up to 8 hours. Serve with the cocktail sauce.

DAY 19: # Redeeming the Past

My mom grew up with three sisters on a farm in rural Michigan. Sun or rain, sleet or snow, the girls would go out each morning to complete their chores before breakfast. They fed pigs, milked animals, and let the chickens out, and when they finished, they went back inside for a breakfast that was always accompanied by a glass of warm goat milk. Yes—*warm*. To this day, my mom refuses any dish made with goat cheese, because the reminder of those breakfasts, the lingering taste she found entirely unpalatable, is something she simply cannot stomach.

It's an unpleasant memory for my mom, but many of us have pasts that are difficult to contend with. As believers, we aren't left to process the contents of our stories on our own. Instead, God has offered to take it all—the pain and disappointment, the chaos and fear, and the terrible, ugly things that happened to and around us—and make something beautiful from them. When we surrender our hearts and experiences, He is big enough to change the song of our mouths (Ps. 40:3), trading any lingering bitter flavors for something that has goodness and purpose in Him.

I don't know your story, but God does. If you haven't before, surrender it to Him today and allow Him to heal where things were broken, bring understanding to places that were difficult, and fill you with gratitude for the people and words that were life-giving. He's big enough to handle your feelings, questions, and the most unsavory parts of your life, so open your heart to Him and let Him make something beautiful of it.

 **PSALM 103:1-5**

DAY 20: Thank Him Anyway

On most mornings, it's still dark when I hear the pitter-patter of my children's feet coming down the hall. They join me in my chair while I finish my coffee and last few pages of reading, and then we head to the kitchen to toast bread, pour cups of milk, and begin stuffing backpacks with lunchboxes and school folders. In a few years, they might be angsty teenagers who want to sleep in, hang out in their rooms, or avoid me at all cost, so for now I'm trying to relish the sweetness of toddlers who just want to be right where Mama is.

Some days, I find myself wishing for that next phase to come more quickly. I want kids who are more independent, who can pour their own milk, wash their own breakfast dishes, and dress themselves for school. I want time to sleep in and the space to shower alone. When those thoughts arise, shame whispers that I should feel guilty for wanting more freedom, as if my desire for some solitude has rendered me ungrateful for the little people who just want to be on my lap, but the truth is, taking care of children *is* work. It's equal parts fulfilling and draining, simultaneously remarkable and monotonous.

When the days feel hard and long, know you're not alone. You can embrace the weight of your circumstances and even look forward to whatever phase of life is on the horizon, but don't miss the beauty of your story while you're in the middle of it. In the everyday offerings of life, there are reasons for gratitude that will settle in your lap, as if God knew we'd need the reminder that He's in that season too. Look for the good (and God!) in your story, and thank Him in exhaustion, thank Him when it's hard, thank Him in all circumstances.

 PSALM 118

DAY 21: Using the Bits and Pieces

I like the challenge of putting leftover ingredients to use. After a week of preparing dinners for my family, I often find a hodgepodge of remnants scattered on my fridge shelves—maybe a cup of broth, a half of a cucumber, or a rind from a used-up wedge of Parmesan—and I wonder, *What could I do with this?* Although it would be easier to throw those odd items in the trash, every once in a while I find it gratifying to concoct something big and wonderful with whatever bits and pieces I have to work with.

To be honest, I often feel just like those bits and pieces. *What could I possibly offer to God? Do my gifts and words and love really count for anything, particularly in light of the millions of slipups I make throughout the week? Wouldn't someone with bigger faith be a better, more useful asset in the kingdom?*

Thankfully, God's economy doesn't work like the world's, where the biggest and best get the most in return; instead, He multiplies our meager offerings and uses even the most unlikely characters to do big, important work. The enemy would like you to believe that God can't use you or that your life isn't valuable enough for impact, but hear me: that's just not true. Throughout the Bible, we read story after story in which God creates purpose for every member of His family, doing immeasurably more with our lives than we could fathom (Eph. 3:20).

In the coming days, ask God to use your life in significant ways for His kingdom. Just offer it up to Him in prayer. You may not see the final outcome of His work, but He will put to use every heart that is bowed in His name. Be a part of the wonderful work He is carrying out, and thank Him in advance for using all the pieces of your life—no matter how small—in ways you can't imagine.

 **LUKE 13:18–21**

DAY 22: # Daily Armor

My work-from-home lifestyle means I rarely go overboard with a daily primping routine, but I have come to rely on a few staples. After all, you'd be surprised what a woman can do with a little dry shampoo and an extra cup of coffee. You might as well hand me a cape.

We all have those tools that help us through the day, and although we don't hesitate to rely on our face cream and iPhones and Spanx, I wonder how often we forget to rely on the resources God has given us. In Ephesians 6, Paul describes the armor of God in a few verses-worth of imagery intended to show believers how they can utilize resources from heaven: faith, truth, righteousness, salvation, God's word, and the gospel of peace. These are tools, weapons even, that provide force and power against the schemes of the enemy and protect us from the darkness of this world.

Today, instead of taking an extra five minutes for your daily dose of caffeine or social media, put on the armor of God. Read the scripture from Ephesians and make it a part of your daily routine. In fact, let's pray:

"Father, thank you for the tools you've given us to fight against the unseen things of this word. We put on the belt of truth, the breastplate of righteousness, and the sandals of the gospel of peace. We pick up our sword, your Word, and our shield, our faith in you, and thank you that you have given us the helmet of salvation. Remind us to rely on these gifts in all circumstances, that we would become a people who are always dressed, always prepared to fight in your name. We're proud to be in your army, and we love you! Amen."

 **EPHESIANS 6:10–20**

DAY 23: Eyes on Jesus

My big kids can never keep their eyes on their own plate. They're much too con-cerned that someone else got the better serving, maybe a couple extra French fries, fewer vegetables, or a bigger slice of cake. I get it, because I've done it my whole life too—always comparing what I have to what I see around me.

God doesn't play favorites, but sometimes we act as if He does. Comparison slips in when we see blessing, provision, and answers to prayer pile up in the lives around us and we begin to wonder, *What have they done to deserve such favor? Why did they see such a powerful breakthrough in their life? What about me?* Rest assured, if your drifting eyes lead to comparison, a discontented heart will follow soon after.

Today, fix your eyes on Jesus and rest in the promise of His provision. His work in the life of your neighbor does not diminish the blessing in yours, and ultimately the testimony of that work is intended to encourage you. He desires for us to cel-ebrate His goodness in every circumstance, so if comparison has left you to won-der if He's forgotten you, don't hesitate to bring that confession to Him. Spend some time reflecting on the work He's done in your life, in both the past and present, and express gratitude for the evidence of that grace. Instead of worrying about what's on everyone else's plate, shift your wandering eyes back to Jesus.

 **LUKE 15:11–32**

DAY 24: Plain as Cream Cheese

You'd be surprised what you can do with a block of cream cheese. Here in the South, we use it in everything: tailgate dips, casseroles, cakes and pies, and even the occasional batch of chicken soup. (God bless those wholesale stores where you can buy twelve blocks at a time!) Cream cheese may not have the cachet that fancier ingredients do, but in the hands of someone who knows their way around a party tray, it's exactly where the magic the happens.

We all bring whatever we have to the table, things like our humor, wisdom, joy, compassion, and imagination. Some of us dance or cook or paint, while others have a way with hammers, shovels, or the spoken word. Some gifts are theatrical and impressive, but others of us display what we feel are only ordinary contributions.

God wants for you to bring *whatever* it is that you've got to Him. Bring your hopes, your talents, your passion, and your love, and spend it generously for the glory of His name. You can stand proud of the beauty in you, no matter how ordinary it may seem in your eyes, because God thinks you are altogether lovely and special. Sister, there's nothing ordinary about God's creation, so offer all you have at His table today, and watch the magic happen.

 **1 TIMOTHY 4:4-5**

DAY 25: Pumpkin Cake

This Pumpkin Cake is one of my dear friend's family recipes, and it's become a favorite in my house too. A tradition in her family was to fill the center well of the cake with any leftover cream cheese frosting, so when you cut into the cake, extra frosting can be spooned on top of warmed slices. We like to serve this cake as breakfast or dessert, and any cake that secretly doubles as a breakfast food is a win in my book. Give it a try, and I think you'll agree.

....

PUMPKIN CAKE

Serves 9 to 10

CAKE

1 cup canola oil

4 large eggs, at room temperature

2 cups canned pumpkin puree

2 cups granulated sugar

2 cups all-purpose flour

2 teaspoons baking powder

2 teaspoons baking soda

1 teaspoon cinnamon

1/4 teaspoon table salt

FROSTING

1/2 cup unsalted butter, at room temperature

8 ounces cream cheese, at room temperature

1 teaspoon vanilla extract

1 pound (3 1/2 cups) confectioners' sugar

TO PREPARE THE CAKE

Preheat the oven to 350°F. Lightly grease and flour a 9-inch tube pan.

In a large bowl or the bowl of a stand mixer, (using a paddle attachment), combine the oil and eggs, stirring to combine. Add the pumpkin and sugar and stir until mixed well. Add the flour, baking powder, baking soda, cinnamon, and salt, and stir just until combined, with no lumps remaining. Spoon the batter into the prepared pan and smooth the top. Bake until the top is puffed, golden, and a toothpick inserted in the center comes out clean, about 50 to 55 minutes. Allow the cake to cool in the pan for 30 minutes, and then carefully remove it to cool completely on a rack.

TO PREPARE THE FROSTING

In a large bowl or the bowl of a stand mixer (using the paddle attachment), cream the butter and cream cheese together until smooth and no lumps remain, about 1 minute. Add the vanilla and stir to combine. Add the confectioners' sugar and beat just until incorporated. You can use a little water or milk, a tablespoon at a time, to thin out the frosting to a pourable consistency if desired. Otherwise, spread thicker frosting on the cake with an offset spatula and serve!

DAY 26: Less Is More

The performer in me has a hard time being content in the here and now. Especially around the holidays, I really struggle with an inner drive to do more and spin a web of wonder and delight for my kids. Can you relate?

In an effort to be more present this time of year, I'm learning to loosen my grip on the nonessentials and make more of each moment by being available. Perhaps less garland, fewer appetizers, and a messier home will yield a happier mom, a less-frazzled Kate. For some of us, cutting back means saying no to some invitations, spending a little more time in our pj's, or trimming down our shopping list, but I believe wholeheartedly that doing less is often the way to get more—more rest, more connection, more Jesus.

I want you to know that in this season when there's pressure to conform to societal norms, it's okay to do and create and perform, but it's also okay to just *not*. Lower the bar a bit and make connection your primary goal. What would that look like in your house? Where can you make more time to be available and emotionally present for one another? Where can you make room for resting in Jesus? Take off some of the pressure where you can, and use that free space to lean in to the beauty this time of year has to offer. If you're unsure where to begin, ask God to inspire ideas for connection, and remember that sometimes doing less means receiving more.

 **LUKE 10:38–42**

DAY 27: Running the Race

A few years ago, I traveled with some girlfriends to run in a marathon. To be clear, by "run," I mean walk, and by "marathon," I mean 5K. Yes, I walked the 5K. Don't you dare make fun of me.

Anyway, all along the race route, there were people cheering us on. They'd hoot and holler, yelling stuff like, "You got this!" or, "You're doing great! Keep going!" Honestly, I had barely moved enough to burn off the creamer from my morning coffee, but all that celebrating and encouragement made me feel like Usain Bolt. At the finish line, there was an even bigger party awaiting the runners, and it was exhilarating. I was proud to have completed the race, but was even more satisfied by all the encouragement I'd encountered along the way.

So often in life, we get caught up in the finish-line moments. We look at our goals and deadlines as the be-all and end-all, forgetting to cheer ourselves along throughout the process. So much of life is spent like that—*in process*. If we're only honoring our efforts at the finish line, that leaves a lot of moments in between to become worn down and ready to quit. It's like running a marathon without a cheerleader—downright exhausting.

Take some time today to celebrate the areas where you are in process. Honor God for the work He is doing in your life, and thank Him in advance for the finish lines He'll walk across with you. You don't need a gold medal to show how far you've come. Instead, remain encouraged by celebrating God's goodness, your progress, and the work that's been done all along the way.

 **ISAIAH 63:7**

DAY 28: Our Place Is Permanent

I can remember lying in bed, pregnant with one of my children, feeling the baby's legs and arms moving and jabbing just beneath the surface of my skin. The hiccups were never convenient, usually happening at two or three in the morning, but the miracle of it all, the flesh and blood that was growing inside of me, kept my sleepless thoughts in perspective; I remained in awe, and grateful. It was a part of the process of motherhood that I relished and wouldn't trade for a thing.

In Isaiah, God uses the mother-child relationship to illustrate His attention toward His people. Not only are we at the forefront of His mind, but our place there is permanent: *I have engraved you on the palms of my hands* (49:16). Although there are plenty of opportunities to buy into the lie that God has forgotten about you or overlooked your needs, scripture is clear that the Father has deep love and affection for His children. He can't forget about us any more than an expectant mother can forget the child in her belly; we're so familiar that our presence is second nature to Him.

Let the verses from Isaiah, selected below, be an encouragement to you today. Your life matters to the Father. He prioritizes your life and never forgets to remember you. You're permanent to Him. Run to Him today with gratitude and affection, loving Him as a child does its mother. Your Father will never leave you—He's always right there.

 **ISAIAH 49:14–16**

DAY 29: Yesterday, Today, and Forever

It's easy to trust God when we're on the winning team. When things go our way and the events of our lives line up like rows of dominoes falling in our favor, belief in His goodness comes easily. We praise Him in victory and rejoice at miracles and breakthroughs, but is our faith secure enough to continue that thankfulness when life isn't going our way? Do we sing the same praise in disappointment, or are the things we believe about Him contingent upon our circumstances?

I'll admit I'm the first to jump ship when things get hard. When faced with loss, unmet expectations, and hopeless situations, I'm prone to believing that God has forgotten about me, that I didn't pray hard enough, or that my needs aren't as important as I think they are. Sister, this is a lie. Hebrews 13:8 says, *Jesus Christ is the same yesterday and today and forever,* meaning that love and kindness, which are in His nature, are unwavering. His affection toward us doesn't shift from day to day, ebbing and flowing based on His mood or our own merit; He is good and loving all the time, always working things out for our benefit (Ps. 107:1).

Take some time this week to record an inventory of God's goodness in your story. Reflect on moments from days, weeks, or months past, jotting down anything that stands out to you. Use those words, your very own experiences, as a testimony to His character, because if He was good yesterday, He'll be good today, and in whatever comes tomorrow as well. His love is unchanging, and that is worth your praise.

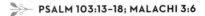 **PSALM 103:13–18; MALACHI 3:6**

DAY 30: ## Personal Truths

The first year Brett and I were married saw more than a handful of disputes. We were two stubborn people attempting to mesh together our ideas, traditions, and behaviors under one roof, and on occasion it ended in conflict. *How will we raise our kids? Where do we invest this money? What will we eat on Christmas morning? Do the bowls go on the top or bottom rack of the dishwasher?* Up until that point, we'd each viewed life from our own frame of reference, and learning to step outside of that to instead see eye to eye presented a challenge that we didn't know how to navigate.

As I get older, I'm reminded that everyone's perspective, the things they've come to believe about life, people, and the world around them, is hugely dependent on the environment they learned in. My understanding of this world isn't the same as yours, because we've each spent our years walking in different pairs of shoes. As believers, we're called to extend grace and understanding to everyone—even people who see the world from a vastly different point of view—and if we attempt to impose our routines and expectations on others, we can expect to be met with disagreement.

Remember that your experience is just that: *yours.* We are each entitled to our own opinions, but when dealing with others, let's rely most heavily on God's truth. How would Jesus respond to a neighbor? What does God say about this situation? How can you share His love with the people in front of you even when you don't agree with them? The world doesn't need more opinions, but it does need more neighbors who look like Jesus, and you can set the tone by being that example of love to the people around you.

Oh, and if you're wondering, the bowls go on the bottom rack of the dishwasher. *Obviously.*

 **EPHESIANS 4:17–32**

DAY 1: It's a Mystery to Me

I have a lot of questions that need answering, like, "Where are half of my socks disappearing to?" "Why are my children's hands infinitely sticky?" "Who hid my car keys in the toy box?" Although I'd really like to be the person who is unbothered by these everyday annoyances, I'm just not. Those daily doses of disorganization make me feel as though I'm on the brink of losing my marbles.

God only gives good gifts, so there's no way He's the creator of these little disruptions, but I do believe He allows them at times to remind us of our dependence on Him. Sometimes it's a flat tire or a rude telemarketer; other times it's a long line at the grocery store or three cereal-bowl spills in one morning. Those minor inconveniences present opportunities to develop patience and perseverance. They are chances to breathe deep, flex that Jesus muscle, and smile through the struggle.

Let this be your reminder this week: God works in mysterious ways. I don't have to know what He's doing in the ruts of everyday life to believe wholeheartedly that He's taking us somewhere good. Instead of being disappointed by the messy parts of your life, ask God how He wishes to sharpen your heart and mind to become more like Jesus through those moments.

 **2 CORINTHIANS 12:1–10**

DAY 2: Christmas Coffee Cake

My mimi used to serve this coffee cake every Christmas morning. She baked it the day before, and we would spend the wee hours of the big day opening stockings and nibbling on bits of homemade cinnamon-spiced cake. Now, with a merry crew of my own to serve on Christmas day, we pop a few candles in the cake and sing "Happy Birthday" to Jesus while my kids sneak pieces of cinnamon sugar crumble off the top. There are a handful of recipes from my childhood that just feel like home, and this is an important one I knew we needed to include in the book.

Christmas Coffee Cake is classic, but its taste and texture are outstanding. The sour cream creates a moist, tender crumb, and the single layer of cinnamon sugar throughout adds a simple and unassuming swirl for an extra bite of sweetness and texture. I highly recommend rewarming individual slices with a schmear of salted butter, and whether you make it on Christmas morning or a random Tuesday, I have no doubt it will fill your heart (and belly) as it does mine.

....

CHRISTMAS COFFEE CAKE

Serves 12

CAKE BATTER

3/4 cup unsalted butter,
    at room temperature

11/2 cups granulated sugar

3 large eggs, at room temperature

11/2 teaspoons vanilla extract

3 cups all-purpose flour

11/2 teaspoons baking powder

11/2 teaspoons baking soda

1/4 teaspoon table salt

11/2 cups sour cream, at room temperature

FILLING

1 cup packed brown sugar

3 teaspoons ground cinnamon

TO PREPARE THE CAKE BATTER

Preheat the oven to 350ºF. With baking spray, lightly grease a tube pan with a removable bottom. In a large bowl or the bowl of a stand mixer, mix the butter, sugar, eggs, and vanilla on medium speed for 2 minutes. In a separate bowl, mix the flour, baking powder, baking soda, and salt together. Add half of the dry ingredients to the butter mixture and stir on low. Add half of the sour cream and stir again. Scrape the sides of the bowl and repeat this process until all the ingredients have been well incorporated.

TO PREPARE THE FILLING

In a small bowl, stir together the brown sugar and cinnamon.

TO PREPARE THE CAKE

Spread one-third of the batter into the bottom of the prepared tube pan and sprinkle one-third of the filling mixture on top. Spoon the remaining batter on top, smooth lightly, and then cover the batter with the remaining filling mixture. Bake for about 50 minutes, or until a toothpick inserted into the center just barely comes out clean. I like to check the cake at 45 minutes, as this cake should not be overbaked. Allow the cake to cool in the pan for 20 minutes, and then remove it to cool completely.

DAY 3: Loving Even When It's Inconvenient

For a long time, I believed that I loved people well. I was nice enough and polite enough, had a handful of friends who didn't look just like me, and regularly volunteered for good causes. In my eyes, I was crushing the love game one Angel Tree Christmas Kid at a time.

Except that I wasn't. Pretty recently, it became blindingly evident to me that this so-called love really only extended as far as it was convenient. I was willing to love, but only when the opportunity suited my schedule and comfort. When it came right down to it, the thought of loving someone at the expense of my own well-being was terrifying. *What if loving my neighbor costs me something I can't give up? What if it means sacrificing bigger pieces of myself than I want to?* At the end of the day, was I really ready to lay it all on the line—my money, my emotions, my pride, and my ease—for the people God had called me to love (read: everyone)?

God's Word is pretty clear about love. We're supposed to spend ourselves endlessly for the pursuit of it. We're to share it with strangers, neighbors, and even the people who hate us. I'm learning that loving as Jesus did isn't always comfortable, and it requires me to show grace toward people who are difficult, seek to understand people who think differently from me, and extend myself on behalf of others, even when there's no immediate personal benefit. Our world needs the kind of love that isn't limited by borders, skin color, dollar signs, or beliefs, and Jesus is our only source.

Who can you love better today? Is there someone in your circle who needs an extra dose of Jesus's kindness? How about outside of your circle? It might take you out of your comfort zone, but you're never alone in doing so. Open your arms wide for people today, and just wait to see how God uses that expression of love.

 **JOHN 13:34–35**

DAY 4: Tying Threads

Although I love a packed party, there's something special about an intimate gathering. My favorite memories are of shared meals around a table where everyone's faces are lit up from the glow of candlelight and laughter is passed around like the oversize platters on the table before us. In those moments, "One more round!" turns into one more story, and no one moves for fear that we'll disrupt the communion that is unfolding right there.

Connection happens when we unravel the threads of our own story and tie them to someone else's. In our homes, the table is the common ground where individuals are welcomed into a larger family, but at the Lord's table, we participate in a different kind of unity. By the breaking of bread and drinking of wine, we step into the mystery and beauty of communion with Christ. We share in His story, tying our threads to His, and partake in the intimate offerings of His presence. It's not just a meal for physical sustenance—it's one that nourishes the deepest parts of us.

Ask God to show you who He's set around your proverbial table, and don't let the treasure of communion or community escape you. There is a magnificent gift waiting from both if you're willing to partake in it.

 **JOHN 6:53–58**

DAY 5: Holy Slow-Down

I love a winter day. The monochrome view of gray skies and bare trees feels like permission to stay cozy inside. Life is rarely quiet these days, but the winter months bring out an inner stillness in me; my need to do more, work more, and be more goes dormant. I'm content to just be still.

God certainly intended for us to produce, but He also set aside time for rest. In Genesis, God spent six days creating but set the seventh aside, making it a holy thing, a blessed day, just for us. Later in the Bible, Jesus explained that the Sabbath isn't our opportunity to be extra spiritual for God's sake—it's an opportunity for Him to fill *us* up.

Rest is a place where spiritual rejuvenation happens. It's about slowing down long enough to make room for His Spirit, recentering in a place of abiding in Him. The Sabbath is so much more than just a physical rest for our bodies; it's a time when we shift our focus from our broken world to Him, and I'm finding that the exchange of our rest for His renewal buoys me all week long.

Where do you feel most at rest? Are you carving out time for spiritual breathers? Pick a time, maybe starting in these bleak winter months, to cozy up, be still, and drink in the love of God. Put your to-do lists and busy tendencies to the side long enough to observe the goodness of God all around you. That holy slowdown is a rest that will carry you all week long.

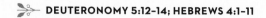 **DEUTERONOMY 5:12–14; HEBREWS 4:1–11**

DAY 6: Setting Realistic Standards

I'll be the first to admit that I have impossible standards, for both myself and others. Settling is not something I do well, because if things could be better, why not try? The trouble is that no one on earth is above reproach, and we're all bound to screw up. Expecting perfection from someone, even if that someone is yourself, is bound to end in disappointment.

Aren't you kind of tired of being at odds with the people in your life? Although there are times when we need to address the issues in others, more often than not we just need to address our own heart. Are you expecting the impossible from the people you love? Are you expecting too much of yourself?

I propose we take lofty expectations away from every relationship. Let's be patient, *bearing with one another in love* (Eph. 4:2), knowing that we're just human. Extend grace to one another, and especially to yourself when you inevitably encounter a failure this week, and rely on God to be the sufficiency you can depend upon.

 **ROMANS 15:1–7**

DAY 7: Spoonfuls of Grace

In video reels and photos of my children's first attempts with food, they spit and gag, cough and pucker at the new flavors and textures found on their spoon. To be honest, it's hysterical, and those photos of chubby babies with mushy peas from their eyebrows to their belly buttons are a reminder of how even simple things like eating are a challenge our first time around.

Although it's not as cute as a baby covered in sweet potatoes, adults can make a mess when they're learning new things too. We fumble through the uncharted territories of apologies and humility and disappointment, because learning to operate with grace in a fallen and broken world is a challenge, a completely unnatural act until Jesus teaches us how. He's like the parent who holds our hand through the process, feeding us spoonfuls of grace to make those difficult moments a bit easier to swallow.

Extend grace to yourself as you engage in new and challenging territory. When facing the embarrassment of a failed idea or relationship, dust yourself off and seek out an opportunity to do it better the next time. Every circumstance can be hard the first (or second! or third!) time around, but Jesus has faced it all and will walk you through it. Ask God to show you how to operate in His goodness, even when things aren't going your way, and remember that His grace is sufficient to cover you in any circumstance you could possibly face this week.

 **HEBREWS 4:16**

DAY 8: Little Cookies, Big Love

Every Christmas season, for as long as I can remember, Mimi made frosted sugar cookies for our family, and as a kid I loved to join her at the counter to play with copper cookie cutters while she cut out shapes from the dough. While the kitchen warmed from the heat of the oven and filled with the scent of butter and vanilla, I'd nibble on remnants of dough and pick at the bits of goodness stuck to the beaters and bowl. Most years, we'd gather around the table to take turns frosting cookies, and those memories of togetherness have become so precious to me.

As an adult, I make those cookies for my own family, and I think about all the time Mimi spent in the kitchen, producing not just cookies, but a tangible reminder of her love. Small acts, like making a batch of cookies or sharing a task around the table, can mark you so profoundly that they continue to bless you even years down the road. I'm grateful to have lived a childhood so rich with those experiences and take comfort knowing that small daily acts for my own children may be similarly filling their little tanks with love.

To the mothers and mimis and women who sow love into the lives of the people around them, I want to say: it makes a difference. Your effort, particularly at this time of year, has the potential to deeply bless lives when done from a spirit of love. I don't think we'll ever know the sum of all the little choices we make, but I feel confident that anything done in love will carry abundant blessing. The little moments of our lives always culminate in stories of big love.

Who loved you in little or big ways? Honor them today with a word of gratitude or a note telling them the difference they've made. Spend time thanking the Father for giving you glimpses of His love, and let that gratitude minister to you today.

 **COLOSSIANS 3:15–17**

DAY 9: Mimi's Frosted Sugar Cookies

These cookies are my most-prized Christmas recipe. If you're without a favorite holiday cookie of your own, I hope you'll consider making Mimi's Frosted Sugar Cookies a part of your Christmas tradition.

....

MIMI'S FROSTED SUGAR COOKIES

Makes 3 to 4 dozen, depending on the size of the cutters

COOKIES

1 cup unsalted butter, at room temperature

2 cups granulated sugar

3 large eggs

1 teaspoon vanilla extract

2 tablespoons milk

5 cups all-purpose flour

1½ teaspoons cream of tartar

1½ teaspoons baking soda

Pinch of table salt

FROSTING

3⁄4 cup unsalted butter, at room temperature

2 pounds (7 cups) confectioners' sugar

2 large pasteurized eggs

3 teaspoons vanilla extract

¼ teaspoon table salt

Milk, as needed

Gel food coloring (optional)

TO PREPARE THE COOKIES

In the bowl of a stand mixer or a large mixing bowl, combine the butter and sugar, creaming on medium speed until the mixture is light and fluffy, about 2 minutes. Add the eggs, vanilla, and milk, and stir to combine for an additional 30 seconds. Scrape the sides of the bowl. In a separate bowl, combine the flour, cream of tartar, baking soda, and salt. Add the dry ingredients to the butter mixture and mix slowly until well incorporated. Scrape the sides of the bowl as needed. Divide the dough into two flat rounds and wrap them in plastic wrap. Chill in the fridge for at least 1 hour or up to three days.

When ready to bake, preheat the oven to 350ºF. Prepare multiple pans by lining them with parchment paper or silicone baking mats.

Generously flour a work surface and roll out one round of dough to ⅛- to ¼-inch thick using a floured rolling pin. Use medium-size cookie cutters to cut out shapes of dough and place them 2 inches apart on the prepared pans. If desired, place the whole pan in the freezer for 5 minutes (or the fridge for 10) to set the shaped dough, and then bake for about 10 minutes, or until the edges of the cookies are well set. Allow the cookies to cool on the pan briefly and then remove them to a rack to cool completely. Gather up the scraps of dough from the cut cookies and gently form them into a disk, working the dough as little as possible and using minimal flour (too much of either will change the texture of the cookies). If the dough gets too warm or sticky, place it back in the fridge to chill a bit. Roll out the disk and cut as many additional cookies as will fit. Free-form the scraps from this round into a last few cookies. Repeat the process with the second disk of dough in the fridge.

TO PREPARE THE FROSTING

In a large bowl, combine the butter, confectioners' sugar, eggs, vanilla, and salt, mixing until well combined. Add milk by the tablespoon until the frosting is thick but smooth, similar to the consistency of a thick cake buttercream. Use gel food coloring to dye the frosting whatever color you'd like and use a knife to spread the frosting on the cookies. Enjoy!

DAY 10: "It Is Good"

We've all experienced that lonely pit of shame and discouragement when we peer into the corners of our lives and see all of our deficiencies, poor choices, and painful experiences. It's easy to feel as though the dark overshadows the light.

Someone once told me that just as God created the light of day and said, "It is good," so also does He delight in the light inside of His children. He doesn't shy away from us because of the messiness of our sin; instead, it's the goodness of His Son *in* us and the beauty of His creation that He is drawn to. Rather than fixate on our shortcomings, our errors, or the places where we're still in process, He treasures the beauty that He put inside us and declares, "It is good."

Sister, I want to remove any shame in you right now, in Jesus's name. You are not defined by who you were, the mistakes you've made, or the places in your heart that seem to have a long way to go. The beauty of Christ in you is all the goodness you'll ever need to be declared "good" in the eyes of our Heavenly Father. Take time to meditate on the cleansing blood of Jesus and ask God to increase His presence in your life. Today, don't fixate on the parts where you're perfectly in process; rest in the things He has declared to be good.

 **2 CORINTHIANS 5:16-21**

DAY 11: Dusting Yourself Off

Famous last words: "Do you want to help?" The last time I uttered that phrase, I wound up with banana-bread batter splattered on the wall and two of my children covered in flour from head to toe. When George turned the mixer up to high speed, he was just trying to help, but how was a four-year-old to know to start on the low setting?

The truth is, we all make a mess sometimes. There's mess in our relationships with friends, family, and coworkers when we fail to communicate with love and intentionality. There's the mess in our homes when we introduce worry, rush, and a never-ending effort to do more and more and more. With the emotional clutter and physical expectations we place upon ourselves, it's adults, not kids, who end up making the most unfortunate messes.

I almost lost it when I saw the banana-bread catastrophe in my kitchen, but a moment of pause reminded me to laugh it off and make it a teachable moment. Thankfully, God offers us that same opportunity. When we make yet another inevitable mess, He doesn't shame us or stay angry forever, but instead dusts the flour off our cheeks and shows us how to do it better the next time. He loves us, messes and all, and if we'll humble ourselves under the wisdom of His instruction, He'll make all those blunders teachable moments.

You can dust yourself off next time you blow it, because God wants to help you in the mess-ups and the areas where you're still in process, so when you find yourself there, call on Him. Ask for His wisdom and instruction in making sense of the chaos, and He will bring order to the mess.

 **ISAIAH 58:11; JOHN 14:26**

DAY 12: Turning Down the Volume

For some of us, silence takes a lot of work, and it is a practice of willpower to intentionally set aside the busyness of life to engage with our hearts in a meaningful way. Women today are so bombarded with information all day long—from our friends, our kids, our phones and computers, and workplaces—that we forget to tune in to the voice in our hearts. Forget what the world is screaming all around you—what is the Holy Spirit saying about the condition of your life right now?

In my head, I know God's words carry more weight than the world's, but I rarely act like it. Instead, I silence His voice to make room for the weightiness that I pick up throughout my day: self-doubt, criticism, comparison, judgment of others, and offense. Instead of slowing down, I move faster, juggling tasks and absorbing all the information until my capacity for connection is reduced to nothing. The noise of this life can wear you out, but I'm here to remind you that there's a still, small voice that is willing and able to sustain you.

Silence it all. Turn down the volume of this world and engage your heart. How are you *really* doing? Which voices get the most air time in your heart? Are there areas where you need to take better care of yourself by relying more deeply on the truth of Christ? He might not try to compete with the noise you surround yourself with, but He's promised to be there whenever you stop to listen. So, shhh . . . What's He saying to you today?

 **1 KINGS 19:11–13**

DAY 13: Birthday Gifts for Jesus

We spent years saving for, planning, and building our home, and it all came together the week before Christmas. I was frustrated by the prospect of moving during the holidays, so even before we toted in boxes and luggage, knick-knacks and furniture, I set up a Christmas tree smack-dab in the middle of our new living room. My husband thought I was crazy (and, okay, I might have been), but absolutely nothing was going to stop me from giving my kids just the tiniest taste of Christmas. There wouldn't be stockings, lights, or gingerbread houses that year, but I was determined to have a tree.

Even though Christmas *looked* different that year, the heartfelt wonder of it all was still there, and I was reminded that the thing that makes the holidays feel so special is love. All that stuff—the elaborate light displays, the tablescapes, the fancy decorations—is wonderful, but ultimately it can easily become one big distraction. I think Jesus is honored on His birthday when we open our hearts to love our people as hard as we can, a gesture requiring none of the décor and razzle-dazzle that the Hallmark Channel would lead you to believe Christmas needs.

Let your heart—your big, wide-open love—be the gift you pour out this year. There's nothing wrong with the spectacle of it all, but it's not nearly as important as we make it out to be. Ask Jesus how He wants to celebrate His birthday this year. If it's a person who pops into your mind, consider how you can make them feel loved this season. If it's a family activity, a need in your community, or even a spiritual gift for yourself, consider that too. Spend a little less effort on the stuff and offer those freed-up bits of your heart to the world around you. I think that's a good gift for Jesus.

 **PROVERBS 3:3–4**

DAY 14: **Wish Lists**

In a photo of Aimee and George from a few years ago, they're sitting next to Santa Claus and a stuffed red-nosed reindeer. George's face is nearly purple, from his screaming in terror at the proximity of this jolly stranger. Aimee stands, arms crossed, with a pout on her face that says, "I'm only doing this because I was promised a candy cane." This Christmas photo is a hilarious nightmare, one you can bet I'll be laughing at and reminding my children of for, like, ever.

When it comes to Jesus, sometimes I have to remind myself that He isn't my own personal Santa Claus. We're all prone to spouting off our wants, hoping we're on the "nice list," so that God will come through this time around by giving us what we want. If we get it, we're elated: *He must be real!* But when we don't see the answers to our prayers, we wonder if He's even out there: *Does He even care? Maybe I wasn't good enough this year?*

Jesus gave us a model for prayer in the New Testament. It's as if He already knew we were going to junk it up with our wordy wish lists. From time to time, I find myself going back to that prayer for a bit of a reset, because I want to shift my heart and desires to better align them with His. I want to honor Him with my words and to experience the fullest measure of power that comes from praying as Jesus did.

If your prayers have felt more like a wish list lately, ask God to shift your heart and make His desires your own. Give praying like Jesus a shot, and remember He's not your Santa Claus. He's your holy friend.

 **MATTHEW 6:9-13**

DAY 15: Filling Our Plates

One December, my friend invited a handful of us over for a cookie exchange. Nothing, I repeat, *nothing* brings my friends to life like a holiday beverage and a nine-foot table brimming with sugar: cutout cookies and frosted brownies, peanut-butter thumbprints and ganache-filled sandwich cookies, gingersnap thins and candy-cane shortbread. In my wildest dreams, the banquet table in heaven is basically a Jesus-hosted cookie exchange, and if I'm wrong, don't you dare tell me. I don't want to know.

The thing I love about cookie exchanges is that you get to take home a taste of what everyone has brought to the table. For one night, you can choose from the delightful tastes and textures that are offered on the table and bring the best of those flavors home with you. You're never stuck with a single kind of cookie, because there's a whole table filled with variety and the opportunity to discover.

Jesus has a table full of possibility too: new seasons, gifts, and promises He's made available to us by His blood. The Bible says that, in Christ, we share in the inheritance of His glory (Col. 1:27). The Christian life is never dull or boring, because we have been given access to layer upon layer of joy, love, peace, and victory, like a table full of wonderful new flavors to experience.

Have you found yourself in a spiritual rut? You will never get to the end of all the beauty and joy that is available to you in Christ, so if you're in need of a fresh taste, just ask for it. Spend time in His Word to fill your plate with reminders of His goodness this morning, and feast on those sweet morsels of His love.

 **PSALM 27:4–14**

Peppermint Brownie Cookies

It's a Christmas miracle: every single member of my family loves these Peppermint Brownie Cookies. I love to bring these to cookie exchanges, school parties, and many other holiday gatherings. Talk about a gift that keeps on giving.

....

PEPPERMINT BROWNIE COOKIES

Makes 24

1/2 cup unsalted butter, cubed

1 cup semisweet chocolate chips

3 large eggs

1/2 cup granulated sugar

1/2 cup packed light brown sugar

1 teaspoon vanilla extract

1 teaspoon peppermint extract

1 cup all-purpose flour

3 tablespoons Dutch-processed cocoa
   powder

1 teaspoon baking powder

Pinch of table salt

Fleur de sel (optional)

Preheat the oven to 350ºF. Line two baking sheets with parchment paper.

Add a cup of water to the bottom of a small saucepan, and place a medium heat-proof glass bowl on top. Add the butter and chocolate chips to the bowl and heat the pan on medium, stirring until melted. Remove the bowl from the heat and allow it to cool slightly.

In a large mixing bowl or the bowl of a stand mixer, whip the eggs, sugar, and brown sugar on medium speed until pale and thickened slightly, about 2 to 3 minutes. Stir in the vanilla and peppermint, and then carefully drizzle in the warm chocolate mixture, stirring all along, to prevent the eggs from cooking. Add the flour, cocoa powder, baking powder, and salt, and then use a rubber spatula to fold the batter until it is uniform throughout.

Portion out 1½-tablespoon-size rounds of batter onto the cookie sheets, spacing the cookies at least 3 inches apart. Bake the pans one at a time for 12 minutes, or until the cookie tops are cracked and the crack lines no longer appear extremely wet. Sprinkle the baked cookies lightly with fleur de sel if desired.

DAY 17: I'll Have What He's Having

There are times when I think I know better than God. You've been there, right? We pray, we reason, we rattle off our lengthy list of wants, making orders as if He's here to serve from some heavenly menu. Although we say we want God's will, realistically, we really just want a short-order cook kind of Jesus.

I'll be honest—I struggle here. Even when I say I value God's plan for my life, I'm often distracted by what's on everyone else's plate, and if their portion looks better than mine, I feel as though I was served someone's leftovers. Instead of resting in God's promises, I fixate on the negativity within my circumstances, losing all track of the contentment and joy I should be finding in Him alone.

You might wrestle with God or question what He's doing in your life, but be careful that your search for understanding doesn't turn into doubting His goodness or demanding answers. Instead, use today's unanswered questions as an opportunity to grow in faith by bringing them to Him in prayer: "God, I trust you—what are you wanting me to believe you for in this season? What is your desire for me today? Show me how to trust you even when I don't understand." Pursue Him, praise Him, and trust Him, even when the steps moving forward seem uncertain. Abide in Him, and allow Him to show you the peace that is offered in His presence.

 **HEBREWS 3**

DAY 18: Waiting for Jesus

Waiting has never been my strong suit. I'm one of those who drive too fast, pay extra for expedited shipping, and sneak extra items on the "10 Items or Less" checkout line at the grocery store. I have friends who wait for things to go on sale, wait to find out the gender of their baby, or willingly sit in a long line at a tollbooth, but this has never been my modus operandi. Brett and I even joke that, if we could, we'd just plug ourselves in for a quick recharge every evening, if it meant skipping the wait of a whole night's sleep.

God's word is clear about the benefits of patience and the promises that come with waiting for Him. I don't think He calls us to this waiting because He's dragging His feet or hasn't made up His mind; instead, I think He gives us that time to fix our eyes on Him, to seek His heart in the dealings of our lives, and to become fully loyal to His will. He longs for connection and relationship with us and knows that our waiting will develop perseverance, trust, and hope.

If you're in a place of waiting for the Lord, don't be discouraged—you're right where you need to be. God is always working on your behalf. He hears your questions, the thoughts you whisper deep within your heart (Ps. 40:1), so keep waiting. He's right there with you.

 **LAMENTATIONS 3:25–27**

DAY 19: # Finding Joy

Joy has become an elusive theme of my life, and I often find myself looking for it around each corner, trying to figure out how to bottle up that magic for myself. I see joy in my toddlers and on the faces of strangers in the airports welcoming home long-awaited family members; I feel it in church, in the crescendo of a powerful song, and even in the confines of my kitchen, that little sanctuary where, every once in a while, I capture a memory of someone I loved through a single bite of food.

I find that joy eludes me when I lose touch with my willingness to receive it. I tend to put my head down and rush from task to task, moment to moment, never really looking up long enough to enjoy it. Rather than stopping to fully embrace the beauty of a moment, I press forward to the next one and the next one. I've found this way of life buries me, and in my rush to acquire more and more good things, I miss out on the fullness of joy available in each moment.

Joy is a holy thing, and when you experience Jesus's brand of real-deal, heart-filling, shout-it-from-the-rooftops kind of joy, you'll know it. It doesn't always come with bells and whistles, but His Word promises that His joy is always glorious and abounding in hope, a tangible offering of His presence (Ps. 16:11). No matter where you are in life, make room for the joy of the Lord, and not just a glimpse of it—ask for the fullness of joy He purchased with His life.

 **JOHN 16:16-24**

DAY 20: Never Home Alone

I love that scene in *Home Alone* where Kevin awakens to find his family gone. He tiptoes through the house calling out for his brother, his cousins and aunts and uncles, only to find they've forgotten him—he's been left home alone. When I was a kid, the possibility of that kind of mistake was equal parts fun and terrifying, but now, as an adult, I see that the fear of being forgotten is still a very real thing for many of us.

I remember the summer after college when a few relationships ended and I was turned down by the graduate program I had banked my future on; I felt forgotten as I watched friends get married, move away, or start jobs, while I was only just beginning to pick through the remnants of my own life. At other times, I've watched as friends waited faithfully for even bigger things—a baby, a physical healing, or a breakthrough in an area they'd been praying through. In the pain of that all waiting, it can be easy to wonder, *"Where is God in all of this? Has He forgotten me?"* None of us are excluded from feeling left behind, and each version of that isolation leaves its own scars.

I'm reminded that Jesus has felt the weight of loneliness. In His humanity, He faced everything we will ever face, and He's promised to walk with us through the shadows of our own dark times until we reach the victories He's paid for. When we find ourselves in seasons of loneliness and waiting, we can rest assured that Jesus knows our heart and will never leave or forsake us.

Are there places you've been feeling alone? Roads that feel all but abandoned by every hope you once felt was secure? You can offer that loneliness and fear to Him and trade them for the confidence of His faithfulness. Today, rest in this hope: you're never alone when your make your home in Jesus.

 **PSALM 17:6–8**

DAY 21: Dusting Off Our Dreams

When Brett and I first married, I bought an expensive bottle of sake with visions of impressing him by preparing an over-the-top Japanese dinner. Somehow the right opportunity just never presented itself, so months turned into years, and by the time I found the bottle in the back of the cabinet, the liquid was no longer good.

I often do the same thing with clothes and pretty cocktail napkins and those expensive face creams from the department store. Always certain the right occasion will present itself, I hold off from utilizing my prized items, and before long they've been forgotten. Now they don't fit, or they've expired, or they're simply out of style. Many of us ration other treasures in our lives too: our gifts, our talents, and our desires. We stifle ideas or hold off from pursuing our dreams because the timing isn't right or it's best suited for another day. Before long, they're dusty and forgotten on the shelf with all the other dreams that died along the way.

What are those hopes that feel out of reach or out of season? Are there gifts and talents you've kept hidden from the world or have resisted discovering yourself? There isn't always a perfect time to start exploring our dreams—sometimes we just need to begin. We can hand our lives over to a creative and wonderful Jesus, who uses them for His purposes in ways we could never imagine.

This week, consider where you may need to dust off dreams you've been saving for a rainy day. God has equipped you to achieve beautiful, remarkable things in this life, so present it all to your Heavenly Father, and watch Him make something wonderful of it all. Today might be the day you've been waiting for, so don't be afraid to dive right in.

 **EPHESIANS 2:10**

DAY 22: A New Song

As believers, we haven't been promised a life without pain or difficulty. Instead, we live with the promise that God will never leave or forsake us and is always working all things for our good. When we walk through seasons of heartache and loss, ones in which it seems as if the whole world is against us, we have the opportunity to grasp hold of those promises and allow the hope we have in Him to shift our perspective, changing the song of our heart.

I'm reminded of David, who, even as a man after God's own heart, saw his own fair share of challenging circumstances. In Psalm 40, just a few verses after describing the desperation and hopelessness of his situation, David thanks God for putting a new song in his mouth. In an instant, God delivered David from the pain of His reality, trading his chords of despair and longing for songs of joy, hope, and life.

We will all work through seasons where the melodies in our hearts are ones of sorrow and hopelessness, but God, in His goodness and mercy, can remove you from that endless playback of pain. We can allow the lyrics of His Word to offer hope and promise for our circumstances, bringing love and peace to the rhythms of our everyday life.

Right now, close your eyes and listen to the song in your heart. If you find yourself longing for a different tune, begin praying for God to change the track. Like David, you may find yourself pressing in deeply and daily for some time, but God will not leave you where He finds you. He did it for David, and He'll do it for you.

 PSALM 40

DAY 23: Vanilla Spiced Pecans

One of my favorite women shared this recipe for Vanilla Spiced Pecans with me years ago, and it became so beloved that we gave small bags of these spiced pecans as favors to our wedding guests. Now I love to prepare these around the holidays, when little bowls of nuts make a welcome offering to guests or a quick homemade gift for teachers, friends, or family.

....

VANILLA SPICED PECANS

Makes 4 cups

⅓ cup granulated sugar

¼ teaspoon table salt

¼ teaspoon ground coriander

¼ teaspoon ground cinnamon

¼ teaspoon ground nutmeg

¼ teaspoon ground allspice

⅛ teaspoon black pepper

2 tablespoons canola oil

1 tablespoon vanilla extract

4 cups shelled pecan halves

Preheat the oven to 325ºF. Line a large rimmed baking sheet with foil and lightly grease it with cooking spray.

In a small bowl, combine the sugar, salt, coriander, cinnamon, nutmeg, allspice, and pepper. In a large bowl, stir together the oil and vanilla, and then toss in the pecans. Add the sugar mixture and toss to evenly coat the nuts. Spread the nuts out on the baking pan and bake for 30 to 35 minutes, stirring every 10 minutes. Once dry and aromatic, remove them from the oven and allow them to cool completely. The nuts will keep in an airtight container for up to three weeks.

DAY 24: Meeting at the Manger

This time of year always elicits warm feelings, as memories of December snowfalls and twinkling lights call up an excitement in my spirit that is so thick, it's almost palpable. As I grow older, I find myself longing to cultivate that same wonder and excitement for my own family—the sounds and smells and experiences that can make this season feel so rich and full of love. I want them to have all the crackling fires, Nat King Cole, and frosted cookies that bring magic to my own recollections.

At the same time, I'm reminded that Christmas is a difficult season for many, and maybe this year that includes you. The lights and presents and songs that make others so merry may just bring you back to memories of painful years past—another reminder of disappointment, loss, and brokenness. Not all of us are holly and jolly this time of year.

I want you to know that, no matter your story, whether you're one Mariah Carey song away from driving your family insane or just aching for this season to be done with, you can bring it all to the foot of the manger. You don't need a tacky sweater, a dazzling light display, or yet another mug of cocoa, because Christmas begins and ends with the miraculous birth of a King. We are all invited to offer our hearts, whether merry or broken, at His feet. In His love, you'll find all the hope and healing your heart so deeply needs, so don't hesitate to give it all to Him. He'll meet you where you are today.

 **ROMANS 15:13**

DAY 25: Happy Birthday

I know some people get all shy and embarrassed when people sing "Happy Birthday" to them, but I've never been that girl. Instead, all the attention and affection just about knocks me over. The singing, the candles, the cake, and confetti all feel like a tangible offering of love, and for the few seconds of that song I soak in every word as if each one is a gift intended just for me.

What do you think it does for Jesus's heart when we celebrate Him? When we talk about His birth or sing songs in a candlelit sanctuary, can't you just see His face glowing in the birthday candles, basking in the affection of His children? I've spent years focused on making Christmas more about tartan and greeting cards and coordinated giftwrap, when, really, it's about lighting His birthday candles to celebrate His birth. This year, I want more of that—less stuff and more Jesus.

Jesus doesn't require fancy gifts or longwinded Hallmark cards; He just wants to feel the glow of your love. Don't miss the coming opportunities to celebrate His birth, His life, and His death, to let Him know how overjoyed you are and how much you love Him. Happy Birthday, Jesus. We love you.

 **MATTHEW 2:10**

DAY 26: The Gift of Presence

Many years ago, when I was a kid, my family and I drove several hours to go to my grandparents' home on Christmas Day. I ate Egg McMuffins and hash browns in the backseat of my mom's car, and if it weren't for my propensity for car sickness, the kid in me would have loved that Christmas morning menu. We rarely took big road trips during the holidays, but our destination and the promise of seeing my grandparents face-to-face on that special day made the miles traveled well worth it.

I love presents, but the one thing I crave more than another bathrobe, scented candle, or Christmas ornament is the gift of *being* present: engaging face-to-face in a life-giving relationship. When you think about it, presence was the original Christmas gift. Jesus left His home in heaven to look humanity in the eye, to share in communion with them, and to love, serve, and die on behalf of them and the millions that were to come. He didn't come to offer gifts of new clothes or shiny toys—He made His presence a forever offering to a world devoid of connection, knowing it was the one gift we could bank our eternities on.

As we unwind from the busyness of Christmas Day, I want to invite you to give yourself and those around you the gift of presence. Dishes and cleanup and adding batteries to all the plastic toys can wait, but love cannot. Have you made enough room for presence today? Are there things you can set aside to make time for loving others, yourself, and the Lord in a meaningful way? Jesus's gift to us on His birthday was Himself—a God made present to a broken and fallen world. Return that gift to Him by setting aside the stuff and engaging with Him and others wholeheartedly today.

 **MATTHEW 1:18-23; LUKE 2:1-20**

DAY 27: Personality Types

I am absolutely fascinated by the Enneagram. Although I've only read a couple of books, I'm a total sucker for those online lists that say things like "Black Friday Shopping According to Your Enneagram Type" or "New Year's Eve Plans Fit for Every Enneagram Number." There's something satisfying about identifying the mentality behind your own actions, of being able to put people and their behaviors neatly into little numbered boxes—I find it to be seriously fun!

The problem comes when we allow our personality type to justify unhealthy behavior. When we write off passivity, aggression, or narcissism as a byproduct of our personality or expect people to laugh off our self-centeredness or codependency as a consequence of our number, we can end up using our "type" as a safety net of excuses to fall back on rather than calling those behaviors what they really are: sin.

As believers, we don't conform to a type or number or wing, because we are to be ever bending more toward Christ. Personality tests are wonderful tools for discovering more about ourselves and the people around us, but ultimately God has the final say about who we are. Look to Him to decide who you are, and honor Him by living a life that looks like Jesus's.

 **EPHESIANS 4:20–24; 1 JOHN 3:2–3**

DAY 28: Only the Taste Counts

I once spent hours making a birthday cake for a friend. Eight thin layers of chocolate cake were topped with a piping of peanut-butter ganache and a drizzle of salted caramel. The edges of the cake were left bare so you could see the exposed layers of the cake, and the top was decorated with extra bits of burnt sugar and roasted peanuts. All throughout dinner, my friends went on and on about how beautiful the cake looked, and I was feeling pretty good about my work.

Except when we finally bit into it, the cake was dry, the ganache was too firm, and the caramel had taken on the flavor of whatever else had been in my refrigerator. I was so disappointed; although from the outside the cake was beautiful, what I found on the inside was left wanting.

It's easy to get too wrapped up in the outward appearances. Often, we can become so invested in how good our performance looks from the outside that we neglect to welcome Jesus into our innermost parts. God didn't intend for us to live a life that just *looks* beautiful; He desires that we enjoy a rich existence, one that is good from the inside out because of His grace and hope and joy.

Are there areas of your life where you've invested more in appearances than peace? Joy? Wholeness? Love? Today, invite God into those spaces and let Him do the beautiful, redemptive work of flavoring your life from the inside out, transforming it into one that looks like Jesus's.

 **2 CORINTHIANS 12:9–10; GALATIANS 1:10**

DAY 29: Great Faith

In Hebrews 11, Abraham's wife, Sarah, is among a few biblical greats who are commended for their big acts of faith. This is the woman who, back in Genesis, laughed when God told her she would bear a child in her old age and attempted to produce a child by her own means instead of believing that God was big enough to accomplish what He had promised. Even though her life was riddled with doubt and unbelief for years, here she is in Hebrews, commended alongside of Noah and Moses and Joseph as a person of great faith.

I'm comforted to know that God celebrates the parts we get right. Sarah might not have obeyed Him at first, but when she did fully place her trust in God, He offered her the blessing of a child. God doesn't remind us of our shortcomings, but, instead, takes pleasure in spotlighting the moments we got it right.

It's natural to doubt, but it's never too late to believe the words of God. He is faithful to what He has promised and will always celebrate your return to belief in Him. You can trust Him to keep His word, every time, knowing that He doesn't intend for you to strive for His promises—if He has promised it, He will accomplish it. Today, if there are areas where you struggle with doubt, just ask Him to help your unbelief. Rest in His promises today.

 **HEBREWS 11:1**

DAY 30: Lavender French 75

New Year's Eve is almost synonymous with champagne, and my absolute favorite champagne cocktail is a French 75. This version features a lavender simple syrup that offers just a hint of fragrance to the cocktail. You can find dried culinary lavender at some specialty stores, but I usually just order it online. Although there's no need to invest in an expensive bottle of bubbly for this drink, I would recommend buying something more dry than sweet.

....

LAVENDER FRENCH 75

Serves 2

LAVENDER SIMPLE SYRUP

(Makes 6 ounces)

1/2 cup water

1/2 cup granulated sugar

1 tablespoon dried culinary lavender

COCKTAILS

3 ounces gin (or vodka)

1 1/2 ounces lavender simple syrup

1 1/2 ounces fresh lemon juice

4 ounces champagne or sparkling wine

2 lemon peel twists (optional)

TO PREPARE THE LAVENDER SIMPLE SYRUP

Combine the water, sugar, and lavender in a small saucepan over medium heat. Stirring occasionally, bring the mixture to a gentle boil. After the sugar has completely dissolved, remove the pan from the heat. Allow the lavender to infuse into the syrup for 20 minutes, and then strain the mixture into a heat-proof container or jar. Refrigerate until cooled and ready to use (you can make this ahead and keep in the fridge for up to two weeks).

TO PREPARE THE COCKTAILS

To a tall cocktail shaker filled with ice, add the gin, lavender syrup, and lemon juice. With the lid on tight, shake vigorously for 20 seconds; strain the mixture into two champagne glasses. Top each with 2 ounces of champagne, and garnish with lemon peel twists, if desired. Cheers!

DAY 31: Fresh Starts

I love a New Year's Eve celebration. Give me all the paper tiaras, bubbling glasses, and metallic streamers. I'll take the late bedtime and rowdy noisemakers if you promise me an epic party and a reason to wear something glittery. For many of us, that final countdown contains all the possibility, promise, and hope that we need for the coming year. We toast to the future, bid farewell to the troubles of the past, and jump at our chance for a reset—to do better, to be stronger, to make more of our coming days than we did with our former ones.

Whether you're celebrating the future or eager to move on from the past, I hope you'll remember that you don't need to wait for a new year to start fresh. We won't find joy in a fulfilled resolution or a fresh calendar page—we find it in the life-giving presence of a good Father who has promised to make all the old things of our lives new (2 Cor. 5:17). He says our future has hope (Jer. 29:11), but He's also promised to clean us up right where we are right now (1 John 1:9). There's no amount of confetti or number of midnight kisses that could make God more ready to fulfill His purposes in your life (Ps. 138:8), because He's already at work on behalf of the people who love Him (Rom. 8:28).

So enjoy your midnight—raise a glass, sing "Auld Lang Syne," and rock that gold jumpsuit as if your life depends on it. But don't forget that the hope for our future, the reset and fresh start you've been waiting for, is found only in the Lord. Celebrate with Him, right now, all the promises and beauty and glory He has already prepared for you.

 **ISAIAH 40:30-31**

❧ Acknowledgments ❧

Many of the stories and recipes found in this book are years in the making, having been shared alongside women who have made endless contributions to my life with their love. To those women: thank you. Birthday cakes and bottles of wine are best enjoyed with you, and I couldn't feel more grateful to call you mine.

A million thanks to Stacey, Katy, Chantal, and the rest of the team at Harper-One for working tirelessly to make this book happen. All of my love to Ann, Averee, Blair, Boo, Catherine, Cherry, Maggie, Rayne, Susu, and Taylor for offering encouragement, wisdom, and discernment for these pages. And hugs and biscuits to Mimi who shared many of her best recipes for this book without a second thought.

Mom, you get your own paragraph because you're my best and longest-running cheerleader. Thank you for always answering your phone and for planting all of your good seeds in my life.

And to Brett, Aimee, George, and Charlie: You feed my heart in the most deeply nourishing ways. So much of what I know to be true about God's love and grace, I've learned through you. I love you.